THE BODY AS
KÖRPER ALS
PROTEST

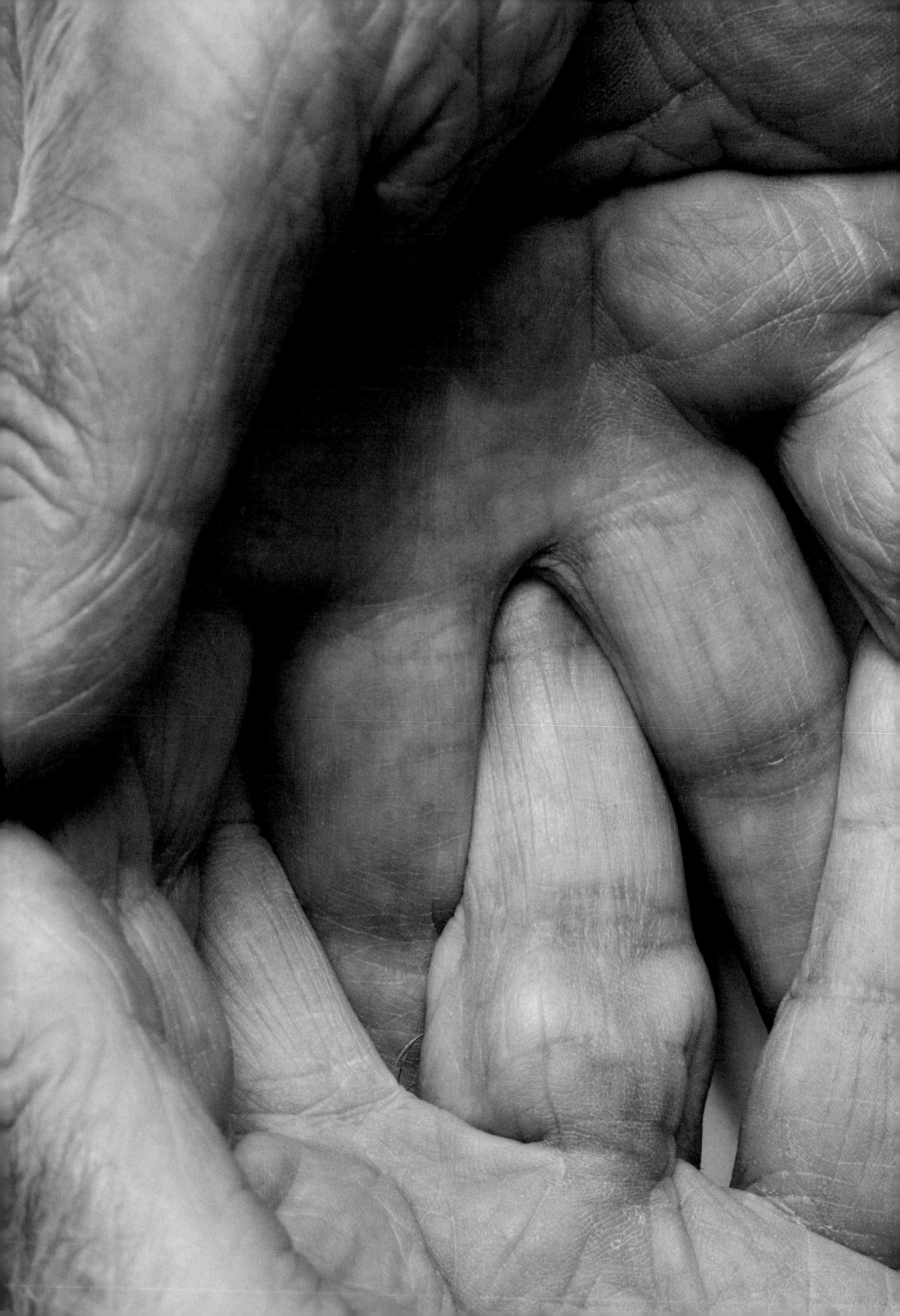

THE BODY AS
KÖRPER ALS
PROTEST

Herausgegeben von Edited by Walter Moser und and Klaus Albrecht Schröder

Texte von Texts by Walter Moser und and Christina Natlacen

ALBERTINA

HATJE
CANTZ

Foreword

Without the artistic achievements of photography, a history of images of the body would be unthinkable. With photography, not only were the norms and rules of previously established iconographies of the human body questioned and expanded, but also, owing to the photographic medium, entirely new modes of representation were created—a situation resulting in part from photography's manifold fields of application, such as art and science.

Against the background of the new possibilities of representation opened up by photography, the exhibition *The Body as Protest* is dedicated to the specific period beginning in 1970 in which the body emerged as a major theme for artists. Not only was the artist's own body rediscovered as a means of artistic expression; its depiction also provided social and political upheavals with a visual form. Feminism, Actionism, the gay-rights movement, as well as the AIDS crisis of the nineteen-eighties—to name only a few aspects—forced a rethinking of the conception, and consequently also the representation, of the body; themes such as gender, sexuality, illness, and age were subjected to visual scrutiny.

These topics found their artistic expression at a moment in which the inherent expressive qualities of photography were being reexamined. In this context, so-called conceptual photography not only understood itself as the *representation* of an object (or, in this case, the body), but, on the basis of the motif, it also began to reflect on its own media specificity and conditions. As a result, conceptual tendencies in photography tend to overlap with specific considerations relating to the body. A cultural history of the body is also a history of the photographic medium and vice versa.

The work of the photographer John Coplans provides a unique testimony to these developments. Over many years, with the help of a razor-sharp and thereby specifically photographic language, he portrayed his own body in fragmented and serially arranged images. The taboo-breaking radicalism with which Coplans staged his naked and aging body should be understood as a reaction to a society in which youthful and flawless bodies were considered an ideal. At the same time, with the fragmented depiction of his body, Coplans also challenges the viewer's perception. The radical fragmentation of the image, by withholding certain visual elements, underscores the way in which photographs per se "only" show sections of "reality."

The exhibition *The Body as Protest* conceived under the direction of Walter Moser places these works by Coplans at the very center of the survey. They are supplemented with outstanding photographic and video works by a number of other international artists. On the one hand, the works of Vito Acconci, Miyako Ishiuchi, Robert Mapplethorpe, Bruce Nauman, Ketty La Rocca, Hannah Villiger, and Hannah Wilke, through pointed juxtapositions, emphasize essential aspects in Coplans's work; on the

Vorwort

Eine Geschichte des Körperbildes ist ohne die künstlerischen Errungenschaften der Fotografie undenkbar. Mit der Fotografie wurden nicht nur Normen und
Regeln bereits etablierter Ikonografien des menschlichen Körpers hinterfragt
und erweitert, sondern auch ganz neue, dem fotografischen Medium geschul-
dete Darstellungsmodi geschaffen – ein Umstand, der sich auch den vielfältigen Anwendungsbereichen der Fotografie wie beispielsweise in Kunst und
Wissenschaft verdankt.

Vor dem Hintergrund solch fotografischer Repräsentationsmöglichkeiten
widmet sich die Ausstellung *Körper als Protest* jenem speziellen Zeitraum ab
1970, in dem der Körper zum Brennpunkt künstlerischen Schaffens wurde.
Nicht nur wurde der eigene Körper als künstlerisches Ausdrucksmittel neu
entdeckt, sondern es wurden auch gesellschaftliche, soziale und politische
Umbrüche anhand seiner Darstellung visualisiert. Feminismus, Aktionismus,
Schwulenbewegung sowie die Aidskrise der 1980er-Jahre – um nur einige
Aspekte zu nennen – forcierten ein Umdenken in der Konzeption und damit
auch in der Darstellung des Körpers; Themen wie Geschlecht, Sexualität, Krank-
heit und Alter wurden visuell hinterfragt.

Diese Inhalte fanden ihren künstlerischen Ausdruck in einer Fotografie, die
zu diesem Zeitpunkt ihre inhärenten Ausdrucksqualitäten neu untersuchte. Die
sogenannte Konzeptfotografie verstand sich hierbei nicht nur als *Abbild* eines
Objekts, das heißt Körpers, sondern reflektierte anhand dieses Motivs gleichzeitig ihre medialen Besonderheiten und Bedingungen. Konzeptuelle Tenden-
zen in der Fotografie überlagern sich dementsprechend mit spezifischen Überlegungen zum Körper. Eine Kulturgeschichte des Körpers ist damit auch eine
Geschichte des fotografischen Mediums und umgekehrt.

Die Werke des Fotografen John Coplans sind einzigartige Zeugnisse dieser
Entwicklungen. Mithilfe einer gestochen scharfen und damit spezifisch fotografischen Bildsprache lichtete er über Jahre hinweg seinen eigenen Körper
in fragmentierten Ansichten ab und ordnete diese seriell an. Die tabubrechen-
de Radikalität, mit der Coplans hierbei seinen nackten und alternden Körper
inszenierte, ist als Antwort auf eine Gesellschaft zu verstehen, in der jugendliche und makellose Körper als Ideal gelten. Gleichzeitig hinterfragt Coplans
mit der fragmentierten Darstellung seines Körpers die Wahrnehmung des
Betrachters beziehungsweise der Betrachterin. So verdeutlichen die radikalen
Ausschnitte, die Letzterem beziehungsweise Letzterer visuelle Elemente vor-
enthalten, dass Fotos per se »nur« Ausschnitte der »Wirklichkeit« wiedergeben
können.

Die unter der Leitung von Walter Moser konzipierte Ausstellung *Körper als
Protest* stellt diese Arbeiten von Coplans in den Mittelpunkt der Schau. Sie
werden durch herausragende Foto- und Videoarbeiten weiterer internationaler
KünstlerInnen ergänzt. Vito Acconci, Miyako Ishiuchi, Robert Mapplethorpe,
Bruce Nauman, Ketty La Rocca, Hannah Villiger und Hannah Wilke unterstrei-
chen anhand gezielter Gegenüberstellungen einerseits essenzielle Aspekte in

other hand, these heterogeneous groups of works illuminate various artistic approaches and themes in a wider, more differentiated context. For the first time in an exhibition, the works of John Coplans are examined from a broad range of perspectives and in a wider artistic field.

With the presentation of the works by John Coplans, this exhibition also addresses a major focus of the Albertina's photography collection. Besides a superb collection of historical photographs, the museum also possesses a significant body of contemporary works. This includes works by exponents of so-called street photography, such as Stephen Shore and Lisette Model; conceptual works by, for instance, Olafur Eliasson; and topographic positions such as the work of Lewis Baltz. With *The Body as Protest* a substantial selection of works from this rich and varied store can now be presented to the public.

I would especially like to thank Christina Natlacen for her insightful essay on the relation of the exhibited artists to Viennese Actionism. Additional thanks go to the lenders: Joree Adilman and Eugene Rutigliano (The Robert Mapplethorpe Foundation), Dr. Julia Friedrich (Museum Ludwig, Cologne), Eric Hattan (The Estate of Hannah Villiger), Georg Kargl (Galerie Georg Kargl), Nick Lesley (Electronic Arts Intermix), Tomoka Aya (The Third Gallery Aya), Dr. Gabriele Schor (SAMMLUNG VERBUND), and Prof. Peter Weiermair. Special thanks are also due to Amanda Means and Linda Law (The John Coplans Trust) for their dedicated support for this project. Last but not least, I owe my deepest thanks to Walter Moser, the chief curator of the Albertina's photography collection, who initiated and conceived this exhibition along with editing and contributing to the scholarly catalogue.

Klaus Albrecht Schröder
Director
Albertina, Vienna

Coplans' Werk, andererseits beleuchten diese heterogenen Werkgruppen verschiedene künstlerische Ansätze und Inhalte in einem darüber hinausreichenden differenzierten Kontext. Erstmalig werden in einer Ausstellung Werke von John Coplans aus vielfältiger Perspektive analysiert und im erweiterten künstlerischen Feld betrachtet.

Mit der Präsentation der Arbeiten von John Coplans widmet sich diese Ausstellung auch einem wesentlichen Schwerpunkt der fotografischen Sammlung der Albertina. So besitzt das Museum neben einer hervorragenden Sammlung an historischen Fotografien auch einen bedeutenden Korpus an zeitgenössischen Arbeiten. Dieser reicht von VertreterInnen der sogenannten Street Photography, wie etwa Stephen Shore und Lisette Model, über konzeptuelle Arbeiten, zum Beispiel von Olafur Eliasson, bis hin zu topografischen Positionen wie Lewis Baltz. Mit *Körper als Protest* kann eine wesentliche Werkgruppe aus diesem vielfältigen Bestand nun der Öffentlichkeit vorgestellt werden.

Besonders danken möchte ich Christina Natlacen für ihren aufschlussreichen Beitrag über das künstlerische Verhältnis der in der Ausstellung gezeigten KünstlerInnen zum Wiener Aktionismus. Mein weiterer Dank gilt den Leihgebern: Joree Adilman und Eugene Rutigliano (The Robert Mapplethorpe Foundation), Dr. Julia Friedrich (Museum Ludwig, Köln), Eric Hattan (The Estate of Hannah Villiger), Georg Kargl (Galerie Georg Kargl), Nick Lesley (Electronic Arts Intermix), Tomoka Aya (The Third Gallery Aya), Dr. Gabriele Schor (SAMMLUNG VERBUND) und Prof. Peter Weiermair. Spezieller Dank gebührt auch Amanda Means und Linda Law (The John Coplans Trust) für ihre engagierte Unterstützung dieses Projekts. Last but not least schulde ich meinen tiefsten Dank Walter Moser, dem Chefkurator der Fotosammlung der Albertina, der diese Ausstellung initiiert und konzipiert sowie den wissenschaftlichen Katalog verfasst hat.

Klaus Albrecht Schröder
Direktor
Albertina, Wien

Walter Moser # The Body as Protest

"Your body is a battleground." When in 1989 Barbara Kruger declared the human body a "battleground," the body had already been at the center of artistic scrutiny for decades. Beginning in the nineteen-fifties at the latest, the body not only became the bearer of a broad range of discourses, it also acted as the means by which these were visualized. Accordingly, social and political upheavals as well as those in matters inherent to art were reflected through artistic practices that raised the body to the center of the work. Its representation was often combined with a specific attitude of protest against dominant social norms and ideals. In this context, the photographer John Coplans has acquired an especially important position. His photographs can be seen as concentrations of theoretical and artistic reflections, which will be examined in the following through targeted comparisons with other important representatives of body-related art. At the same time, a range of themes such as self-staging, conceptual photography, feminism, body language, but also transience will be analyzed in an expanded artistic field. In addition, a differentiated picture of the critical representation of the human body since 1970 will be presented.

The photographer John Coplans, born in London in 1920, is among the most fascinating figures to emerge in recent art and photographic history. As the art critic, editor of the famous magazine *Artforum,* and director of the Akron Art Museum, Coplans had already made his presence felt in the art world in a number of fields when he eventually turned to photography

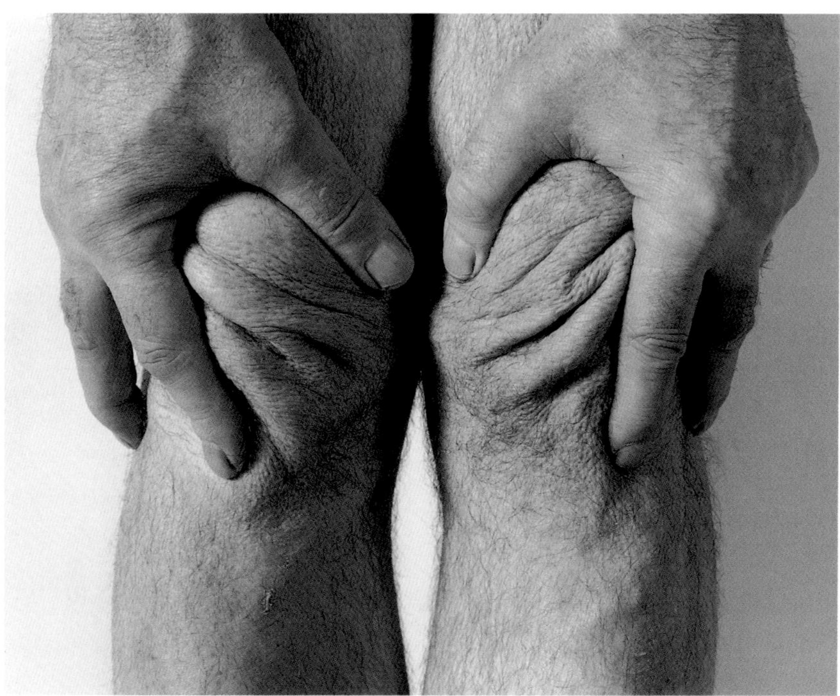

Abb. Fig. 1   John Coplans, *Hands Squeezing Knees,* 1985

Walter Moser

Körper als Protest

»Your body is a battleground.« Als Barbara Kruger den menschlichen Körper 1989 zum »Schlachtfeld« erklärte, stellte dieser den Mittelpunkt einer bereits seit Jahrzehnten geführten künstlerischen Auseinandersetzung dar. Nicht nur war der Körper spätestens seit den 1950er-Jahren Träger unterschiedlichster Diskurse, sondern fungierte auch als Mittel, um diese zu visualisieren. So wurden gesellschaftliche, politische, aber auch kunstimmanente Umwälzungen durch künstlerische Praktiken, die den Körper zum Zentrum ihrer Arbeit erhoben, reflektiert. Seine Darstellung war nicht selten mit einer spezifischen Protesthaltung gegen herrschende gesellschaftliche Normen und Ideale verbunden. Dem Fotografen John Coplans kommt innerhalb dieses Kontextes eine außerordentlich wichtige Bedeutung zu. Seine Fotografien können als Verdichtungen theoretischer und künstlerischer Überlegungen verstanden werden, die im Folgenden durch gezielte Vergleiche mit anderen wichtigen VertreterInnen körperbezogener Kunst herausgearbeitet werden sollen. Hierbei werden so unterschiedliche Themen wie beispielsweise Selbstinszenierung, Konzeptfotografie, Feminismus, »body language« oder auch Vergänglichkeit in einem erweiterten künstlerischen Feld analysiert. Darüber hinaus wird ein differenziertes Bild der kritischen Darstellung des menschlichen Körpers seit 1970 vorgestellt.

Der 1920 in London geborene Fotograf John Coplans gehört zu den faszinierendsten Figuren der rezenteren Kunst- und Fotogeschichte. Als Herausgeber des berühmten Magazins *Artforum,* als Kunstkritiker und als Museumsdirektor des Akron Art Museum war Coplans bereits in vielfacher Hinsicht in der Kunstwelt in Erscheinung getreten,[1] als er sich im Alter von 64 Jahren der Fotografie zuwandte. Nach einer kurzen Auseinandersetzung mit Porträtfotografie konzentrierte er sich auf ein Thema, das er fortan bis zu seinem Tod künstlerisch behandeln sollte: auf die Darstellung seines eigenen nackten Körpers. In großformatigen, seriell konzipierten und präzise ausgeleuchteten Fotografien lichtete er diesen auf monumental-skulpturale Weise ab (Kat. 4–12). Nicht nur visualisierte er seinen Körper fragmentiert, sondern dokumentierte in schonungslosen Darstellungen seinen Alterungsprozess. Durch die radikale Wiedergabe eines »unperfekten« Körpers widersetzte sich Coplans der herrschenden künstlerischen und gesellschaftlichen Konvention, die jugendliche und makellose Körper als Inbegriff eines künstlerischen Ideals betrachtet. Seine Fotos lassen sich jedoch nicht nur im Hinblick auf die deutliche Repräsentation des alternden Körpers als Protest gegen ein Tabu verstehen; auch die direkte Darstellung der eigenen Nacktheit widerspricht klassischen Selbstinszenierungen von Künstlern. Während Selbstdarstellungen von männlichen Künstlern als Akt äußerst rar sind, wird genau dieser bei Coplans zum primären Thema.[2] Vor neutralem Hintergrund im Studio abgelichtet, fokussiert der Fotograf auf Form, Oberfläche und Pose des Körpers, den er so in der Tradition des Minimalismus streng formal beziehungsweise auf das Wesentliche reduziert wiedergibt. Visuell isoliert und auf sich selbst konzentriert wird er zum alleinigen Mittelpunkt der Werke.

at the age of sixty-four.[1] After a brief experiment with portrait photography, he subsequently concentrated on a subject that would form the center of his artistic production up to his death: the representation of his own naked body. In large-format, serially conceived, and precisely lit photographs, he depicted this in a monumental and sculptural manner (cat. 4–12). Coplans not only visualized his body in a fragmentary way, he also provided an unsparing representation of his aging process. In his radical depiction of an "imperfect" body, he opposes the dominant artistic and social convention that views youthful and flawless bodies as the epitome of an artistic ideal. Even so, his photos should not only be seen in relation to the unsparing depiction of the aging body as a protest against a taboo; the direct representation of his own nakedness also contradicts classical self-representations of artists. While nude self-representations of male artists are extremely rare, this is precisely what formed Coplans's primary subject.[2] Photographed in the studio against a neutral background, the photographer focuses on the body's form, surface, and pose, reducing it in the tradition of minimalism to its essentials in a strictly formal way. Visually isolated, and concentrated on itself, the body becomes the sole focus of the work.

The Body as Artistic Focus

The strategy of using the body for artistic and socio-political investigations was not fundamentally new, however. When Coplans began making his photos in 1984, a broad spectrum of artists had been declaring the body as the object of often radical artistic interrogations for decades. In the wake of Abstract Expressionism, movements such as Happenings and Fluxus, but also Viennese Actionism, treated the body in an entirely new way by placing it at the center of their work. Various representatives of Body Art—including such famous artists as Bruce Nauman, Vito Acconci, and Hannah Wilke—subsequently drew attention to an artistic reorientation in which the artist's own body was understood as a fundamental component of the work.[3] The artist's body thus became the immediate object of the work that could be used in a variety of ways: as a painterly support, as raw material that could be manipulated and destroyed at will, and as a medium of potentially expressive qualities that could be systematically formed and investigated. Aside from the fundamental concentration on the artist's own body, it is particularly the latter aspect of expressivity that can be recognized as an important characteristic in Coplans's photographic works. For the photographer, skin and flesh represent raw materials that can be worked on and formed at will. While in some photos he presses together the skin over his knees, in a further image he (de)forms his upper body, which is visualized as a relief-like structure (figs. 1, 2).

One of the key protagonists who, beginning in the nineteen-sixties, had a major impact on this artistic approach is the American artist Bruce Nau-

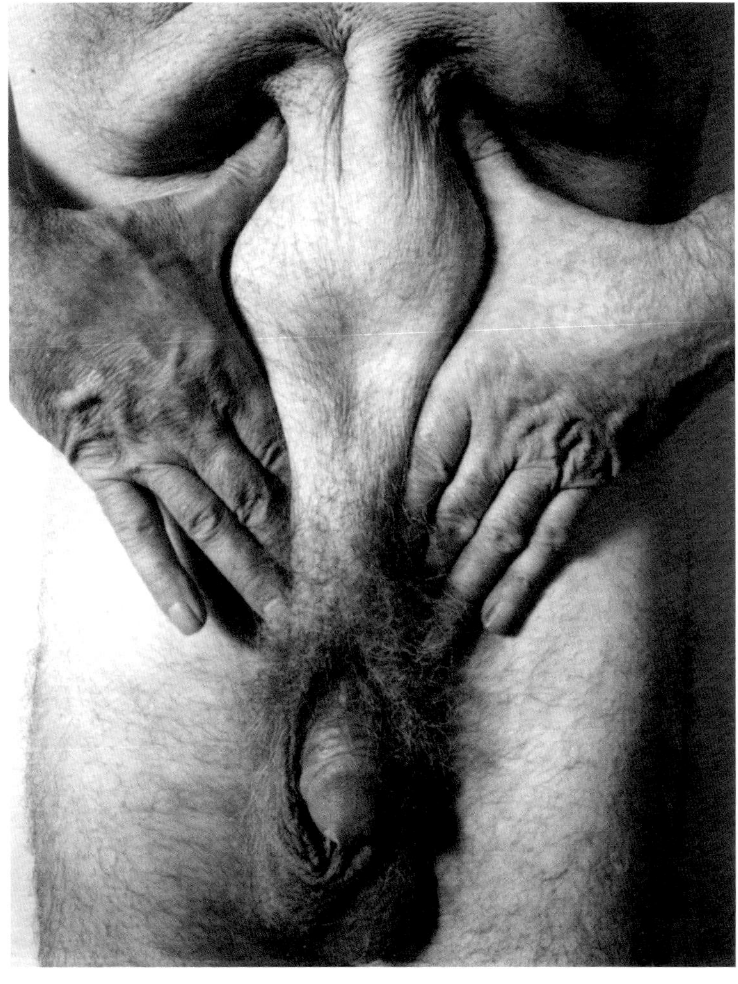

Abb. Fig. 2   John Coplans, *Untitled Platinum Print, No. 1,* 1984

Körper als künstlerischer Fokus

Die Strategie, den Körper für künstlerische und gesellschaftspolitische Ausei-
nandersetzungen zu nutzen, war grundsätzlich nicht neu. Als Coplans 1984
begann, seine Fotos aufzunehmen, hatten verschiedenste KünstlerInnen den
Körper bereits jahrzehntelang zum Gegenstand oftmals radikaler künstlerischer
Auseinandersetzungen erklärt. Bewegungen wie Happening und Fluxus in der
Nachfolge des abstrakten Expressionismus, aber selbstverständlich auch der
Wiener Aktionismus verhandelten den Körper insofern völlig neu, als sie ihn
in den Mittelpunkt ihrer Kunst stellten. Unterschiedliche VertreterInnen der
Body Art – darunter so bekannte KünstlerInnen wie Bruce Nauman, Vito Acconci
und Hannah Wilke – verdeutlichten in Folge eine künstlerische Neuorientierung,
bei welcher der eigene Körper als elementarer Bestandteil des künstlerischen
Werkes begriffen wurde.[3] Der Körper des Künstlers oder der Künstlerin wurde zum unmittelbaren Gegenstand, der in vielerlei Hinsicht genutzt werden
konnte: Als Träger für Bemalung, als bloßes Material, das beliebig bearbeitet
und zerstört wurde, sowie als Medium potenzieller expressiver Ausdrucksqualitäten, die systematisch geformt und untersucht werden konnten. Abgesehen
von der grundsätzlichen Konzentration auf den eigenen Körper lässt sich
besonders der zuletzt genannte Aspekt der Expressivität als wichtiges Merkmal von Coplans' Fotoarbeiten erkennen. Haut und Fleisch stellen für den
Fotografen bloße Materialien dar, die beliebig bearbeitet und geformt werden
können. Während er dementsprechend in manchen Fotos die Haut über seinen

man. In video works such as *Thighing* (1967), *Pinch Neck* (1968), but also in the silk-screen prints *Studies for Holograms* (1970) made after Polaroids by the photographer Jack Fulton, Nauman provides a rigorous analysis of the expressive potential of his own body (cat. 1, 13). The revolutionary nature of his work has often been remarked on: by utilizing his body as an artistic material he reorders the relationship between artist and work, just as he redefines art per se. In Nauman's performances not only the role of the artist as the explicit producer of works is presented, but his body is also exemplified as an object. The body produces the work and at the same time represents it, whereby the originally separated entities of artist, body, and work are visually merged together.[4] An equally relevant aspect of Nauman's work is the simultaneous objectification of the body, behind which the artist as person withdraws. As such, the representation of the artist's own body does not serve an interrogation of the artist as person, or the visual exploration of the self. Nauman visualizes this artistic approach most clearly with the help of his face. Here, the face is grasped as a material that has become detached from the artist as person, and whose potential expressive possibilities are systematically explored.[5] Nauman commented pragmatically on this approach in relation to his series *Studies for Holograms:* "The idea of making faces had to do with thinking about the body as something that you can manipulate. . . . That's really all the faces were about—just making a bunch of arbitrary faces."[6]

The primary emphasis on the bodily is also made clear in video works in which Nauman shows the body only in fragments. In his video work *Thighing* for example, in which "only" his upper leg can be seen, he presses and kneads this into different forms and shapes.

This form of self-representation, in which the artist's own body represents the object and, as expressive material, becomes uncoupled from the artist's self, is an equally essential aspect of Coplans's works. However, while Nauman disappears behind arbitrary grimaces and body fragments in order to objectify his body, Coplans concentrates on the rendering of single body parts. Through the stylistic device of fragmentation, he visually separates his body from his face. In none of his photos is his head to be seen. As in Nauman's video *Thighing,* an identification with/of the artist as person is made impossible; the investigation of different expressions is only undertaken with the body, not with the help of the face.

Self-Staging as Performative Act

In relation to Coplans's work, an interesting context for Nauman's five-part series *Studies for Holograms* is provided by Jean-Luc Godard's famous film *À bout de souffle (Breathless)* (figs. 3–6). In a central scene of the French film from 1960 the two protagonists, Jean-Paul Belmondo and Jean Seberg, begin to pull a series of grimaces. These do not serve the incarnation of

Knien zusammenpresst, (ver)formt er in einem weiteren Bild seinen Oberkörper, der als reliefartige Struktur visualisiert wird (Abb. 1, 2).

Der amerikanische Künstler Bruce Nauman ist einer jener zentralen Protagonisten, die ab den 1960er-Jahren diesen künstlerischen Zugang maßgeblich prägten. In Videoarbeiten wie *Thighing* (1967), *Pinch Neck* (1968), aber auch in den nach Polaroids des Fotografen Jack Fulton entstandenen Siebdrucken *Studies for Holograms* (1970) beschäftigte sich Nauman konsequent mit den künstlerischen Ausdrucksmöglichkeiten seines eigenen Körpers (Kat. 1, 13). Das Revolutionäre seiner Arbeiten ist oft betont worden: Mit dem Einsatz seines Körpers als künstlerischem Material ordnete er das Verhältnis von Künstler und Werk neu, genauso wie er Kunst per se neu definierte. So wurde bei seinen Performances nicht nur die Rolle des Künstlers als explizitem Produzenten von Werken vorgeführt, sondern sein Körper auch als Objekt exemplifiziert. Der Körper produziert das Werk und stellt es gleichzeitig dar, womit die ursprünglich getrennten Instanzen von Künstler, Körper und Werk visuell miteinander verschmelzen.[4] Als ebenso relevant für Naumans Werk erweist sich die gleichzeitig stattfindende Objektivierung des Körpers, hinter der die Person des Künstlers zurücktritt. So dient die Darstellung des eigenen Körpers nicht einer künstlerischen Befragung der eigenen Person oder der visuellen Ergründung des Selbst. Am deutlichsten visualisiert Nauman diesen künstlerischen Zugang mithilfe des Gesichts. Dieses wird als von der eigenen Person losgelöstes Material aufgefasst, dessen potenzielle Ausdrucksmöglichkeiten systematisch erforscht werden.[5] Nauman hat diesen Zugang in Bezug auf seine Serie *Studies for Holograms* pragmatisch kommentiert: »The idea of making faces had to do with thinking about the body as something that you can manipulate. […] That's really all the faces were about – just making a bunch of arbitrary faces.«[6]

Auch Videoarbeiten, in denen Nauman nur Körperfragmente zeigt, verdeutlichen die primäre Betonung des Körperlichen. In seiner Videoarbeit *Thighing*, in der »nur« sein Oberschenkel zu sehen ist, drückt und knetet er diesen beispielsweise zu unterschiedlichen Formen und Gestalten.

Diese Form der Selbstdarstellung, bei welcher der eigene Körper des Künstlers das Objekt darstellt und als expressives Material vom Selbst der Person entkoppelt wird, ist ein ebenso essenzieller Aspekt in Coplans' Arbeiten. Während Nauman sowohl hinter arbiträren Grimassen als auch Körperfragmenten verschwindet, um seinen Körper zu objektivieren, konzentriert sich Coplans auf die Wiedergabe von einzelnen Körperteilen. Durch das Stilmittel der Fragmentierung trennt er seinen Körper visuell vom dazugehörigen Gesicht ab. Sein Kopf ist auf keinem seiner Fotos zu sehen. Wie in Naumans Video *Thighing* wird so eine Identifizierung (mit) der Person verunmöglicht, die Untersuchung unterschiedlicher Ausdrücke nur mit dem Körper, nicht aber mithilfe des Gesichts durchgeführt.

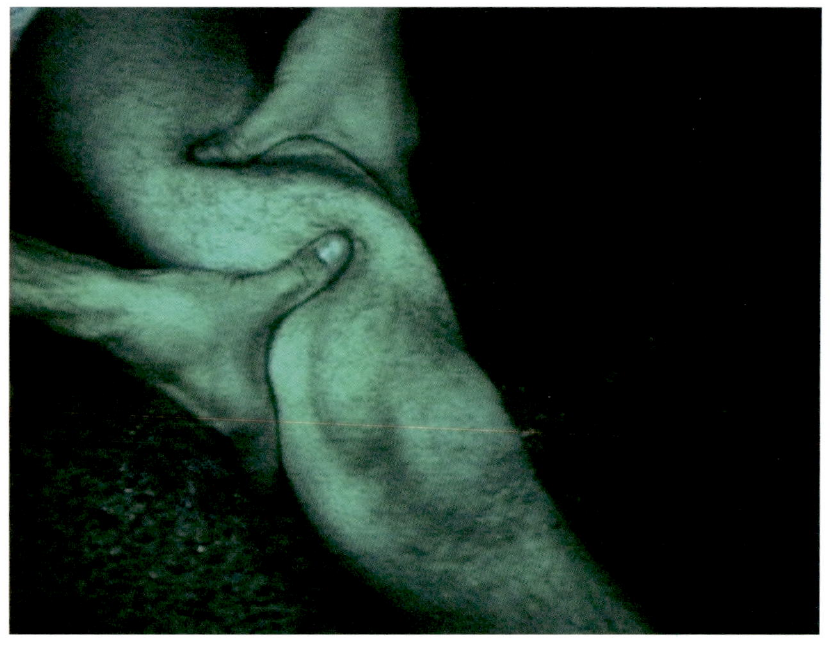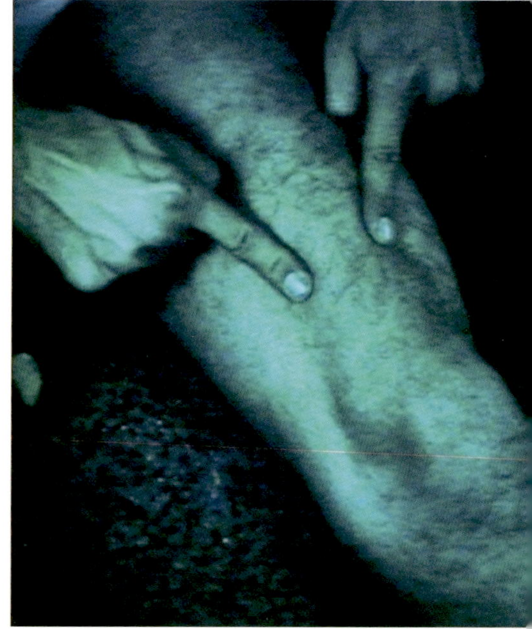

1   Bruce Nauman, *Thighing (Blue),* 1967, Video video, Courtesy Electronic Arts Intermix (EAI), New York

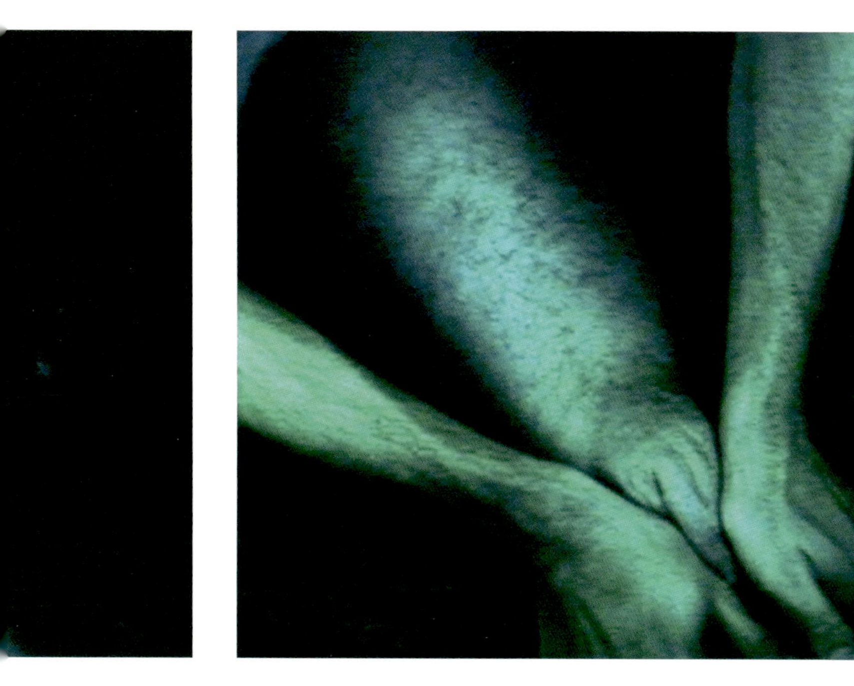

another role or person, however; instead, as in Nauman's works, they are portrayed as arbitrary and impersonal faces. Hence, anticipating Nauman, Godard's influential film visualizes a series of human expressive possibilities without portraying these as determined by the subjective emotional worlds of his protagonists.[7] Moreover, the rejection of natural facial expressions disconcerts the viewer, who feels that he or she being mocked or made fun of. And because the viewer is unable to translate the expression into a logically coherent semantics, it becomes impossible—as with Nauman—to identify with what is being shown.

Interestingly, the unsettling of the viewer in relation to Nauman's work was the subject of an exhibition review in *Artforum* from 1971—hence, precisely the year John Coplans took on the post as the art magazine's editor-in-chief: "Perhaps this is why Nauman chose to do facial contortions . . . both because we have an immediate sense of what it would feel like to distort one's face in those ways, and so that we feel somewhat mocked by having faces made at us."[8] With regard to the mocking and disconcerting effect of their contortions, Coplans's photographs are in no way less remarkable than the works of Nauman—with the notable difference that Coplans creates this impression with his body alone, not with his face. Coplans defamiliarizes his body with seemingly absurd gestures and poses for which the viewer is unable to find a logical explanation (fig. 7). Instead, the viewer is confronted with the mocking and ironic representations of a body that, like the photos of Nauman's grimaces, have an unsettling effect.

Beyond these similarities in the ironic defamiliarization of the body, the comparison with Godard's work also accentuates the crucial aspect of the time-based pictorial conception in Nauman's work. In *Studies for Holograms*, for example, the serial lining up of separate motifs is based on a linear, temporal, and in this sense filmic, principle that suggests to the viewer the process-like variations of a face. This intention becomes all the more clear once we consider that *Studies for Holograms* is based on the video performance *Pinch Neck,* in which the grimaces actually appear in the form of a video-based moving image. For *Studies for Holograms* Nauman privileged the medium of photography since it allowed him to concentrate on specific expressions at selected moments.[9] In addition, these photos were not made by Nauman alone, but with the help of the photographer Jack Fulton, who recorded the expressions staged for the camera with a Polaroid camera. Nauman's photos thus mark a conceptual approach to photography that is indebted to time-based (video) performance.

This photographic practice should be seen in the context of photography's relation to performance. As is well known, performance artists have always had recourse to the medium of photography to document and record their performances, although photography and performance actually stand

Selbstinszenierung als performativer Akt

Es erweist sich in Bezug auf Coplans' Werk als interessant, die fünfteilige Serie *Studies for Holograms* von Nauman im Kontext von Jean-Luc Godards berühmtem Film *À bout de souffle* zu sehen (Abb. 3–6). In einer zentralen Szene des 1960 entstandenen französischen Films schneiden die beiden Protagonisten Jean-Paul Belmondo und Jean Seberg verschiedenste Grimassen. Diese dienen nicht etwa der Verkörperung einer anderen Rolle oder Person, sondern werden wie in den Arbeiten Naumans als von der Person getrennte beziehungsweise arbiträre Expressionen geschildert. Godard visualisiert in seinem einflussreichen Film damit bereits vor Nauman eine Reihe menschlicher Ausdrucksmöglichkeiten, ohne diese als Resultate von innersubjektiven Gefühlswelten seiner Protagonisten zu schildern.[7] Die Abkehr von einem natürlichen Gesichtsausdruck schreckt darüber hinaus den Betrachter beziehungsweise die Betrachterin ab, scheinen sie sich doch über diese/n lustig zu machen oder zu spotten [im Folgenden wird aus Gründen der besseren Lesbarkeit stellvertretend für beide Geschlechter der Begriff »der Betrachter« verwendet]. Der Betrachter kann den Ausdruck nicht in eine logisch-kohärente Semantik überführen, wodurch – wie bei Nauman – eine Identifizierung mit dem Dargestellten unmöglich wird.

Es ist interessant, dass dieser Aspekt der Verunsicherung des Betrachters Naumans Werk bereits 1971 in *Artforum,* also genau in dem Jahr, in welchem John Coplans den Posten des Chefredakteurs bei dem Kunstmagazin übernahm, in einer Ausstellungskritik festgehalten wurde: »Perhaps this is why Nauman chose to do facial contortions […], both because we have an immediate sense of what it would feel like to distort one's face in those ways, and so that we feel somewhat mocked by having faces made at us […].«[8] Im Hinblick auf den spöttischen und beunruhigenden Effekt der Verzerrungen stehen Coplans' Fotografien den Arbeiten Naumans um nichts nach – mit dem relevanten Unterschied, dass Coplans diesen Eindruck nur mit seinem Körper, aber nicht mit seinem Gesicht erzeugt. So verfremdet Coplans seinen Körper mit scheinbar lächerlichen Gesten und Posen, die sich der Betrachter nicht logisch erklären kann (Abb. 7). Er wird mit spöttischen und ironischen Darstellungen des Körpers konfrontiert, die genauso wie die Fotos von Naumans Grimassen eine verunsichernde Wirkung haben.

Über diese inhaltliche Kongruenz in Bezug auf ironische Körperverfremdungen hinaus akzentuiert der Vergleich mit Godards Arbeit auch den wesentlichen Aspekt der zeitlich basierten Bildkonzeption in Naumans Werk. So basiert in *Studies for Holograms* die Aneinanderreihung der einzelnen Motive zu einer Bildserie auf einem zeitlich-linearen und in diesem Sinne filmischen Prinzip, das dem Betrachter die prozesshafte Veränderung eines Gesichtes suggeriert. Diese Intention wird umso deutlicher, wenn man bedenkt, dass *Studies for Holograms* auf seiner Videoperformance *Pinch Neck* basiert, in welcher die Grimassen tatsächlich als videobasiertes Bewegungsbild gezeigt

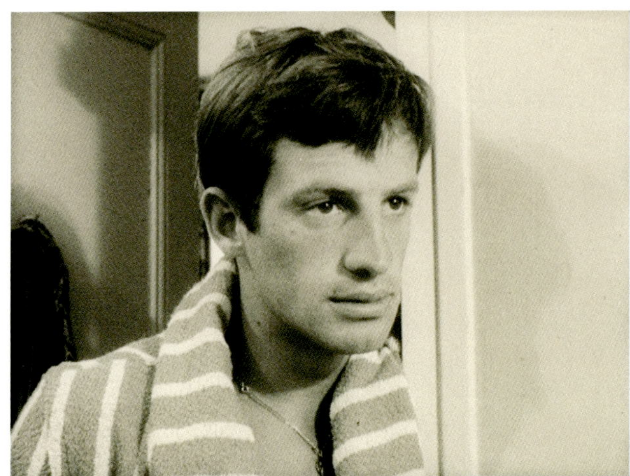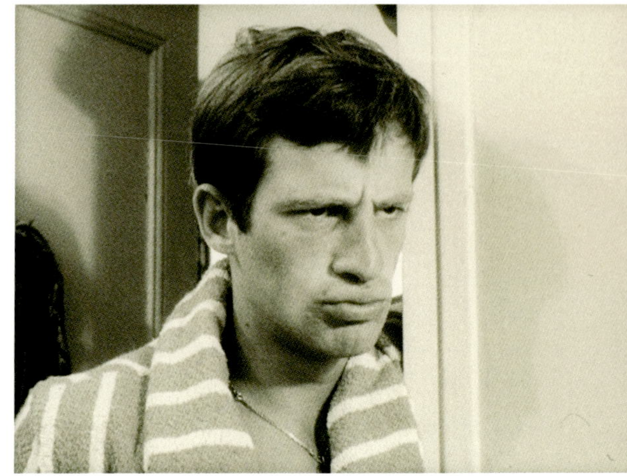

Abb. Figs. 3–6   Jean Luc Godard, *À bout de souffle (Breathless),* Frankreich France, 1960 (Kadervergrößerungen frame enlargements)

in a contradictory relationship to one another—performance is process-based, ephemeral, and immediate; photography is static, durable, and (due to its mediation by a photographer) indirect.[10] Nevertheless, with the help of photography, documents could be made that present durable traces of past performances. This relationship between photography and time-based performance increased in complexity with the appearance of Body Art: not only did performance artists often stage themselves directly for the camera; the photographic medium was also—as for instance in Nauman's works—utilized skillfully and discursively for their artistic intentions.[11]

A conceptual and time-based mode of photography is also fundamental to Coplans's photographs, whose media reflexivity goes far beyond Nauman's requirements. To describe Coplans's mode of image production it is appropriate to use the term "performativity." Despite the many different ways this term has been used, it always implies a temporal or process-based action through which sense is generated.[12] For a theory of photography, this term, which was originally derived from "performance," is especially valuable, since it allows photography to be seen as a discursive *process* and not merely as the automatic product of a technical apparatus. Coplans's photos are performative to the extent that they rest on a time-based production process that is visibly inscribed in the image. For his self-representations, Coplans worked with both an assistant, who operated the camera's shutter release, as well as a video camera and monitor, with which he could control the framing of each image. When Coplans assumed different poses, and thereby pressed the body into different forms, he could also immediately check them as representations on the screen. Hence, underlying the actual image production is an elaborate process of self-staging that creates the image even before the shutter release is pressed. The images are based on a temporal act, during which the body is staged. The image is thus already generated before it is fixed as a photo. The actual shot "only" terminates the staging, but at the same time allows the motif to appear. This performative aspect comes to light especially in the photos in which Coplans, in a single image, shows his body three times from different perspectives. The movement from position to position suggests a bodily movement, and thus a temporal change. In this way the performative process underlying the photos becomes clearly visible.

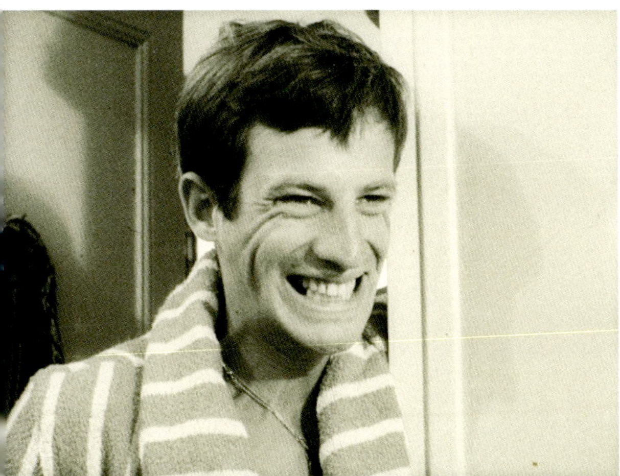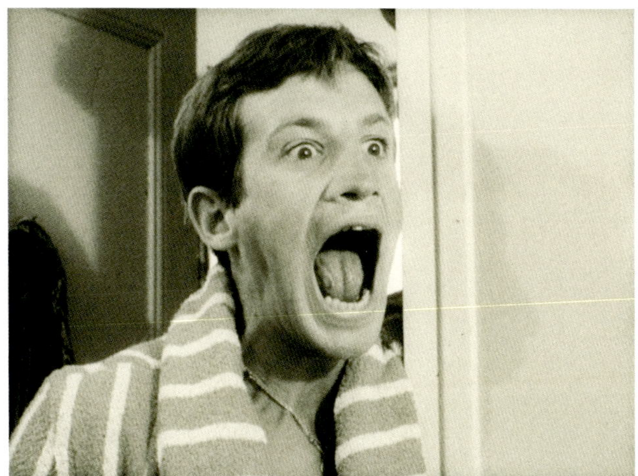

werden. Für *Studies for Holograms* bevorzugte er das Medium der Fotografie, erlaubte es ihm doch die zeitlich punktuelle Konzentration auf spezifische Ausdrücke.[9] Zudem fertigte Nauman diese Fotos nicht alleine an, sondern mithilfe des Fotografen Jack Fulton, der die für die Fotokamera inszenierten Expressionen mit einer Polaroidkamera festhielt. Die Fotos von Nauman markieren damit einen konzeptuellen Zugang zur Fotografie, der einer zeitlich basierten (Video)Performance geschuldet ist.

Diese fotografische Praxis muss im Kontext des Verhältnisses von Fotografie zu Performance gesehen werden. Es ist bekannt, dass Performance-Künstler schon immer auf das Medium der Fotografie zur Dokumentation und Aufzeichnung ihrer Aufführungen zurückgriffen, obwohl Fotografie und Performance eigentlich in einem widersprüchlichen Verhältnis zueinander stehen: Performance ist prozesshaft, ephemer und unmittelbar; Fotografie ist statisch, dauerhaft und (aufgrund der Vermittlung durch einen Fotografen) indirekt.[10] Nichtsdestotrotz konnten mithilfe der Fotografie Dokumente geschaffen werden, die dauerhafte Spuren vergangener Performances präsentieren. Diese Beziehung von Fotografie und zeitlich orientierten Aufführungen nahm mit dem Aufkommen der Body Art an Komplexität zu: Nicht nur inszenierten sich Performance-KünstlerInnen oftmals direkt für die Fotokamera, sondern das fotografische Medium wurde auch – wie etwa bei Nauman – gekonnt und diskursiv für ihre künstlerischen Intentionen eingesetzt.[11]

Eine konzeptuelle und zeitbasierte Art der Fotografie erweist sich auch für Coplans' Fotografien als elementar, wobei hier die Medienreflexivität jedoch weit über Naumans Ansprüche hinausgeht. Es bietet sich an, für Coplans' Art der Bildproduktion den Begriff der »Performativität« zu bedienen. So vielfach dieser Begriff auch verwendet wird, meint er doch immer eine zeitliche beziehungsweise prozesshafte Handlung, über welche Sinn generiert wird.[12] Für eine Theorie der Fotografie ist dieser ursprünglich von »Performance« abgeleitete Begriff besonders wertvoll, erlaubt er es doch, Fotografie als diskursiven Generierungs*prozess* und nicht bloß als automatisches Produkt eines technischen Apparates zu sehen. Coplans' Fotos sind nun insofern performativ, als sie auf einem zeitlich basierten Entstehungsprozess beruhen, der sich sichtbar in das Bild einschreibt. Coplans arbeitete bei seinen Selbstinszenierungen sowohl mit einer Assistentin, die den Kameraauslöser bediente, als auch mit einer Videokamera und einem Bildschirm, über welchen er jegliche Bildeinstellungen kontrollieren konnte. Wenn nun Coplans unterschiedliche Posen

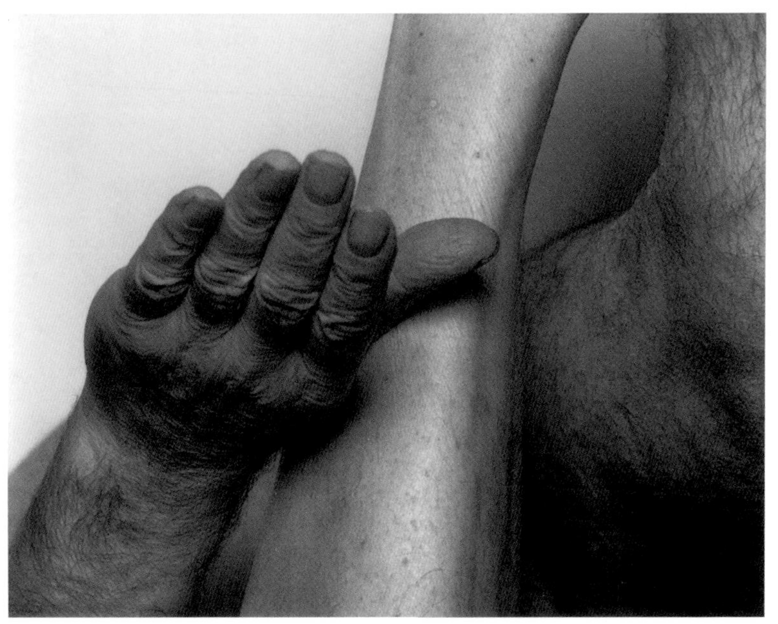
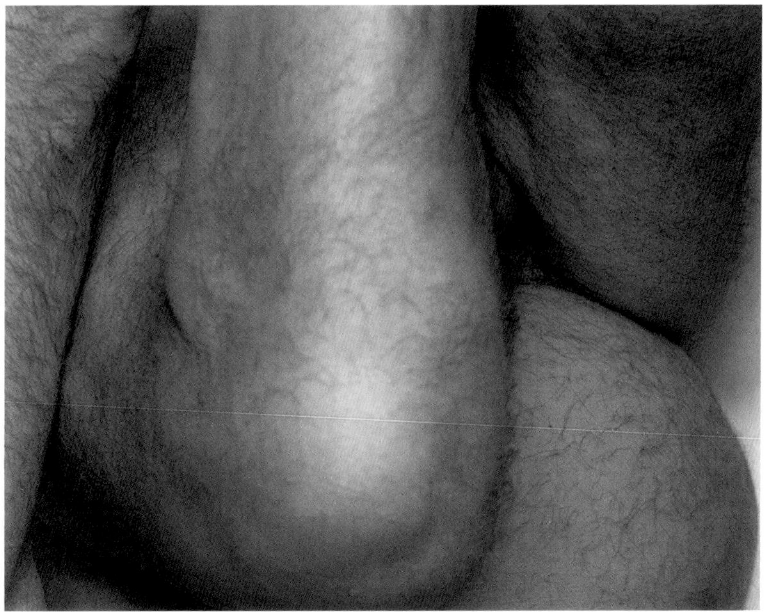
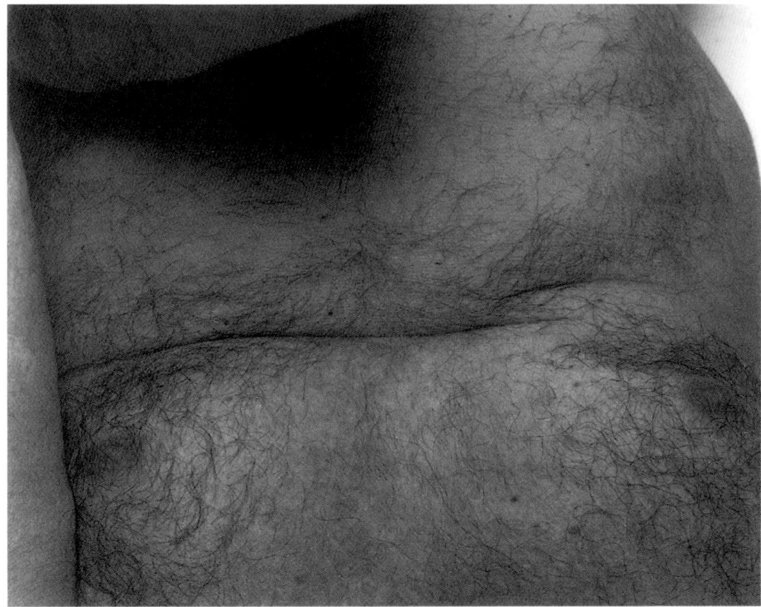

Abb. Fig. 7 John Coplans, *Upside Down, No. 1,* 1992

einnahm und den Körper dabei zu Formen presste, konnte er diese als Abbild
sofort am Bildschirm überprüfen. Der eigentlichen Bildproduktion liegt somit
ein aufwendiger Selbstinszenierungsprozess zugrunde, der das Bild erzeugt,
bevor noch auf den Auslöser gedrückt wird. Die Bilder basieren auf einem
zeitlichen Akt, während welchem der Körper inszeniert wird. Das Bild wird
damit aber bereits generiert, noch bevor es als Foto fixiert wird. Die tatsächli-
che Aufnahme schließt dementsprechend die Inszenierung »nur« noch ab,
bringt aber das Motiv erst zur Erscheinung. Dieser performative Aspekt tritt
besonders in jenen Fotos zutage, in denen Coplans in einem Foto seinen
Körper dreimal aus unterschiedlichen Perspektiven ablichtet. Die Veränderung
von Position zu Position suggeriert körperliche Bewegung und damit zeitliche
Veränderung. Der performative Prozess, der den Fotos zugrunde liegt, wird so
deutlich sichtbar.

Fotografie als Konzept

Diese Relevanz von Zeitlichkeit muss in Coplans' Werk auch in Bezug auf die
Präsentation der Fotos gesehen werden. Diese basieren vielfach nicht auf
singulären Darstellungen eines einheitlichen Körpers, sondern ganz im Gegenteil auf der seriellen Anordnung einzelner Körperfragmente. Will der Betrachter den Körper von Coplans rekonstruieren, muss er seinen Blick über mehrere Bilder gleiten lassen und die einzelnen Teile imaginär zusammensetzen. Ein
solches Prinzip der Serie beziehungsweise Montage, bei dem einzelne Fragmente zu einem neuen Ganzen zusammengesetzt werden, kann als Stilmittel
unterschiedlicher Bestrebungen der Konzeptfotografie gesehen werden.[13] Speziell Ed Ruschas 1966 erschienenes und in Folge sehr einflussreiches Buch
Every Building on the Sunset Strip, in dem er die Gebäude des Sunset Strip in
Los Angeles abfotografierte und zu einem Panoramaformat zusammenfügte,
kann hierfür als richtungsweisendes Beispiel genannt werden (Abb. 8).[14] Dieses
Buch war nicht nur revolutionär, weil es in der Tradition der Pop-Art technisch
scheinbar unperfekte Bilder zeigte, sondern darüber hinaus diese Einzelbilder
zu einem horizontalen Band montierte. Die räumlichen und zeitlichen Grenzen
des herkömmlichen Einzelbildes wurden auf diese Weise erweitert, wurde dem
Betrachter doch eine Art filmische Kamerafahrt suggeriert, die auf einem zeitlichen und weniger auf einem räumlichen Prinzip beruht. Wie bei Coplans'
Werken muss der Betrachter seinen Blick gleiten lassen, wenn er den Inhalt
erfassen will.

Coplans arbeitet hierbei freilich stärker mit visuellen Brüchen, was an Fotoarbeiten von David Hockney erinnert. So konstruiert Coplans seinen visuellen
Körper durch die Aneinanderreihung einzelner Bildausschnitte, die er so miteinander kombiniert, dass in dem jeweiligen Folgebild ein Element des vorhe-
rigen Bildes wiedererkennbar ist. Durch diese Wiederholungen bildlicher Elemente kann der Betrachter die Fotos zwar kombinieren, leichte perspektivische
Verschiebungen von Bild zu Bild ergeben jedoch Anschlussfehler. Eben dieses

Photography as Concept

In Coplans's work the relevance of temporality should also be seen in relation to the photos' presentation. In many cases this is not based on singular representations of a unified body but, quite the contrary, on the serial arrangement of body fragments. In order to reconstruct Coplans's body, the viewer must scan a number of pictures and recompose the separate parts in his or her imagination. Such a series or montage principle, in which single fragments are assembled to form a new whole, can be seen as a stylistic device at the center of a number of tendencies in conceptual photography.[13] Particularly Ed Ruscha's extremely influential book *Every Building on the Sunset Strip* from 1966, in which he made photographs of the buildings on the Sunset Strip in Los Angeles and subsequently assembled them into a panorama format, can be seen as pioneering in this respect (fig. 8).[14] This book was revolutionary not only because it contained images that seemed to lack technical perfection in the tradition of Pop Art but, moreover, because it lined up these single images into a horizontal strip. In this way, the spatial and temporal limits of the conventional image were expanded, indeed suggested to the viewer a kind of filmic tracking shot, one that rested more on a temporal than on a spatial principle. As with Coplans's works, in order to grasp the content, it is necessary to let our gaze drift over the image.

Coplans, admittedly, works to a greater degree with visual breaks than Ruscha, which recalls certain photographic works by David Hockney. Coplans constructs his visual body by lining up single pictorial details that he combines in such a way that each subsequent image contains an element from the previous one. Through the repetition of these pictorial elements, the viewer is able to combine the different parts, but the minor perspectival displacements occurring from image to image create a visual disturbance. Precisely this stylistic device is also used by David Hockney. Like Coplans, Hockney, with the help of montage, does not create a logically coherent body, but visualizes it as fractured and fragmented (fig. 9). While Coplans arranges only a few photos at a slight distance from one another, Hockney combines a multitude of single images within a larger tableau. Building on this principle, the photos of Coplans and Hockney function like structural avant-garde films, which, due to the apparent bridging errors in the montage, draw attention to their ontological structure.

Such a reflective use of media in Coplans's work should also be seen in the context of an ontology of the photographic image. With this strategy our attention is drawn to the fact that the photographic image is always based on fragments or details, and that pictorial reality is per se constructed. Due to the imperfect sutures, the viewer scanning the pictures is unable to receive a coherent pictorial reality and, as a result, finds him or herself constantly challenged. This also inevitably draws attention to the visual limits of the pictorial detail on which the photographic image is based.

Stilmittel nutzt auch David Hockney. Wie Coplans erzeugt Hockney mithilfe
der Montage keinen kohärent-logischen Körper, sondern visualisiert ihn brüchig
und fragmentiert (Abb. 9). Während Coplans jedoch wenige Fotos in räumlichem
Abstand zueinander anordnet, kombiniert Hockney eine Vielzahl von Einzelbildern in einem größeren Tableau. Auf diesem Prinzip aufbauend, funktionieren
die Fotos von Coplans und Hockney wie strukturelle Avantgardefilme, die durch
scheinbare Anschlussfehler bei der Montage eben deren ontologische Struktur deutlich machen.

Eine solche mediale Selbstbezüglichkeit beziehungsweise Selbstthemati-
sierung muss bei Coplans auch im Kontext einer Ontologie des fotografischen
Bildes gesehen werden. So führt seine Strategie deutlich vor Augen, dass das
fotografische Bild immer auf Ausschnitten beruht und die Bildwirklichkeit per
se konstruiert ist. Der Betrachter, der mit seinem Blick die Bilder scannt, kann
aufgrund der fehlerhaften Schnittstellen keine kohärente Bildwirklichkeit rezi-
pieren, sondern wird ständig irritiert. Die visuelle Begrenzung des Ausschnittes,
auf dem das fotografische Bild basiert, wird so unweigerlich thematisiert.

Die Präzision, mit der Coplans hierbei die einzelnen Körperteile visuell
fragmentiert, sowie der erläuterte Inszenierungsprozess verdeutlichen, dass der
Fotograf seine Selbstdarstellung explizit als Bild konzipiert. Dieser Sachverhalt,
so banal er erscheinen mag, ist insofern wesentlich als Fotografien von Künstlern der Body Art ihren Fokus oftmals auf das Objekt beziehungsweise den
Körper, nicht aber in gleichem Maße auf das Bild legen. Der inszenierte Körper
spielt die primäre Rolle, das Bild selbst wird diesem Inhalt untergeordnet. In
Coplans' Arbeiten werden Fotos im Gegensatz dazu durch den konzeptuellen
Zugang nicht nur in ihrer eigenen Medialität reflektiert, sondern auch die Art
der Darstellung des Körpers selbst wird thematisiert. Anders gesagt: Die Fotografien zeigen nicht nur einen Körper, sondern reflektieren diesen bereits als
Abbild und damit in seinem Status als Bild. Diese Strategie wird speziell dann
sichtbar, wenn sich Coplans Posen aneignet, die sich auf klassische Darstellungen der Kunstgeschichte beziehen. So nimmt er beispielsweise für ein in
drei Teile zerlegtes Querformat eine horizontale Liegeposition ein, in der er mit
einer Hand sein Geschlecht verdeckt (Abb. 10). Diese Pose weist eindeutig
Reminiszenzen an Werke der klassischen Kunstgeschichte wie etwa Giorgiones
Venus auf. Die Übernahme einer eindeutig weiblich konnotierten Pose durch
einen männlichen Körper erzeugt einen semantischen Widerspruch zwischen
klassischem Vorbild und (Re)Inszenierung, welche die Konstruktion von Ge-
schlechtern in Medien konterkariert. Coplans verdeutlicht, dass (geschlechtliche)
Körper immer auch durch Fotografien beziehungsweise Bilder konstruiert werden. Die grundsätzliche künstlerische Untersuchung des Körpers als geschlechtliche Konstruktion in Bildern war freilich keine Erfindung Coplans, sondern
basiert auf den Errungenschaften einer der wesentlichsten Bewegungen der
zweiten Hälfte des 20. Jahrhunderts: dem Feminismus.

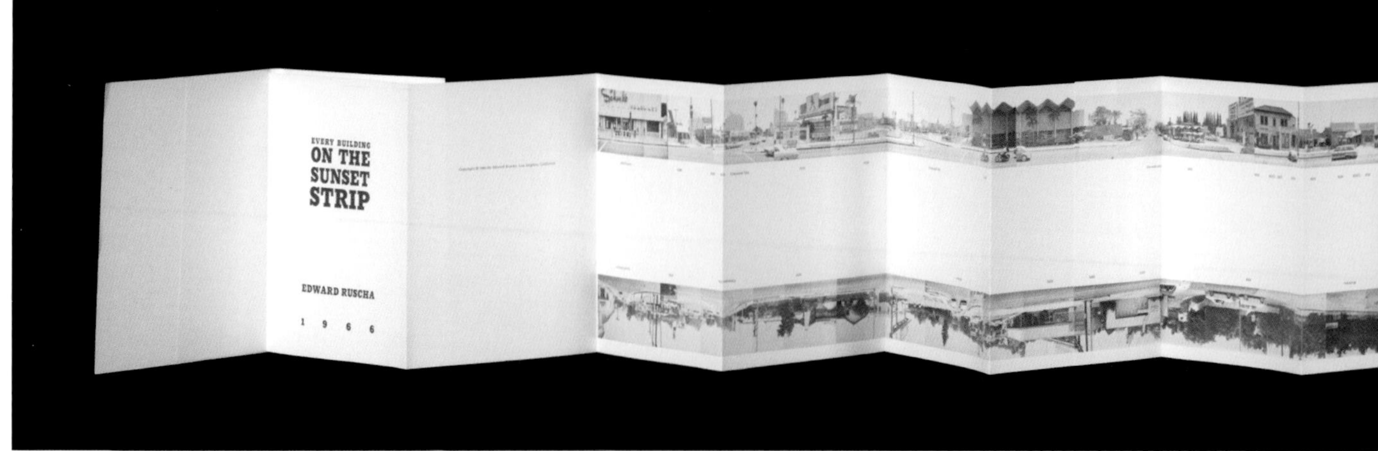

Abb. Fig. 8   Ed Ruscha, *Every Building on the Sunset Strip,* 1966

The precision with which Coplans visually fragments the individual body parts, as well as the staging process already outlined above, make clear that the photographer conceives his self-representation explicitly as an image. This situation, as banal as it might seem, is crucial insofar as the photographs of the artists of Body Art often place the focus on the object, or rather the body, but not to the same extent on the image. The staged body plays the primary role; the image itself is subordinated to this content. In Coplans's works, by contrast, photos, due to the artist's conceptual approach, are not only reflected in their mediality; the manner of the body's representation is also treated as a theme. In other words, the photographs not only show a body, but also already reflect this as a representation, and thereby in its status as an image. This strategy becomes particularly visible when Coplans adopts poses that refer to classical representations found in art history. For example, in a horizontal-format photo split into thee parts he assumes a horizontal lying position in which he covers his sex with one of his hands (fig. 10). This pose clearly evokes associations with works of classical art history such as Giorgione's *Venus.* The adoption of a clearly female-connoted pose by a male body creates a semantic contradiction between the classical source image and the (re-)staging, which goes against the media construction of gender. Coplans makes clear that (gendered) bodies are always also constructed through images. The fundamental artistic investigation of the body as a gender construction in images was of course not Coplans's invention, but was based on the achievements of one of the key movements of the second half of the twentieth century: feminism.

Feminist (Visual) Strategies

Despite the heterogeneity of the works by feminist artists from the nineteen-fifties on, as well as the complexity of their content, these works address not only the female body per se, but always also expressly its visual representation.[15] The female body is the medium through which a wide variety of reflections on its socio-cultural meaning as well as on its integration into the prevailing social norms can be made transparent. Slogans such as "The Private Is Political" or "Your Body Is a Battleground" illustrate the political impetus with which the female body is enlisted for the visual examination of identity, gender, social affiliation, and social roles. It was

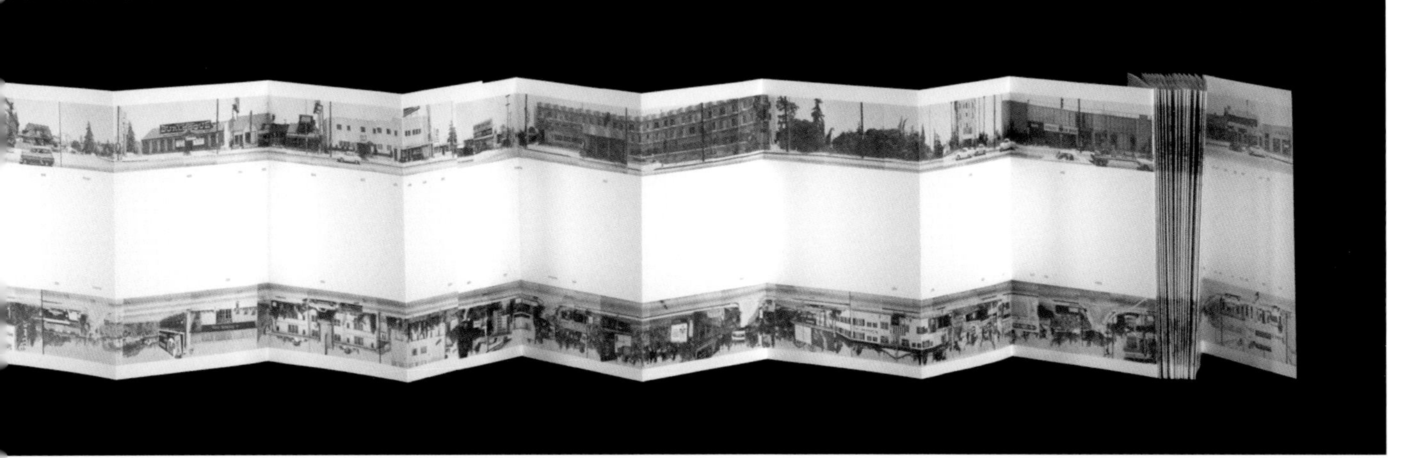

Feministische (Bild)Strategien

So heterogen sich die Werke von feministischen Künstlerinnen ab den 1950er-Jahren präsentieren und so vielschichtig ihre Inhalte sind, setzen sich ihre Arbeiten nicht nur mit dem weiblichen Körper per se, sondern immer auch dezidiert mit dessen bildlicher Repräsentation auseinander.[15] Der weibliche Körper ist hierbei das Medium, an dem sich sowohl verschiedenste Überlegungen zu seiner soziokulturellen Bedeutung sowie zu seiner Einbindung in bestehende gesellschaftliche Normen transparent machen lassen. Slogans wie »The private is political« oder »Your body is a battleground« verdeutlichen den politischen Impetus, mit dem der weibliche Körper zur visuellen Hinterfragung von Identität, Geschlecht, sozialer Zugehörigkeit und gesellschaftlicher Rolle herangezogen wird. Es ist eine logische Schlussfolgerung, dass sich feministische Positionen hierbei auch mit Darstellungen von Weiblichkeit auseinandersetzen, tritt darin doch der Widerspruch zwischen Selbstwahrnehmung und vorwiegend männlich dominierter Fremdwahrnehmung besonders deutlich zutage. Bilder der klassischen Kunstgeschichte werden hierbei genauso einer künstlerischen Untersuchung unterzogen wie Abbildungen in alltäglichen Massenmedien. In der 1974 entstandenen Videoarbeit *Gestures* thematisiert Hannah Wilke eben diese Aspekte (Kat. 2). Der Vergleich ihrer Arbeit zu Naumans *Pulling Mouth* und *Studies for Holograms* liegt nahe, beschäftigen sich beide Werke doch gleichermaßen mit dem Ausdruckspotenzial des Gesichts. In oftmals repetitiven Handlungen zupft, zieht, reibt und schlägt Wilke mit ihren Händen ihr Gesicht, wodurch sie verschiedenste Möglichkeiten menschlichen Ausdrucks durchdekliniert. Mit den Gebärden und Mimiken, die Wilke hierbei vollführt, spielt sie typisch weiblich konnotierte Gesten durch, die sie jedoch oftmals als von außen aufgezwungen und nicht als selbst gegeben schildert. So verdeutlicht die Aggressivität, mit der Wilke ihr Gesicht zu bestimmten Ausdrucksformen zwingt, eine körperliche Disziplinierung, die dezidiert fremdbestimmt ist. Hannah Wilkes Selbstinszenierung zeigt damit einen weiblichen Körper, der nicht zwingend ihr eigener ist, sondern der geformt wird. Die Visualisierung einer solchen Differenz kann gleichzeitig als Kommentar über Bilder und Medien gelesen werden, die diese genormten Darstellungen von Weiblichkeit erst konstruieren. Dieser Aspekt stellt den wesentlichsten Unterschied zu Naumans Videoarbeit dar, der an einem solchen Bruch nicht interessiert ist. Verkörpern Naumans Arbeiten in erster Linie Erweiterungen künstlerischer

therefore only a matter of consequence for feminist positions to also address representations of femininity, since it is here that the contradiction between self-perception and a predominantly male outside perception comes to light especially clearly. In this context, the works of classical art history are of as much interest as images from everyday mass media. In her video work *Gestures* from 1974, Hannah Wilke addresses precisely this aspect (cat. 2). Obvious comparisons for Wilke's work are Nauman's *Pulling Mouth* and *Studies for Holograms*, since both works deal in a similar way with the expressive potential of the face. In often repetitive actions Wilke plucks, pulls, rubs, and slaps her face with her hands, whereby she runs through a range of possibilities of human expression. With the gestures and expressions that Wilke executes here, she acts out a typically female-connoted body language, which she often portrays as being imposed from outside and not as self-given. Accordingly, the aggressiveness with which Wilke forces her face to take on certain expressions highlights a physical disciplining of the body that is expressly determined from outside. Hannah Wilke's self-staging shows a female body that is not strictly her own but, rather, is formed. The visualization of such a difference can also be read as a commentary on the images and media that initially construct these standardized representations of femininity. This aspect represents the most essential difference to Nauman's video work, which is not interested in such a split. If Nauman's works primarily embody extensions of artistic norms, Wilke's examination of the representation of femininity is intended as a socio-political protest from the outset.[16]

In the early nineteen-eighties, when Coplans made his first photos, the existential feminism of the early sixties had already become transformed into a discursive and media-reflexive strategy that was equally influential for male artists. Urs Lüthi, Jürgen Klauke, and Lucas Samaras are a few of the prominent artists who, in the tradition of feminism, have used self-staging to address representations of male gender roles.[17] Here, reenactments and repetitions of female-connoted signs draw attention to a new image of masculinity, whose normativity had long become fractured.[18] Reflections on male identity, which performatively constructs the subject through repetitions and the adoption of social concepts, not only form the content of such artistic investigations; they are also at the source of a series of "masculinities studies," which in recent years have begun to a flourish in a broad range of publications.[19] This is important to mention at this point insofar as at the end of the seventies, when John Coplans produced his first self-representations, reflections on masculinity were being theoretically formulated for the first time.[20] As different as the approaches of individual theorists have been, there is a general consensus that masculinity, like femininity, is not stable and unchanging, but fraught with tensions and contradictions.

Normen, so ist Wilkes Auseinandersetzung mit der Darstellung von Weiblichkeit von vornherein als gesellschaftspolitischer Protest intendiert.[16]

In den frühen 1980er-Jahren, als Coplans seine ersten Fotos aufnahm, hatte sich der existenzielle Feminismus der frühen Sechzigerjahre bereits zu einer diskursiven und medienreflexiven Strategie gewandelt, die männliche Künstler gleichermaßen beeinflusste. Urs Lüthi, Jürgen Klauke und Lucas Samaras gehören zu jenen bekannten Künstlern, die sich in der Tradition des Feminismus anhand von Selbstinszenierungen mit der Darstellung männlicher Rollenbilder auseinandersetzten.[17] »Reenactments« und Wiederholungen von weiblich konnotierten Zeichen verdeutlichen hier ein neues Männlichkeitsbild, dessen Normativität längst brüchig geworden war.[18] Überlegungen zur männlichen Identität, die das Subjekt durch Wiederholungen und Übernahmen gesellschaftlicher Konzepte performativ konstruiert, ist nicht nur Inhalt künstlerischer Auseinandersetzungen, sondern auch Thema einer Reihe von »masculinities studies«, die in den letzten Jahren in einer Vielzahl von Publikationen eine theoretische Hochblüte erlebten.[19] Dies ist an dieser Stelle insofern wichtig, als Ende der Siebzigerjahre, als John Coplans seine ersten Selbstdarstellungen anfertigte, Überlegungen zur Männlichkeit erstmals theoretisch formuliert wurden.[20] So unterschiedlich die Zugänge einzelner Theoretiker sind, herrscht dennoch die grundsätzliche Übereinkunft, dass Männlichkeit ebenso wie Weiblichkeit keine stabile und unveränderliche Instanz darstellt, sondern widersprüchlich und spannungsreich konstruiert wird.

Dem Performance-Künstler Vito Acconci ist in diesem Zusammenhang eine Vorreiterrolle zuzurechnen, der als einer der ersten Body-Art-Künstler solche Konstruktionen von Männlichkeit hinterfragt hat.[21] In seinen berühmten Videoperformances wie *Openings* (1970) oder *Conversion* (1971) wird dies deutlich sichtbar (Kat. 3). So zupft er sich beispielsweise in *Openings* vor laufender Kamera seine Körperbehaarung aus, was zu einer visuellen Transformation von einem Männerkörper zu einem weiblichen (unbehaarten) Körper führt. Die Darstellung von Männlichkeit (und Weiblichkeit) wird als durch visuelle Zeichen konstruiert vorgeführt, bei der der Körper der Träger eben dieser Zeichen ist. Die imaginäre Verwandlung über die Geschlechtergrenzen hinweg reformuliert ein Bild von Männlichkeit, indem es seine klassische Darstellung dekonstruiert.

Coplans, der als Chefredakteur von *Artforum* die feministische Auseinandersetzung mit normierten Rollenbildern unmittelbar verfolgte,[22] veranschaulicht in seinen Fotografien eine ähnliche Strategie wie seine erwähnten männlichen Kollegen, geht aber aufgrund seines bereits erklärten konzeptuellen Zugangs und seinen theoretischen Überlegungen weit über diese hinaus. Coplans nimmt für seine Fotografien nicht nur eine Vielzahl an weiblich konnotierten Posen ein, sondern presst seinen Körper auch zu Formen, die explizit an weibliche Geschlechtsteile erinnern (Abb. 2). Die Integration solcher normalerweise als weiblich verstandenen Zeichen in einen Männerkörper veranschaulicht einen semantischen Widerspruch. In diesem Kontext muss auch die Darstellung des

In this connection, the performance artist Vito Acconci—who, as one of the first Body Art artists, challenged such constructions of masculinity—should be seen as a pioneer.[21] This becomes clear in his famous video performances such as *Openings* (1970) or *Conversion* (1971) (cat. 3). In *Openings* for example, Acconci plucked out his body hair in front of a running camera, leading to a visual transformation from his conspicuously male body to a female (hairless) body. In this work, the representation of masculinity (and femininity) is presented as constructed by visual signs, whereby the body is the bearer of precisely these signs. The imaginary transformation beyond the gender boundaries reformulates the image of masculinity by deconstructing its classical representation.

Coplans, who as editor-in-chief of *Artforum* directly followed the feminist critique of standardized gender roles,[22] demonstrates in his photographs a strategy similar to that of his male colleagues mentioned above. However, due to his conceptual approach and his theoretical reflections, he goes much further. For his photographs Coplans not only assumed a multitude of female-connoted poses, but also pressed his body into forms that explicitly recall female genitalia (fig. 2). The integration of such signs that are normally understood as female into a male body creates a semantic contradiction. Also to be seen in this context is the representation of the body without a head or face and thus without individuality. Such a staging of the body without a head was normally used for the representation of female nudes.[23] With the adoption of such female-connoted visual languages, Coplans makes clear that the male body is also a (media) construct.

Body Language

While Acconci, for the visualization of media constructions of the body, makes use of body hair designated as male sign, Coplans uses poses and gestures to challenge simplistic depictions of masculinity. His absurd and comic poses ironize and parody an ideal representation of masculinity.[24] That Coplans's work also concentrates on the depiction of gestures seems only logical, since it is precisely through gesture that masculinity is constructed. Gestures and poses are acquired culturally and function both sociologically and linguistically as a means of communication that is always encoded.[25] Standardized poses and gestures can be read and interpreted as visual signs, and precisely in this way stabilize (preformed and repeated) concepts of masculinity.

Coplans opposes such a norm by visualizing bodies that cannot be integrated into a preformed schema. This can be seen in a concrete way in his pictures of his hands. In extreme close-ups the hands become abstract visual forms that depict or convey nothing other than themselves. It is essential to see this aspect in connection with language. Coplans him-

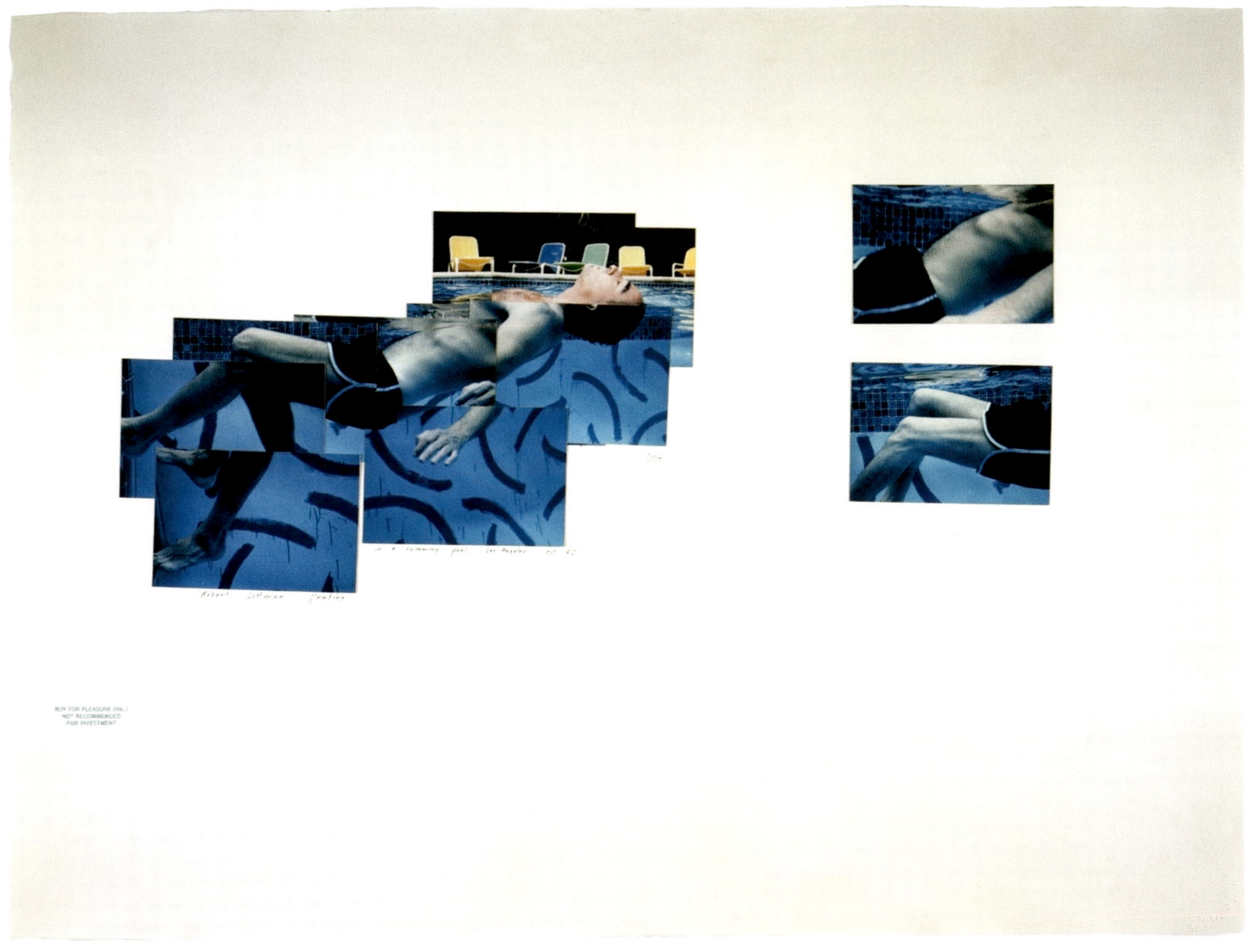

Abb. Fig. 9   David Hockney, *Robert Littman Floating in My Pool, Oct. 1982,* fotografische Collage photographic collage

Körpers ohne Kopf beziehungsweise Gesicht und damit ohne Individualität gesehen werden. Eine solche Inszenierung des Körpers ohne Kopf wurde normalerweise für die Darstellung weiblicher Akte verwendet.[23] Mit der Übernahme solcher weiblich konnotierter Bildsprachen verdeutlicht Coplans somit auch den männlichen Körper als (medial) konstruiert.

»Body language«

Während sich Acconci zur Visualisierung medialer Körperkonstruktionen des als männlich definierten Zeichens der Körperbehaarung bedient, nutzt Coplans Posen und Gesten, um vereinfachende Darstellungen von Männlichkeit zu hinterfragen. Absurd-komische Posen ironisieren und parodieren so eine ideale Darstellung von Männlichkeit.[24] Dass sich Coplans hierfür auch auf die Wiedergabe von Gesten konzentriert, erscheint als logische Schlussfolgerung, wird doch Männlichkeit über eben diese konstruiert. Gesten wie auch Posen werden kulturell erlernt und funktionieren gleichermaßen soziologisch wie auch linguistisch als Kommunikationsmittel, die immer codiert sind.[25] Normierte Posen und Gesten können als visuelle Zeichen gelesen und interpretiert werden und stabilisieren eben dadurch (vorgeformte und wiederholte) Konzepte von Männlichkeit.

Coplans widersetzt sich einer solchen Norm, indem er Körper visualisiert, die in kein passendes Schema eingeordnet werden können. Konkret verdeutlichen dies Fotos von seinen Händen. In extremen Close-ups werden sie zu

self has emphasized that his intention with these pictures was not to create linguistic signs or even a sign language, but to produce photos that could only be perceived visually, which is to say, could not be read.[26] For Coplans, this issue should be understood in distinction to photographs that often function in a narrative way, or even contain written text.[27] In this connection, Coplans himself has mentioned works by the photographer Duane Michals. Against the background of narratively informed images, however, the series *You You* (1974) by Ketty La Rocca, who, like Coplans, investigates gender-specific themes, provides a more interesting context (cat. 17). In this series Ketty La Rocca runs through a broad range of gestures by means of a hand. From the clenched fist to the open palm, different types of gesture are presented. The narrative aspect arises in these photos not only through the fact that the gestures can in part be read (like the fist in the sense of an aggressive protest), but also through the fact that they are presented between two additional (male) hands, whose position constantly remains the same. In her work La Rocca makes use of the method of pictorial series, which presents the motifs as a temporal development while also underscoring the narrative component. With each new gesture between the hands, the context of the individual pictures changes. La Rocca thereby implies a set of relationships between two people, or, more specifically, between a woman and man, which is portrayed as ranging from threatening to aggressive. The gestures serve the visualization of interpersonal communication, which the artist wanted to be understood as independent of language.[28] While, through language, communication can be regulated and controlled, inherent to body language in her opinion is an immediacy that makes the non-verbalizable transparent and visible.[29] Body language thus visualizes aspects of interpersonal relations that are often hidden by being regulated by verbal language, which only allows certain meanings to appear. Gestural signs and their functions make social structures and relations transparent that cannot otherwise be recognized. La Rocca combines this kind of sign language in with written words; she thus adds the personal pronoun "you" to the image. The linguistic reference to the other exemplifies a female self-understanding that, as with Wilke, is determined from outside. The "I" is always visualized as the self that is defined through the other. In La Rocca's work the artist's own (female) body is the support in which the (male) other in the truest sense of the word inscribes himself.

Although Coplans likewise investigates gender identity through language and visual body signs, his work is conceived differently from that of La Rocca. Unlike the Italian artist, Coplans does not use legible gestures, but rather, as already described, unintelligible poses and gestures. The resulting emphasis on the purely visual, before any linguistic formulation, recalls the works of Art Informel in which immediate visual sensation had priority

abstrakten visuellen Gebilden, die nichts zeigen oder vermitteln außer sich selbst. Es ist essenziell, diesen Aspekt in Zusammenhang mit Sprache zu sehen. So hat Coplans selbst betont, dass er mit diesen Bildern keinesfalls linguistische Zeichen oder gar eine Zeichensprache wiedergeben wolle, sondern vielmehr versuche, Fotos zu produzieren, die nur visuell wahrgenommen, nicht aber gelesen werden können.[26] Diesen Sachverhalt wollte er im Unterschied zu Fotografien verstanden wissen, die oftmals narrativ funktionieren oder mit tatsächlich geschriebenem Text versehen sind.[27] Coplans selbst nennt in diesem Zusammenhang Werke des Fotografen Duane Michals. Die Serie *You You* (1974) von Ketty La Rocca eröffnet vor dem Hintergrund erzählerischer Bildwirklichkeiten jedoch einen interessanteren Kontext, untersucht sie doch wie Coplans geschlechtsspezifische Themen (Kat. 17). In dieser Serie dekliniert Ketty La Rocca mittels einer Hand eine Reihe verschiedenster Gesten durch. Von der geballten Faust bis zur offenen Handfläche werden unterschiedliche Ausdrucksweisen von Gesten vorgeführt. Der erzählerische Aspekt ergibt sich bei diesen Fotos nicht nur dadurch, dass die Gesten ansatzweise linguistisch lesbar sind (wie die Faust im Sinne eines aggressiven Protests), sondern dadurch, dass sie zwischen zwei weiteren (männlichen) Händen präsentiert werden, deren Haltung jedoch fortwährend gleichbleibt. La Rocca bedient sich in ihrer Arbeit des Mittels der Bildserie, welche die Motive als zeitlich fortlaufende Veränderung präsentiert und darüber hinaus die erzählerische Komponente unterstreicht. Durch die jeweils unterschiedliche Geste zwischen den Händen ändert sich der jeweilige inhaltliche Kontext der Einzelbilder. La Rocca deutet damit ein Beziehungsgefüge zwischen zwei Menschen beziehungsweise Frau und Mann an, das von bedrohlich bis aggressiv geschildert wird. Die Gesten dienen der Visualisierung zwischenmenschlicher Kommunikation, welche die Künstlerin als unabhängig von Sprache verstanden wissen wollte.[28] Während Kommunikation durch Sprache reguliert und kontrolliert werden kann, haftet der Körpersprache ihrer Meinung nach ein unmittelbareres Moment an, das Nonverbalisierbares transparent und sichtbar macht.[29] Körpersprache visualisiert dementsprechend Inhalte zwischenmenschlicher Beziehungen, die durch die inhaltliche Regulierung der Sprache oftmals verdeckt werden. Gestische Zeichen und deren Funktion machen soziale Strukturen und Verhältnisse transparent, die ansonsten nicht erkennbar sind. Diese Art der Zeichensprache wird bei La Rocca mit geschriebenen Wörtern kombiniert, so fügt sie das Personalpronomen »you« dem Bild hinzu. Der linguistische Verweis auf den Anderen verdeutlicht damit ein weibliches Selbstverständnis, das wie bei Wilke fremdbestimmt ist. Das Ich wird immer auch als das durch das Andere definierte Selbst visualisiert. Der eigene (weibliche) Körper ist bei La Rocca der Träger, in dem sich der (männliche) Andere im wahrsten Sinne des Wortes einschreibt.

    Coplans untersucht geschlechtliche Identität zwar ebenfalls durch Sprache und visuelle Körperzeichen, konzipiert seine Werke jedoch anders als La Rocca.

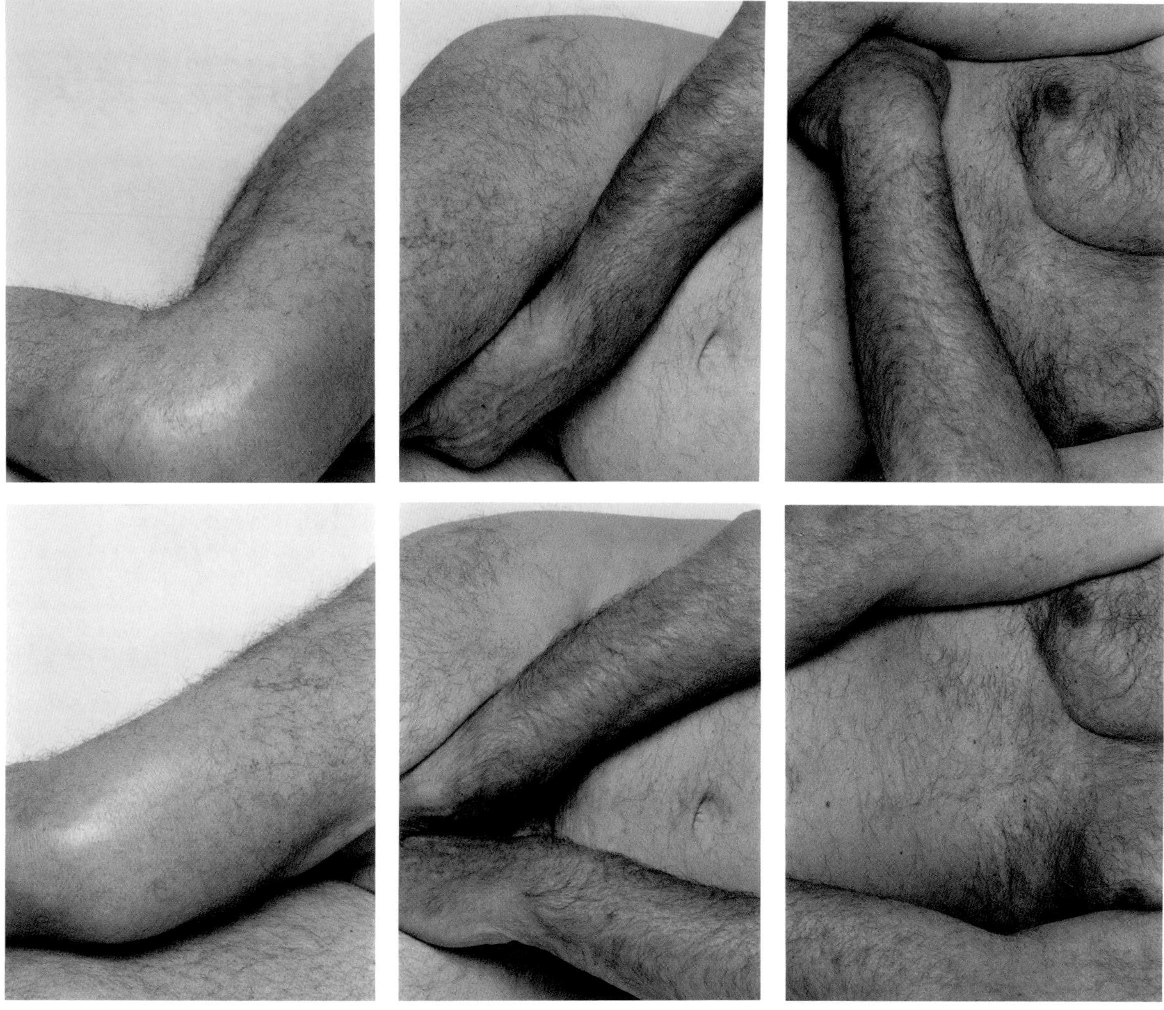

Abb. Fig. 10   John Coplans, *Reclining Figures, No. 1,* 1996

over any textualization. Through the negation of a photographic narrativity,
Coplans is able to concentrate on the body's visual expressive potential.
This should be seen, however, in connection with the construction of a
standardized masculinity. As has already been mentioned, visual and linguistic signs represent content and sense, and thereby stabilize standardized gender images. When Coplans adopted poses and gestures that
eluded linguistic legibility, he brought the deconstruction of an image of
masculinity rigorously to its conclusion. Where the images reject con-
sciously selected gender roles and avoid both visual and linguistic catego-
rization, Coplans destroys a standardized image of masculinity, which he
situates in his photographs outside (visual) culture and language.

Sculptural Body Fragments

This strategy of deconstruction is not only conveyed through the represented body, but equally through the aforementioned conceptual stylistic
device of fragmentation with which Coplans divides his body visually into
separate parts that are then recombined. This formal aspect should be
reemphasized here, since it shows how the represented body and the images that record it are structurally linked. In other words, the dissolution
of the standardized image of masculinity as content finds its formal response in the body's fragmentation into a number of pictorial details.

Im Unterschied zu der italienischen Künstlerin nutzt der Fotograf nicht wie bereits beschrieben lesbare Gesten, sondern im Gegensatz dazu unverständliche Posen und Gesten. Die so erreichte Betonung des rein Visuellen vor jeder sprachlichen beziehungsweise linguistischen Formulierung erinnert an die Kunstströmung des Informels, bei welcher die unmittelbare visuelle Empfindung Priorität vor jeder inhaltlichen Textualisierung hat. Durch die Verneinung einer fotografischen Narrativität kann sich Coplans auf visuelle Ausdruckspotenziale des Körpers konzentrieren. Dies muss jedoch in Zusammenhang mit der Konstruktion einer normierten Männlichkeit gesehen werden. Es wurde bereits bemerkt, dass visuelle und sprachliche Zeichen Inhalt und Sinn repräsentieren und dadurch normierte Geschlechterbilder stabilisieren. Wenn Coplans nun Posen und Gesten einnimmt, die sich einer sprachlichen Lesbarkeit entziehen, führt er die Dekonstruktion eines Männlichkeitsbildes konsequent an ihr Ende. Denn dort, wo sich die Bilder von bewusst gewählten Vorbildern abwenden und sich weder visuell noch sprachlich kategorisieren lassen, zerstört Coplans ein normiertes Männerbild, das er in seinen Fotografien außerhalb von (visueller) Kultur und Sprache verortet.

Skulpturale Körperfragmente

Diese Strategie der Dekonstruktion wird nicht nur durch den dargestellten Körper vermittelt, sondern gleichermaßen durch das bereits angesprochene konzeptuelle Stilmittel der Fragmentierung, bei der Coplans seinen Körper in visuelle Einzelteile zerlegt, die wieder kombiniert werden. Dieser formale Aspekt muss an dieser Stelle nochmals betont werden, belegt er doch, dass der dargestellte Körper und die Bilder, die ihn fassen, strukturell miteinander verbunden sind. Anders gesagt: Die inhaltliche Auflösung des normierten Männerbildes findet seine formale Antwort in der Fragmentierung des Körpers durch unterschiedliche Bildausschnitte. Silvia Eiblmayr hat dieses Konzept, bei dem Geschlechtlichkeit als (Ab)Bild durch die Selbstinszenierung mitreflektiert wird, als eigentliches Merkmal feministischer Künstlerinnen herausgearbeitet.[30] Für die Autorin wird hierbei der Bildkörper metaphorisch mit dem tatsächlichen (weiblichen) Körper gleichgesetzt.[31] Richtet sich der Protest feministischer Künstlerinnen nun gegen weibliche Rollenbilder, betrifft dies nicht nur den Inhalt, sondern auch das Material des Bildes. Die Dekonstruktion weiblicher Körper findet so ihre formale Antwort in der tatsächlichen Zerstörung des Bild(material)es. In diesem Zusammenhang muss auch die Bildsprache der Schweizer Künstlerin Hannah Villiger verstanden werden. In ihren Fotoarbeiten zerlegt Villiger wie Coplans ihren einheitlichen Körper durch die visuelle Fragmentierung in Einzelbilder (Kat. 14, 15). Im Unterschied zu Coplans arbeitet Villiger jedoch nicht mithilfe einer Assistentin, sondern fotografiert sich mit einer Polaroidkamera, die sie im ausgestreckten Arm hält. Der Blick durch die Kamera auf den eigenen Körper wird bei Coplans genau kontrolliert, während Villiger ihre Bilder rein durch die Geste, mit der sie ihre Kamera auf sich selbst

Silvia Eiblmayr sees this concept, in which gender as image or representation is reflected alongside through the self-staging, as the fundamental characteristic of feminist artists.[30] For the author the pictorial body is metaphorically equated with the actual (female) body.[31] If the protest of feminist artists is directed against female gender roles, this is not only a matter of content, but also concerns the image's materiality. Hence, the deconstruction of the female body finds its formal response in the actual destruction of the pictorial (material). The pictorial language of the Swiss artist Hannah Villiger should also be seen in this connection. In her photographic works, Villiger, like Coplans, disassembles her unified body through visual fragmentation into single images (cat. 14, 15). Unlike Coplans, however, Villiger does not work with the help of an assistant, but photographs herself with a Polaroid camera that she holds in her outstretched hand. While in Coplans's work the view through the camera onto the body is precisely controlled, Villiger produces her pictures purely through the gesture with which she points her camera at herself. The various parts are arranged by the artist in such a way that they create completely new forms, allowing her body, in contrast to Coplans's body, to become only partially recognizable. The deconstruction of the representation of the female body as content thus finds its formal response in the actual destruction of a unified pictorial body.[32]

In both Coplans's and Villiger's work the abstraction that experiences the body as a visual image is often interpreted with regard to its sculptural qualities.[33] This comparison is suggestive: the three-dimensional body, through its transformation into a temporally fixed and two-dimensional image acquires a static quality that recalls immobile sculptures. Not only the pose, but also the visual emphasis on plasticity and the body's treatment as raw material, supports this comparison. Furthermore, this view is not negated by the fact that these pictures often only show body fragments. Indeed for Coplans the *Belvedere Torso* was as much a frame of reference as photographs of sculptures by Constantin Brancusi.[34] In addition, the body's precise lighting and the black-and-white film material used by Coplans evoke sculptural surface qualities: the body seems to bear traces of a chisel.

As much as such a pictorial form corresponds to a classical tradition, the representation of the old, wrinkled, and transient body directs itself all the more clearly against a classical rendering. Coplans himself has described this artistic approach as a rejection of an idealized depiction of the male body, as typified for example in the photographs of Robert Mapplethorpe.[35] In his photos Mapplethorpe made use of a pictorial language that combines a classical body ideal with sculptural qualities (cat. 18–20). Flawless and perfect, fragmented male bodies are presented that seem to be modeled from light and shadow. In principle, such a pictorial language

richtet, anfertigt. Die Einzelteile werden von der Künstlerin so arrangiert, dass sie völlig neue Formen bilden, welche ihren Körper im Gegensatz zu Coplans' Körper nur noch andeutungsweise erkennen lassen. Die inhaltliche Dekonstruktion der Darstellung des weiblichen Körpers findet so ihre formale Antwort in der tatsächlichen Zerstörung eines einheitlichen Bildkörpers.[32]

Die Abstraktion, welche der Körper als visuelles Bild erfährt, wurde bei Coplans und Villiger oftmals im Hinblick auf ihre skulpturalen Qualitäten interpretiert.[33] Dieser Vergleich liegt nahe: So bekommt der dreidimensionale Körper durch seine Transformation in ein zeitlich fixiertes und zweidimensionales Bild ein statisches Moment, das an unbewegliche Skulpturen erinnert. Nicht nur die Pose, sondern auch die visuelle Betonung der Plastizität sowie die Bearbeitung des Körpers als wäre er bloßes Material bestätigen diesen Vergleich. Dass oftmals nur Körperfragmente in den Bildern zu sehen sind, tut dieser Überlegung keinen Abbruch. Im Gegenteil: Der Torso vom Belvedere wurde für Coplans ebenso als Bezugsrahmen herangezogen wie Fotografien der Skulpturen von Constantin Brancusi.[34] Die präzise Beleuchtung des Körpers und das schwarzweiße Filmmaterial, mit dem Coplans arbeitet, evozieren darüber hinaus skulpturale Oberflächenqualitäten. Der Körper erscheint gemeißelt.

So sehr eine solche Bildform einer klassischen Tradition entspricht, so deutlich richtet sich die Darstellung des alten, faltigen und vergänglichen Körpers gegen seine klassische Wiedergabe. Coplans selbst hat diesen künstlerischen Zugang als Abkehr einer idealisierten Wiedergabe von Männerkörpern beschrieben, wie sie beispielsweise Fotografien von Robert Mapplethorpe exemplifizieren.[35] Mapplethorpe hat in seinen Fotos eine Bildsprache umgesetzt, die ein klassizistisches Körperideal mit skulpturalen Qualitäten verbindet (Kat. 18–20). Makellos und perfekt werden fragmentierte Männerkörper dargeboten, die durch Licht und Schatten modelliert scheinen. Eine solche Bildsprache war prinzipiell nicht neu und lässt sich bereits bei so berühmten Vorläufern wie Edward Weston oder George Platt Lynes finden, die die skulpturale Visualisierung männlicher Körper ebenfalls mit einer fragmentarischen Bildsprache zu verbinden wussten. Radikal anders an Mapplethorpes Fotos war jedoch die Deutlichkeit und Unmittelbarkeit, mit der Mapplethorpe seine vorwiegend afroamerikanischen Modelle als (homo)sexuell begehrbare Körper präsentierte.[36] Die klassische Formensprache stellt hierbei einen kunsthistorischen Anknüpfungspunkt dar, der die oftmals expliziten Darstellungen legitimierte. Mapplethorpe verschaffte damit einer schwulen Subkultur Sichtbarkeit, die im Zuge von Bürgerrechtsbewegungen immer deutlicher erkennbar wurde. Die Frage, ob seine Bilder nur ein privates sexuelles Begehren verkörpern oder von vorneherein auch politisch intendiert waren, sei dahingestellt; die kulturellen Strukturen, in welchen Mapplethorpe arbeitete, machten diese Fotos jedenfalls zu einem kontroversen Politikum, das die politische Rechte bekanntlich zur Einstellung finanzieller Unterstützung für kulturelle Projekte bewegte. Den Fotos hat dieser Umstand nicht geschadet: Bis heute haftet Mapplethorpes Bildern

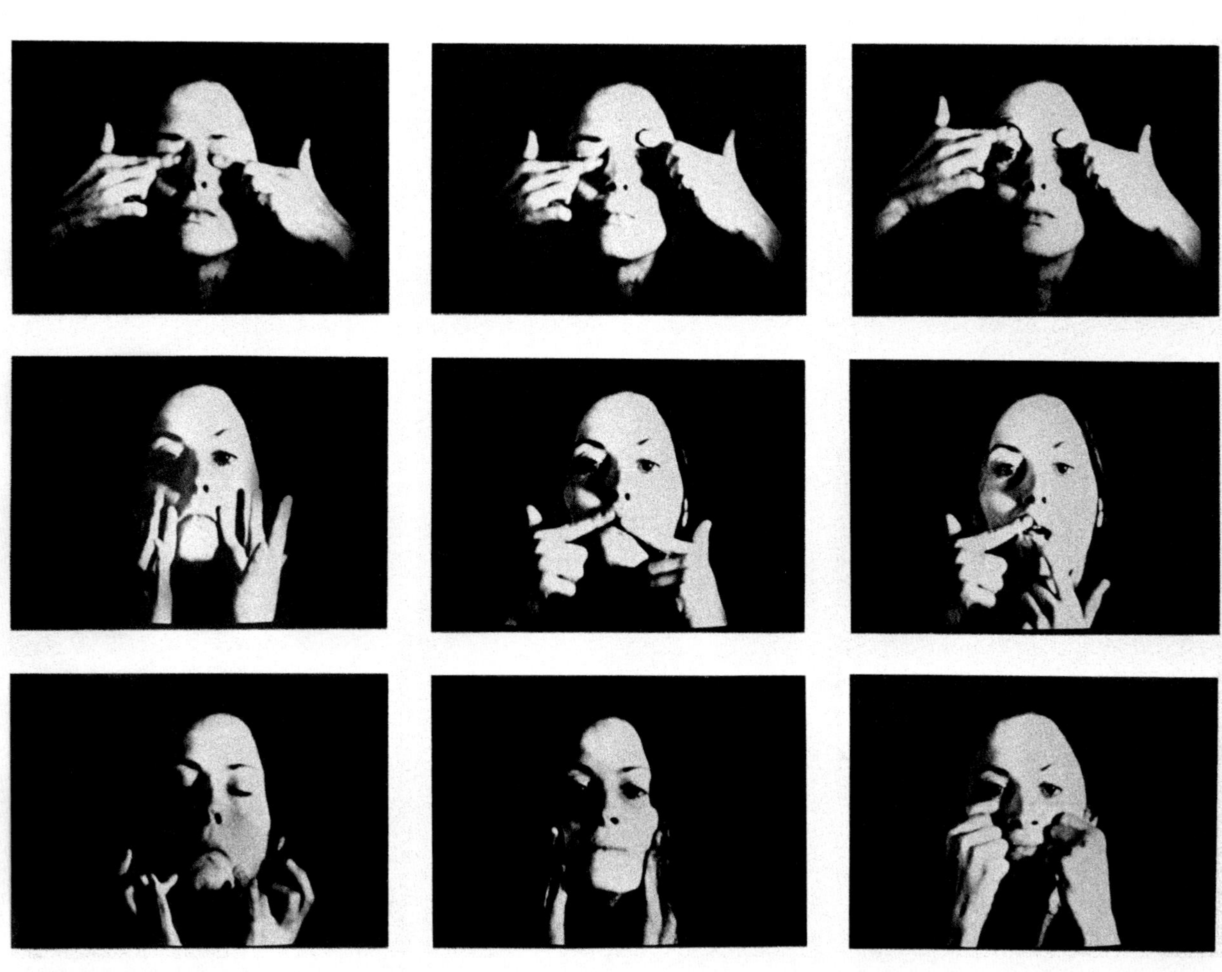

2 Hannah Wilke, *Gestures*, 1974–1976

was not new; indeed it can already be found in the works of such famous predecessors as Edward Weston or George Platt Lynes, who likewise knew how to combine a sculptural visualization of male bodes with a fragmentary pictorial language. What set Mapplethorpe's photos radically apart was the clarity and immediacy with which he presented his predominantly African-American models as (homo)sexually desirable bodies.[36] At the same time, the classical formal language represents an art-historical reference that legitimates the frequently explicit representations. In this way Mapplethorpe obtained visibility for a gay subculture, which became ever more clearly recognizable in the course of the civil rights movements. Whether his pictures merely embody a private sexual desire or were intended as political from the outset remains an open question; at all events, the cultural structures in which Mapplethorpe worked gave these photos a political charge that famously moved the political right to suspend financial support for cultural projects. This circumstance did no harm to the photos, however: up to today, due to his motifs, Mapplethorpe's pictures still contain an element of resistance—even if for some time now his works are no longer found in gay subculture but in the lofty art establishment.

As much as Mapplethorpe's photos are inscribed with a political gesture, they still conform to a society in which youth and beauty embody an ideal, while the representation of old age is excluded. It was particularly against this aspect that Coplans's critique was directed:

> The principal thing is the question of how our culture views age: that old is ugly. Take a photographer like Robert Mapplethorpe. Every single photograph of his is about classical notions of beauty, of young beautiful black men, young beautiful gay women. He selects subjects who are essentially interesting and good-looking and extremely physical. I can't stand them. They grate my teeth.[37]

Although the artists of Body Art recognized gender and race as signs of social difference, age—an equally crucial aspect for social belonging—was nevertheless largely omitted.[38] Against this background, Coplans's photographs bear similarities with certain sculptures by Auguste Rodin.[39] As early as 1889 Rodin famously caused a scandal by representing the writer Victor Hugo not as young and idealized, but as old, and in this sense "realistic." That this theme has subsequently lost none of its force is demonstrated by the photos of John Coplans. In a society in which young flawless bodies represent the epitome of a beauty ideal, and age is largely repudiated or considered a physical "defect" that can be corrected at any time with plastic surgery, Coplans's photos have become mirrors that clearly show the viewer what the latter does not want to see. Accordingly, the direct representation of old age in Coplans's photos still appears as a

aufgrund seiner Motive ein widerständiges Element an – auch wenn seine
Arbeiten freilich längst nicht mehr in der schwulen Subkultur, sondern im hohen
Kunstbetrieb zu finden sind.

So sehr Mapplethorpes Fotos eine politische Geste eingeschrieben ist, so
konform gehen seine Fotos mit einer Gesellschaft, in der Jugend und Schön-
heit ein Ideal verkörpern, die Darstellung des Alters jedoch ausgeschlossen
wird. Gegen diesen Aspekt richtet sich Coplans' Kritik:

> The principal thing is the question of how our culture views age: that old is
> ugly. Take a photographer like Robert Mapplethorpe. Every single photograph
> of his is about classical notions of beauty, of young beautiful black men,
> young beautiful gay women. He selects subjects who are essentially inter-
> esting and good-looking and extremely physical. I can't stand them. They
> grate my teeth. [37]

Künstler der Body Art haben zwar Geschlecht und Rasse als Zeichen sozialer
Differenz erkannt, das Alter, ein ebenso wesentlicher Aspekt für gesellschaftliche Zugehörigkeit, wurde jedoch weitgehend ausgespart.[38] Vor diesem Hintergrund lassen Coplans' Fotografien eher Ähnlichkeiten mit Skulpturen von Auguste Rodin erkennen.[39] So sorgte Rodin bekanntlich bereits 1889 für einen
Skandal, als er den Schriftsteller Victor Hugo nicht jung und idealisiert, sondern
alt und in diesem Sinne »realistisch« darstellte. Dass dieses Thema seither nicht
an Brisanz verloren hat, bezeugen die Fotos von John Coplans. In einer Gesellschaft, in der junge und makellose Körper Inbegriffe eines Schönheitsideals
darstellen, Alter weitgehend verleugnet und als körperlicher »Defekt« angesehen
wird, der sich durch plastische Chirurgie jederzeit korrigieren lässt, werden
seine Fotos zu Spiegeln, die dem Betrachter deutlich zeigen, was dieser nicht
sehen will. Die unmittelbare Darstellung des Alters erscheint damit bis heute
als provokanter Inhalt von Coplans' Fotos. Ihre Brisanz wird durch den Umstand
verstärkt, dass sein Körper von Jahr zu Jahr beziehungsweise Serie zu Serie
faltiger, schlaffer und haariger wird. Durch die präzise und »schonungslose«
Beleuchtung der Haut werden die Spuren der Vergänglichkeit deutlich sichtbar.

Haut als Zeichen der Vergänglichkeit

Der Haut wurde von jeher ein besonderer Bezug zum Körper zugeschrieben.
Nicht nur markiert sie die Grenze zwischen dem Selbst und dem Außen, sondern sie ist auch Träger sozialer Zeichen.[40] Mit der Darstellung der faltigen
und von Pigmentflecken überzogenen Haut markiert Coplans den Körper unweigerlich als alt. Neben dieser inhaltlichen Komponente ist die Haut ein es-
senzielles formal-ästhetisches Mittel. Durch ihre präzise Beleuchtung und ihre
Wiedergabe in großen Formaten wird der Körper beinahe abstrakt. Es wurde
oben bereits darauf hingewiesen, dass feministische Künstlerinnen die Darstellung normierter Weiblichkeit vielfach durch die materielle Auflösung des

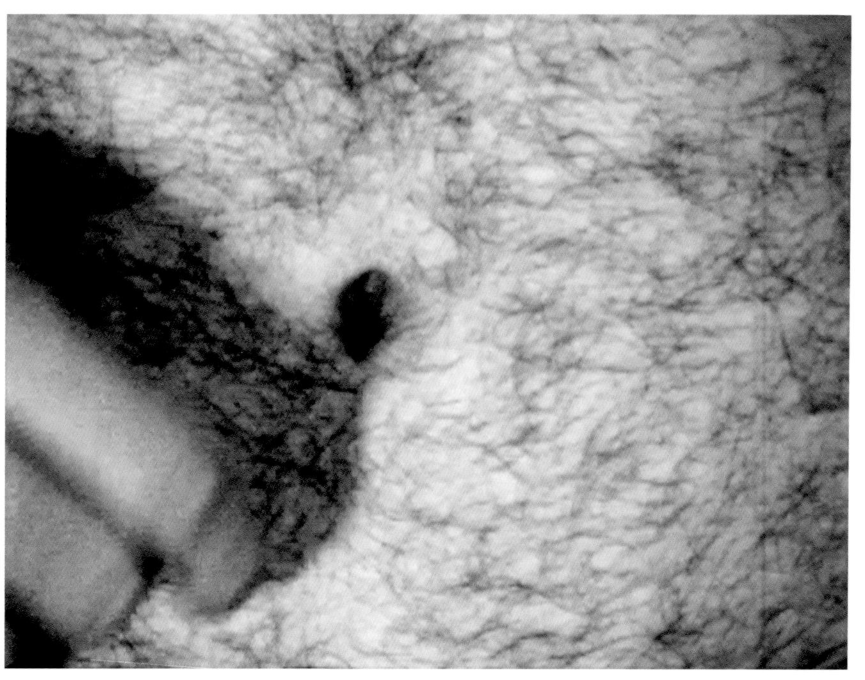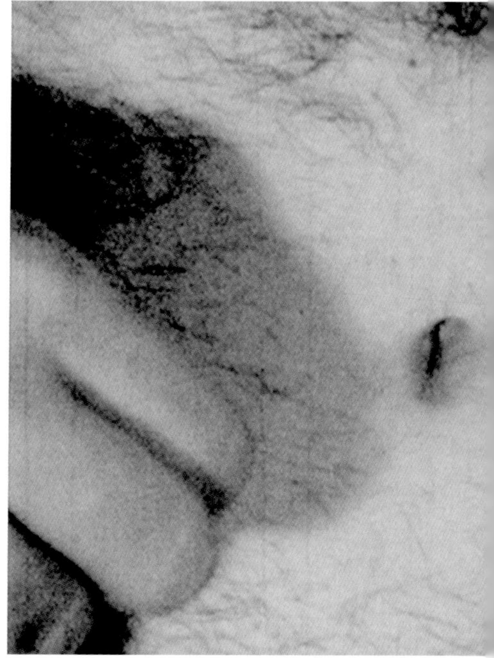

3 Vito Acconci, *Openings,* 1970, Video video, Courtesy Electronic Arts Intermix (EAI), New York

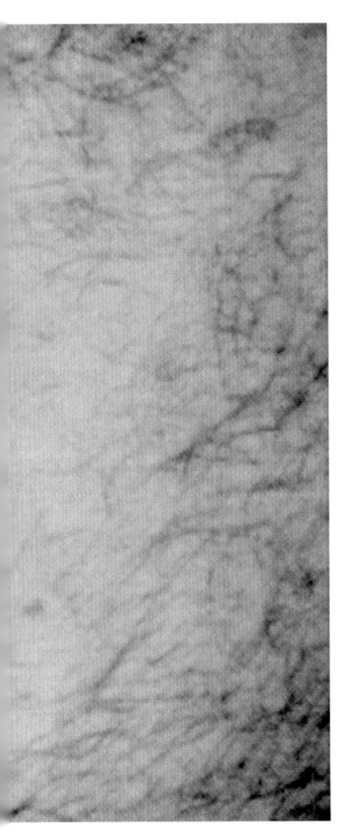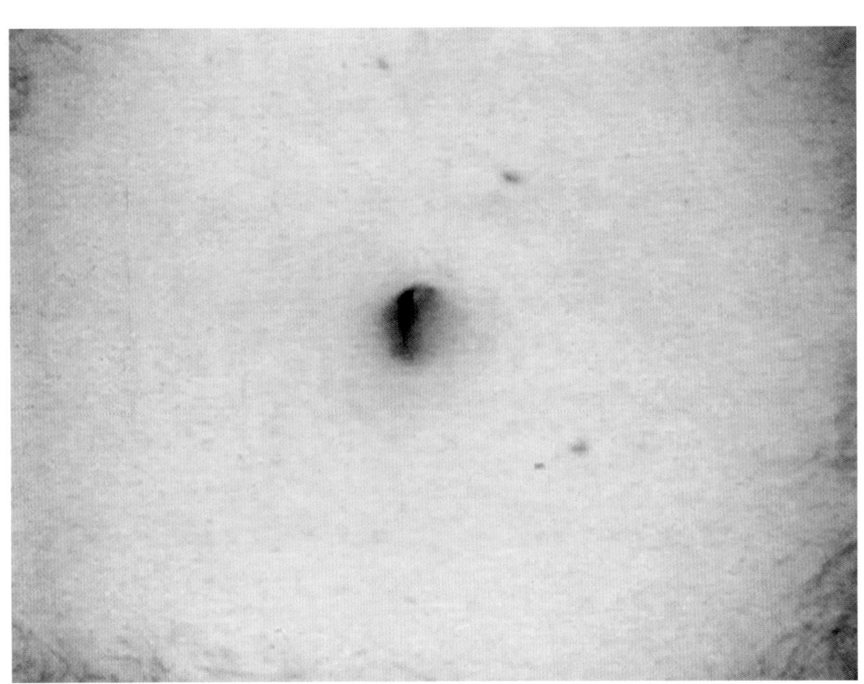

provocation. And their force has been further strengthened through the circumstance that from year to year and from series to series his body became increasingly wrinkled, flabby, and hairy. Through the precise and "unsparing" lighting of the skin, the traces of transience were made clearly visible.

The Skin as a Sign of Transience

The skin has long been ascribed a special relationship to the body. It not only marks the threshold between the self and the outside, it is also the bearer of social signs.[40] With the representation of wrinkled skin covered in pigment spots, Coplans unmistakably designates the body as old. Besides this content component, the skin is also an essential formal-aesthetic device. Through its precise lighting and its large-scale representation, the body is made nearly abstract. It has already been pointed out above that feminist artists often challenged the representation of standardized femininity through the material dissolution of the image. This is relevant again at this point since Coplans embodies such a strategy in two ways: on the one hand he breaks up, as has already been mentioned, the unified image of the body into a number of (pictorial) parts; on the other hand, he dissolves the body in a further step through the abstracting of the surface of the skin. While standing directly in front of the pictures, the viewer only sees the skin dissolved into abstract structures—only when the viewer steps back does the visually structured plane assemble into parts of the body. Skin is thus structurally linked with the picture surface; the body's materiality is suggested through the photos. The body's dissolution through the pictorial fragment finds its continuation in the visual dissolution of the pictorial motif.

In the context of such a pictorial language the photographic series *1906 to the Skin* (1991–93) by the Japanese photographer Miyako Ishiuchi occupies a special position (cat. 21–26). For this series Ishiuchi photographed the 1906-born dancer Kazuo Ohno, whom she depicts in a way that superficially recalls Coplans's work: not only does she render the dancer's body anonymous by not representing his face, but she also visually fragments his body into single parts. The aspect of the performative staging is likewise clearly inscribed in these pictures. Accordingly, single photos represent poses and gestures whose visible body tension is clearly derived from dance. Ishiuchi's primary interest, however, is the theme of skin, which she treats in a systematic way in a multitude of pictures. The structural link between skin and photography articulated in Coplans's work is here significantly heightened. Thus in a number of pictures, the dancer's wrinkled skin occupies the entire frame, whereby the surface of the photos not only renders the materiality of the aged skin, but is visually transformed into it. The temporal process of aging and of inevitable physical decline

Bildes hinterfragen. Dies ist an dieser Stelle nochmals relevant, weil Coplans eine solche Strategie zweifach verkörpert: Einerseits bricht er, wie bereits angesprochen, das einheitliche Bild des Körpers in mehrere (Bild)teile auf, andererseits löst er den Körper in einem weiteren Schritt durch die Abstrahierung der Hautoberfläche auf. Steht der Betrachter direkt vor den Bildern, sieht er nur die in abstrakte Strukturen aufgelöste Haut – erst wenn er sich von den Bildern entfernt, setzt sich die visuell strukturierte Fläche zu Körperteilen zusammen. Die Haut wird so strukturell mit der Bildoberfläche verbunden, die Materialität des Körpers durch die Fotos suggeriert. Die Auflösung des Körpers mithilfe des Bildausschnittes findet damit ihre Fortsetzung in der visuellen Auflösung des Bildmotivs.

Im Kontext einer solchen Bildsprache nimmt die Fotoserie *1906 to the Skin* (1991–1993) der japanischen Fotografin Miyako Ishiuchi eine Sonderstellung ein (Kat. 21–26). Für diese Serie fotografierte Ishiuchi den 1906 geborenen Tänzer Kazuo Ohno, den sie auf eine Art und Weise darstellte, die oberflächlich an Coplans' Arbeiten erinnert: Nicht nur anonymisiert sie den Körper des Tänzers, indem sie sein Gesicht nicht darstellt, sondern fragmentiert auch seinen Körper in visuelle Einzelteile. Der Aspekt der performativen Inszenierung schreibt sich ebenfalls deutlich in diese Bilder ein. So repräsentieren einzelne Fotos Posen und Gesten, deren sichtbare Körperspannung eindeutig dem Tanz geschuldet ist. Ishiuchis primäres Interesse gilt jedoch dem Thema Haut, das sie in einer Vielzahl von Bildern systematisch behandelt. Die strukturelle Verknüpfung von Haut und Fotografie, wie sie bei Coplans betont wurde, wird hier deutlich zugespitzt. So nimmt die faltige Haut des Tänzers in manchen Bildern den gesamten Ausschnitt ein, womit die Oberfläche der Fotos die Materialität der alten Haut nicht nur wiedergibt, sondern sich visuell in diese transformiert. Der zeitliche Prozess der Alterung und des unweigerlichen körperlichen Vergehens wurde nie deutlicher sichtbar. Ishiuchis Bildsprache ist hierbei wie auch die von Coplans explizit fotografisch. Beide Künstler lichten ihr Motiv »straight«, also unumwunden und direkt ab. Die indexikalische Qualität der Fotografie wird damit deutlich vorgeführt, kann doch nur dieses Medium die Haut mit einer derartigen Präzision und Schärfe wiedergeben. Nicht nur in formalästhetischer Hinsicht, sondern auch in Bezug auf das Thema Vergänglichkeit erscheint die Verwendung des fotografischen Mediums schlüssig.

Der Fotografie wurde seit jeher ein besonderer Bezug zu Vergänglichkeit und Tod zugeschrieben. Es war Roland Barthes, der dieses Verhältnis von Fotografie, Vergänglichkeit, Zeit und Tod in seinem berühmten Buch *Die helle Kammer* formuliert hat.[41] Nach Barthes wird beim Aufnahmeakt ein Motiv durch die fotografische Fixierung eines Augenblickes dem zeitlichen Ablauf entrissen und verweist damit immer in die Vergangenheit. So hat sich das Objekt, die Person, tatsächlich zu einem vergangenen Zeitpunkt vor der Kamera befunden (»Es ist so gewesen«). Im Bild präsent anwesend, liegt dieser Moment nichtsdestotrotz bereits in der Vergangenheit. Indem jedes Foto, sobald es aufgenom-

has never been more clearly visible. Here, as with Coplans too, Ishiuchi's visual language is explicitly photographic. Both artists light their motif "straight," which is to say, directly and without tricks. The indexical quality of photography is thus clearly presented, since only this medium can render the skin with such precision and sharpness. Photography seems the appropriate medium, not only from a formal aesthetic point of view, but also in relation to the theme of transience.

Photography has long been attributed a special relationship to transience and death. It was Roland Barthes who formulated this relationship between photography, transience, time, and death in his famous book *Camera Lucida*.[41] According to Barthes, in the act of taking a picture, a motif is wrested from the passage of time through the photographic fixing of a moment, and therefore always refers to the past. In a past moment in time, the object, the person, found themselves thusly in front of the camera ("this-has-been"). Currently present in the picture, this moment nevertheless already resides in the past. Each photo, as soon as it is taken, already belongs to the past—it embodies a transience that already points to death. Many of the photos discussed here have a direct relation to death. For years John Coplans documented his own physical decline and thereby visualized, like Miyako Ishiuchi, the theme of temporal transience. Hannah Villiger began to photograph and make a theme of her body once she became ill. In the nineteen-eighties, in the context of the AIDS crisis, even Robert Mapplethorpe's photos of perfect, flawless, and untouchable bodies acquired a certain fragility that contrasts with the timelessness of their pictorial language. To the clear representation of transience, as rendered in the works of Ishiuchi and Coplans, we can add the aforementioned gestures of protest. Despite the range of the individual artistic strategies, they are all the visual expression of a specific resistance that serves a making-visible of taboo or hidden aspects. When, in closing, we speak of the visualization of transience, it is also a matter of the visualization of death—still one of the greatest social taboos. Precisely the photos that deal with this theme show how protest can also be directed against one's own body. In defiance of all theories of the subject, these pictures make clear that identity is essentially marked by the body. The body is the limit of one's being—at least in a temporal dimension. This has been visualized most clearly by Ketty La Rocca: with the image of a fist inserted into an X-ray of her head in the spot of her deadly brain tumor (cat. 16).

men wird, der Vergangenheit zugehörig ist, verkörpert es eine Vergänglichkeit, die bereits auf den Tod verweist. Viele der hier besprochenen Fotos stehen in direktem Bezug zum Tod: John Coplans dokumentierte über Jahre hinweg seinen eigenen körperlichen Verfall und visualisierte damit wie Miyako Ishiuchi das Thema der zeitlichen Vergänglichkeit. Hannah Villiger begann ihren Körper zu fotografieren und thematisieren, als sie erkrankte. Selbst Robert Mapplethorpes Fotos von perfekten, makellosen und unantastbaren Körpern bekamen in den 1980er-Jahren im Kontext der Aidskrise eine Brüchigkeit, die in Kontrast zu der Zeitlosigkeit ihrer Bildsprache steht. Die deutliche Darstellung der Vergänglichkeit, wie sie in den Werken von Ishiuchi und Coplans dargestellt wird, kann den bisher genannten Gesten des Protests hinzugefügt werden. So unterschiedlich sich die einzelnen künstlerischen Strategien darstellen, sind sie doch allesamt visueller Ausdruck eines spezifischen Widerstandes, welcher der Sichtbarmachung tabuisierter oder verborgener Aspekte dient. Wenn abschließend von der Sichtbarkeit der Vergänglichkeit die Rede ist, geht es hierbei auch um die Visualisierung des Todes, einem der bis heute größten gesellschaftlichen Tabus. Gerade die Fotos, die dieses Thema behandeln, belegen, dass sich der Protest auch gegen den eigenen Körper richten kann. Aller Subjekttheorien zum Trotz verdeutlichen diese Bilder, dass die eigene Identität wesentlich durch den Körper geprägt wird. Nicht zuletzt begrenzt der Körper – zumindest in zeitlicher Dimension – das eigene Sein. Am deutlichsten hat dies Ketty La Rocca visualisiert: mit einer Faust, die sie in einer Röntgenfotografie ihres Kopfes an die Stelle ihres tödlichen Gehirntumors montiert hat (Kat. 16).

The author would like to thank Monika Faber and Roland Fischer-Briand, Austrian Film Museum, Vienna, for their professional advice.

1   Coplans was among the first art theorists to address Pop Art, and as early as 1967 published a book on Roy Lichtenstein. In 1970 and 1971 he curated exhibitions on such famous artists as Andy Warhol, Richard Serra, and Donald Judd. The theme of photography also played a key role in his theoretical production. Coplans not only wrote texts on the photojournalist Weegee, but also published articles on the historical landscape photographer Carleton Watkins. From 1971 to 1979 Coplans was editor-in-chief of the art magazine *Artforum,* for which important photography theorists such as Rosalind Krauss and Max Kozloff also wrote at the time. Although their texts display different approaches to photography, they share a concern with the medium's ontology. Theoretical approaches that address the qualities of the medium as such are clearly reflected in Coplans's photos. For a biography of Coplans see John Coplans, *A Body* (New York, 2002), pp. 150–67. His articles are collected in Stuart Morgan, ed., *John Coplans: Provocations* (London, 1996).

2   However, the self-representations of naked artists can already be found in the earlier history of art and photography: Albrecht Dürer, Egon Schiele, and Richard Gerstl are famous examples in painting; Eadweard Muybridge, Rudolf Koppitz, and Thomas Eakins are prominent representatives in the history of photography. Such representations of nakedness were often legitimated by the content, however. Thus, for example, the photos of Muybridge were made under the aegis of science, whereas the self-representation of Eakins served as an artist's study. Such connotations cannot be found in Coplans's photos. On the representation of the male nude in photography with examples of artists' self-portraits see John Pultz, *The Body and the Lens: Photography 1839 to the Present* (London, 1995); Peter Weiermair, *Das verborgene Bild: Geschichte des männlichen Akts in der Fotografie des 19. und 20. Jahrhunderts* (Vienna, 1987); see also Emmanuel Cooper, *Fully Exposed: The Male Nude in Photography* (London, 1990).

3   For an overview see Thomas Dreher, *Performance Art nach 1945: Aktionstheater und Intermedia* (Munich, 2001); RoseLee Goldberg, *Performance Art: From Futurism to the Present* (London,

2011 [1979]); Peter Noever, ed., *Out of Actions: Aktionismus, Body Art & Performance 1949–1979,* exh. cat. MAK—Österreichisches Museum für angewandte Kunst, Vienna (Ostfildern, 1998).

4   On this see Robert C. Morgan, ed., *Bruce Nauman* (Baltimore, 2002); Joan Simon, ed., *Bruce Nauman* (Basel, 1994); Coosje van Bruggen, *Bruce Nauman* (New York, 1988).

5   The investigation of bodily expressions with the help of grimaces in Nauman's work has led to comparisons with the works of artists ranging from Franz Xaver Messerschmidt to Egon Schiele. Another important comparison can be made with the photographs made by the French physiologist Guillaume Duchenne de Boulogne between 1852 and 1856. In experiments using an electric probe, Duchenne stimulated a variety of facial muscles, which were thus made to contract. The facial expressions thereby created were the result of an artificial influence, not an inner emotion. The various facial expressions were recorded in a series of famous photographs. See Robert A. Sobieszek, *Ghost in the Shell,* exh. cat. Los Angeles County Museum of Art (Cambridge [Mass.], 1999), pp. 260–83.

6   Quoted in Christopher Cordes, *Bruce Nauman: Prints 1970–89* (New York, 1989), p. 25.

7   The grimaces served Godard as a stylistic device that is used regularly in the film. Thus on the one hand, in a self-reflexive way, the director treats the theatrical aspect of acting as such; on the other hand, it also serves him from a narrative point of view. Thus the character played by Belmondo disappears not only behind arbitrary masks, but also behind gestures and expressions borrowed from Humphrey Bogart—this should be considered as a filmic strategy that acts as a reference to American cinema, which was so important for Godard's work.

8   Kenneth Baker in a review of Bruce Nauman, Robert Ryman, Jack Tworkov, et al. in *Artforum* (April 1971), pp. 77–81, here p. 77.

9   Cordes 1989 (see note 6), pp. 25–26.

10 On the theme of performance and photography see Christian Janecke, ed., *Performance und Bild: Performance als Bild* (Berlin, 2004).

11 See Alice Maude-Roxby, *Live Art on Camera: Performance and Photography* (Southampton, 2007).

12 See Sybille Krämer, *Performativität und Medialität* (Munich, 2004); Erika Fischer-Lichte, *Ästhetik des Performativen* (Frankfurt am Main, 2010); and esp. also Ludger Schwarte, ed., *Bild-Perfor-*

manz (Munich, 2011).

13 Serial strategies can be found for example in the work of photographers such as Bernd and Hilla Becher, Duane Michals, but also Ray K. Metzker. Prior to his career as a photographer John Coplans wrote a book on serialism in painting in which he dealt with this artistic principle in theoretical terms. See John Coplans, *Serial Imagery* (Pasadena, 1968).

14 John Coplans mentions this example himself in an interview with Jean-François Chevrier. See Coplans 2002 (see note 1), p. 172.

15 See Rebecca Schneider, *The Explicit Body in Performance* (New York, 1997); Jane Wark, *Radical Gestures: Feminism and Performance Art in North America* (Montreal and Kingston, 2009); Silvia Eiblmayr, *Die Frau als Bild: Der weibliche Körper in der Kunst des 20. Jahrhunderts* (Berlin, 1993). The strategy of challenging representations of the female body did not appear with the Body Art artists of the nineteen-sixties, but as early as the twenties, such as in the work of the artist Claude Cahun. On this see Gen Doy, *Claude Cahun* (London, 2007); Inka Graeve Ingelmann, ed., *Female Trouble: Die Kamera als Spiegel und Bühne weiblicher Inszenierungen,* exh. cat. Pinakothek der Moderne, Munich (Ostfildern, 2008).

16 This circumstance was recognized as paradigmatic of one of the most essential differences between male and female representatives of Body Art. Female artists often intend their artworks to be more socio-political than do their male colleagues. See Amelia Jones, *Body Art: Performing the Subject* (Minneapolis, 1998), pp. 146–50.

17 On this see, for instance, Bernhard Schwenk, "Dressed to Kill? Arbus, Goldin, Klauke, Lüthi, Mapplethorpe, Melhus, Molinier," in Ingelmann 2008 (see note 15), pp. 86–111.

18 In her influential book *Male Trouble,* Abigail Solomon-Godeau has attested, on the basis of Neoclassical painting, that male identity and its representation were already contradictory in classical art history and in this sense fragile. See Abigail Solomon-Godeau, *Male Trouble: A Crisis in Representation* (London, 1997).

19 See, for instance, R. W. Connell, *Masculinities* (Cambridge, 2005); Peter Lehman, ed., *Masculinity: Bodies, Movies, Sculpture* (New York, 2001); Todd W. Reeser, *Masculinities in Theory* (Chichester [West Sussex], 2010).

20 See Peter F. Murphy, *Feminism and Masculinities* (Oxford, 2004), esp. pp. 7–18.

Der Autor bedankt sich bei Monika Faber und Roland Fischer-Briand, Österreichisches Filmmuseum, Wien, für fachliche Hinweise.

1 Coplans gehörte zu den ersten Kunsttheoretikern, die sich mit Pop-Art auseinandersetzten und publizierte bereits 1967 ein Buch zu Roy Lichtenstein. 1970 und 1971 kuratierte er Ausstellungen zu so berühmten Künstlern wie Andy Warhol, Richard Serra und Donald Judd. Auch das Thema Fotografie spielte in seinem theoretischen Schaffen eine wesentliche Rolle. Coplans schrieb nicht nur Texte zu dem Reportagefotografen Weegee, sondern veröffentlichte auch Aufsätze über den historischen Landschaftsfotografen Carleton Watkins. Von 1971 bis 1979 war Coplans Chefredakteur des Kunstmagazins *Artforum,* für das zu dieser Zeit auch bedeutende Fototheoretiker wie etwa Rosalind Krauss und Max Kozloff schrieben. Obwohl ihre Texte unterschiedliche Zugänge zur Fotografie aufweisen, beschäftigen sie sich doch gleichermaßen mit der Ontologie des Mediums. Theoretische Zugänge, die sich mit den Qualitäten des Mediums an sich auseinandersetzen, spiegeln sich deutlich in Coplans' Fotos wieder. Vgl. zu einer Biografie von Coplans: John Coplans, *A Body,* New York 2002, S. 150–167. Seine Aufsätze wurden gesammelt abgedruckt in Stuart Morgan (Hrsg.), *John Coplans. Provocations,* London 1996.
2 Selbstinszenierungen nackter Künstler lassen sich aber bereits früher in der Kunst- und Fotogeschichte feststellen. Albrecht Dürer, Egon Schiele und Richard Gerstl sind berühmte Beispiele hierfür in der Malerei, Eadweard Muybridge, Rudolf Koppitz und Thomas Eakins sind prominente Vertreter aus der Fotogeschichte. Die Darstellung der Nacktheit wurde jedoch nicht selten inhaltlich legitimiert. So entstanden beispielsweise die Fotos von Muybridge unter dem Deckmantel der Wissenschaft, während die Selbstdarstellung von Eakins als Künstlervorlage diente. Die Fotos von Coplans lassen indes keine Konnotationen dieser Art erkennen. Vgl. zur männlichen Aktdarstellung in der Fotografie mit Beispielen von Künstlerselbstporträts: John Pultz, *The Body and the Lens. Photography 1839 to the Present,* London 1995. Peter Weiermair, *Das verborgene Bild. Geschichte des männlichen Akts in der Fotografie des 19. und 20. Jahrhunderts,* Wien 1987. Siehe auch Emmanuel Cooper, *Fully Exposed. The Male Nude in Photography,* London 1990.
3 Für einen Überblick siehe Thomas Dreher, *Performance Art nach 1945. Aktionstheater und Intermedia,* München 2001. RoseLee Goldberg, *Performance Art.*

From Futurism to the Present, London 2011 [1979]. Peter Noever (Hrsg.), *Out of Actions. Aktionismus, Body Art & Performance 1949–1979,* Ausst.-Kat. MAK – Österreichisches Museum für angewandte Kunst, Wien, Ostfildern 1998.
4 Vgl. hierzu Robert C. Morgan (Hrsg.), *Bruce Nauman,* Baltimore 2002. Joan Simon (Hrsg.), *Bruce Nauman,* Basel 1994. Coosje van Bruggen, *Bruce Nauman,* New York 1988.
5 Die Untersuchung körperlicher Expressionen mithilfe der Grimasse in Naumans Werk hat zu Vergleichen mit Arbeiten von Franz Xaver Messerschmidt bis hin zu jenen von Egon Schiele geführt. Einen wesentlichen Vergleich stellen auch die zwischen 1852 und 1856 entstanden Fotografien des französischen Physiologen Guillaume Duchenne de Boulogne dar. Duchenne reizte bei Versuchen durch Stromstöße verschiedenste Gesichtsmuskeln, die daraufhin kontrahierten. Die so erzeugten Gesichtsausdrücke waren Resultate eines künstlichen Einflusses, nicht aber einer inneren Gefühlsregung. In einer Reihe berühmter Fotografien wurden diese unterschiedlichen Gesichtsausdrücke festgehalten. Vgl. Robert A. Sobieszek, *Ghost in the Shell,* Ausst.-Kat. Los Angeles County Museum of Art, Cambridge (Massachusetts) 1999, S. 260–283.
6 Zit. n.: Christopher Cordes, *Bruce Nauman. Prints 1970–89,* New York 1989, S. 25.
7 Die Grimasse dient Godard als ein Stilmittel, das im Film laufend zum Einsatz kommt. Der Regisseur thematisiert damit einerseits auf selbstreflexive Weise den theatralen Aspekt des Schauspielens an sich. Andererseits dient es ihm auch in narrativer Hinsicht. So verschwindet der Charakter, den Belmondo darstellt, nicht nur hinter arbiträren Masken, sondern auch hinter Gesten und Mimiken, die er von Humphrey Bogart übernimmt – dies ist als eine filmische Strategie zu betrachten, die als Referenz auf das für Godards Werk wichtige amerikanische Kino fungiert.
8 Kenneth Baker in einer Ausstellungskritik zu Bruce Nauman, Robert Ryman, Jack Tworkov u. a., in: *Artforum,* April 1971, S. 77–81, hier S. 77.
9 Cordes 1989 (wie Anm. 6), S. 25 f.
10 Vgl. zum Thema Performance und Fotografie Christian Janecke (Hrsg.), *Performance und Bild. Performance als Bild,* Berlin 2004.
11 Vgl. Alice Maude-Roxby, *Live Art on Camera. Performance and Photography,* Southampton 2007.
12 Vgl. Sybille Krämer, *Performativität und Medialität,* München 2004. Erika Fischer-Lichte, *Ästhetik des Performativen,* Frank-

furt am Main 2010. Siehe im Besonderen auch Ludger Schwarte (Hrsg.), *Bild-Performanz,* München 2011.
13 Serielle Strategien sind beispielsweise prägend für Fotografen wie Bernd und Hilla Becher, Duane Michals, aber auch Ray K. Metzker. Vor seiner Karriere als Fotograf hat John Coplans ein Buch über Serialität in der Malerei verfasst, in dem er sich theoretisch bereits mit diesem künstlerischen Prinzip auseinandersetzte. John Coplans, *Serial Imagery,* Pasadena 1968.
14 John Coplans erwähnt dieses Beispiel selbst in einem Interview mit Jean-François Chevrier. Siehe Coplans 2002 (wie Anm. 1), S. 172.
15 Vgl. Rebecca Schneider, *The Explicit Body in Performance,* New York 1997. Jane Wark, *Radical Gestures. Feminism and Performance Art in North America,* Montreal und Kingston 2009. Silvia Eiblmayr, *Die Frau als Bild. Der weibliche Körper in der Kunst des 20. Jahrhunderts,* Berlin 1993. Die Strategie, den weiblichen Körper als Abbildung zu hinterfragen, tritt nicht erst mit den Body-Art-Künstlerinnen der 1960er-Jahre auf, sondern bereits in den 1920ern, wie beispielsweise bei der Künstlerin Claude Cahun. Vgl hierzu Gen Doy, *Claude Cahun,* London 2007. Inka Graeve Ingelmann (Hrsg.), *Female Trouble. Die Kamera als Spiegel und Bühne weiblicher Inszenierungen,* Ausst.-Kat. Pinakothek der Moderne, München, Ostfildern 2008.
16 Dieser Sachverhalt wurde paradigmatisch als einer der wesentlichsten Unterschiede zwischen männlichen und weiblichen Vertretern der Body Art erkannt. Weibliche Künstlerinnen intendieren ihre Kunstwerke oftmals gesellschaftspolitischer als ihre männlichen Kollegen. Vgl. Amelia Jones, *Body Art. Performing the Subject,* Minneapolis 1998. S. 146–150.
17 Vgl. hierzu beispielsweise Bernhard Schwenk, »Dressed to Kill? Arbus, Goldin, Klauke, Lüthi, Mapplethorpe, Melhus, Molinier«, in: München 2008 (wie Anm. 15), S. 86–111.
18 Abigail Solomon-Godeau hat in ihrem einflussreichen Buch *Male Trouble* anhand klassizistischer Malerei belegt, dass männliche Identität und ihre Darstellung schon in der klassischen Kunstgeschichte widersprüchlich und in diesem Sinne brüchig waren. Vgl. Abigail Solomon-Godeau, *Male Trouble. A Crisis in Representation,* London 1997.
19 Vgl. etwa R. W. Connell, *Masculinities,* Cambridge 2005. Peter Lehman (Hrsg.), *Masculinity. Bodies, Movies, Sculpture,* New York 2001. Todd W. Reeser, *Masculinities in Theory,* Chichester (West Sussex) 2010.
20 Vgl. Peter F. Murphy, *Feminism and Mas-

21 In her well-known book *Body Art: Performing the Subject*, Amelia Jones has pointed out that Acconci's challenging of male normative identity served precisely its restoration. See Jones 1998 (see note 16), pp. 103–50, esp. pp. 136–46. In her book *What the Body Costs: Desire, History, and Performance*, Jane Blocker investigates the sexist aspects in Acconci's work against the background of Jones's research. See Jane Blocker, *What the Body Costs: Desire, History, and Performance* (Minnesota, 2004).

22 A well-known controversy in *Artforum*, which interestingly was unleashed in 1974 when Coplans was editor-in-chief, is a clear example of feminist artists' interrogation of the representation of women. In the November issue a photo of the American artist Lynda Benglis was printed in which she poses naked with a dildo between her legs. The force of this motif was further heightened by the circumstance that she assumes a pose that is clearly borrowed from male macho poses. The photo, which is concerned with precisely such gender roles and stereotypes, unleashed a scandal that brought Benglis accusations of vulgarity and pornography. This self-representation has subsequently become an example for the prejudiced views of art critics whose critique of Benglis frequently involved stereotypical attitudes.

23 Particularly in the nineteen-twenties, as for instance in the works of Man Ray, female bodies were transformed into abstract sculptures whose flawless surfaces conveyed a timeless pictorial language.

24 John Coplans himself named the painter Philip Guston as a model for his ironic and humorous representation of masculinity. See John Coplans in *John Coplans: Autoportraits*, exh. cat. Centre de la Vieille Charité, Marseille (Arles, 1989), pp. 14–15.

25 See Marcus Mrass, *Gesten und Gebärden: Begriffsbestimmung und -verwendung in Hinblick auf kunsthistorische Untersuchungen* (Regensburg, 2005).

26 See Coplans 2002 (see note 1), pp. 170–71.

27 See ibid., p. 172.

28 Elena Del Becaro, *Intermedialità al femminile: L'opera di Ketty La Rocca* (Rome, 2008), pp. 155–56.

29 See ibid., p. 156.

30 See Eiblmayr 1993 (see note 15).

31 See ibid., p. 141.

32 The description of such a fragmentary visual language cannot avoid treating the "crisis of the subject" heralded particularly in the nineteen-nineties. These considerations are based on analytical concepts that view the subject not as a normative authority, but as a deeply contradictory, suggestible entity susceptible to control by structures. In his theory of the mirror stage, the French psychoanalyst Jacques Lacan has provided the adequate explanatory model that is often cited in texts on body representations. At the core of this theory is the moment in which the small child recognizes that it can only perceive itself as fragmented or fractured, but not complete (as in the mirror). As a consequence of its search for identity, the subject attempts to remedy this lack and to attain unity. Lacan's considerations turn out to be ideal for visual material insofar as he frequently relates his theories to visual perceptions. His theory that the subject per se is fractured and split finds its visual expression in the self-perception of a fragmentary body. The pictures of Hannah Villiger and John Coplans lend themselves to this sort of psychoanalytical interpretation since they show the artists' own bodies not integrally, but dismantled into individual parts and fragments. The subject is visualized as split in the truest sense of the word. On this subject see Norbert Haas, ed., *Das Werk von Jacques Lacan, Das Seminar: Buch I (1953-1954): Freuds technische Schriften* (Vienna et al. 1990); translated as Jacques-Alain Miller, ed., *The Seminar of Jacques Lacan: Book I 1953–1954: Freud's Papers on Technique,* trans. John Forrester (New York, 1991); see also Peter Widmer, *Subversion des Begehrens: Eine Einführung in Jacques Lacans Werk* (Vienna, 2009). For an analysis of Coplans's work, on the basis of the psychoanalytical considerations of Jacques Lacan see Melody D. Davis, *The Male Nude in Contemporary Photography* (Philadelphia, 1991), p. 63. For a Lacanian analysis of the work of Hannah Villiger see Griselda Pollock, "Der Körper, mein Körper, ihr Körper," in *Hannah Villiger,* ed. Jolanda Bucher and Eric Hattan (Zurich, 2001), pp. 200–02.

33 On the relationship between sculpture and Coplans's photographs see Jean-François Chevrier, "Archaism in Times of Reproduction," in *John Coplans: Self Portrait Hand/Foot,* exh. cat. Museum Boijmans Van Beuningen (Rotterdam, 1990). On the other hand, two books explore Hannah Villiger's works in the context of sculpture: *Hannah Villiger: Skulptural,* exh. cat. Museum für Gegenwartskunst (Basel, 1989); see in addition Herta Wolf, ed., *Skulpturen, Fragmente,* exh. cat. Wiener Secession, Vienna (Zurich, 1992).

34 See Chevrier 1990 (see note 33), p. 6. See also Christina Natlacen, *Am Beispiel Dieter Appelt, John Coplans und Arno Rafael Minkkinen: Zur Komplexität männlicher Selbstdarstellung in der zeitgenössischen Fotografie,* diploma thesis, Universität Wien, 2001, pp. 57–61.

35 See Coplans 2002 (see note 1), p. 175.

36 The representation of African-American models as explicitly sexual bodies that are often rendered anonymous through the visual fragmentation of the body has led to accusations of Mapplethorpe serving colonialist racist stereotypes. The articles on this theme written by Kobena Mercer remain the most differentiated to date. See Kobena Mercer, "Just Looking for Trouble: Robert Mapplethorpe and Fantasies of Race," in *Sex Exposed: Sexuality and the Pornography Debate*, ed. Lynne Segal and Mary McIntosh (New Jersey, 1992); Kobena Mercer, "Skin Head Sex Thing: Racial Difference and the Homoerotic Imaginary," in *How Do I Look? Queer Film and Video* (Seattle, 1991); and also Gen Doy, *Black Visual Culture: Modernity and Postmodernity* (New York, 2000), pp. 156–203.

37 Coplans 2002 (see note 1), p. 175.

38 Here Hannah Wilke represents an exception. In *Portrait of the Artist with Her Mother, Selma Butter* from the series *So Help Me Hannah,* the artist depicts her old mother with cancer. In the nineteen-nineties the photographer Melanie Manchot likewise photographed the body of her aging mother. For a comparison between the photos of Manchot and Coplans see Chris Townsend, *Vile Bodies: Photography and the Crisis of Looking* (New York, 1998), pp. 97–104.

39 See Coplans 2002 (see note 1), p. 175.

40 See Claudia Benthien, *Haut—Literaturgeschichte—Körperbilder—Grenzdiskurse* (Hamburg, 1999). On artists' examinations of skin, such as in the work of VALIE EXPORT or Jenny Holzer, see *Auf den Leib geschrieben,* exh. cat. Kunsthalle Wien (Vienna, 1995).

41 Roland Barthes, *Die helle Kammer* (Frankfurt am Main, 1989); translated from the French as *Camera Lucida: Reflections on Photography,* trans. Richard Howard (New York, 1981).

culinities, Oxford 2004, besonders S. 7–18.

21 Amelia Jones hat in ihrem bekannten Buch *Body Art. Performing the Subject* darauf hingewiesen, dass Acconcis Hinterfragung von männlicher normativer Identität zur Wiederherstellung eben dieser dient. Vgl. Jones 1998 (wie Anm. 16), S. 103–150, besonders S. 136–146. Jane Blocker untersucht in ihrem Buch *What the Body Costs. Desire, History, and Performance* vor dem Hintergrund von Jones' Forschungen die sexistischen Aspekte in Acconcis Werk. Vgl. Jane Blocker, *What the Body Costs. Desire, History, and Performance,* Minnesota 2004.

22 Eine bekannte Kontroverse in *Artforum,* die interessanterweise 1974 ausgelöst wurde, als Coplans Chefredakteur war, ist ein deutliches Beispiel für die Auseinandersetzung feministischer Künstlerinnen mit der Darstellung von Frauen: In der Novemberausgabe wurde ein Foto der amerikanischen Künstlerin Lynda Benglis abgedruckt, auf dem sie nackt und mit einem Dildo zwischen ihren Beinen posiert. Die Brisanz dieses Motivs wird durch den Umstand verstärkt, dass sie eine Pose einnimmt, die eindeutig an machoartige Inszenierungen von Männern angelehnt ist. Dieses Foto, das sich mit genau solchen Rollenbildern und Stereotypen auseinandersetzt, löste einen Skandal aus, der Benglis den Vorwurf der Vulgarität und des Pornografischen einbrachte. Diese Selbstdarstellung ist darüber hinaus zu einem Beispiel für die voreingenommene Anschauung von Kunstkritikern selbst geworden, die bei ihrer Kritik an Benglis oftmals stereotype Sichtweisen transportierten.

23 Speziell in den 1920er-Jahren, wie etwa bei Man Ray, wurden weibliche Körper in abstrakte Skulpturen transformiert, deren makellose Oberflächen eine zeitlose Bildsprache vermittelten.

24 John Coplans selbst hat den Maler Philip Guston als Vorbild für seine ironisch-humoristische Darstellung von Männlichkeit genannt. Vgl. John Coplans in *John Coplans. Autoportraits,* Ausst.-Kat. Centre de la Vieille Charité Marseille, Arles 1989, S. 14 f.

25 Vgl. Marcus Mrass, *Gesten und Gebärden. Begriffsbestimmung und -verwendung in Hinblick auf kunsthistorische Untersuchungen,* Regensburg 2005.

26 Vgl. Coplans 2002 (wie Anm. 1), S. 170 f.

27 Vgl. ebd, S. 172.

28 Elena Del Becaro, *Intermedialità al femminile. L'opera di Ketty La Rocca,* Rom 2008, S. 155 f.

29 Vgl. ebd., S. 156.

30 Vgl. Eiblmayr 1993 (wie Anm. 15).

31 Vgl. ebd., S. 141.

32 Die Beschreibung einer solchen fragmentarischen Bildsprache kommt freilich nicht umhin, die speziell in den 1990er-Jahren beschworene »Krise des Subjekts« zu thematisieren. Diese Überlegungen basieren auf analytischen Konzepten, welche das Subjekt nicht als normative Autorität, sondern als zutiefst widersprüchliche, beeinflussbare und durch Strukturen geregelte Instanz erklären. Der französische Psychoanalytiker Jacques Lacan hat in seinem Spiegelgleichnis hierfür das adäquate Erklärungsmodell geliefert, das auch in Texten zu Körperdarstellungen häufig zitiert wird. In diesem Gleichnis ist jener Moment zentral, in dem das Kleinkind erkennt, das es sich nur fragmentiert beziehungsweise zerstückelt, aber nicht komplett (wie im Spiegel) wahrnehmen kann. Das Subjekt versucht infolge seiner Identitätsfindung diesen Mangel zu beheben und zu seiner Gesamtheit zu gelangen. Lacans Überlegungen bieten sich insofern ideal für Bildmaterial an, als er seine Theorien vielfach über visuelle Wahrnehmungen schildert. Seine Theorie, dass das Subjekt per se uneinheitlich und gespalten ist, findet seinen visuellen Ausdruck in der Selbstwahrnehmung eines fragmentierten Körpers. Die Bilder von Hannah Villiger und John Coplans bieten sich für eine solche psychoanalytische Interpretation an, zeigen sie ihre eigenen Körper doch nicht ganzheitlich, sondern in Einzelteile und Fragmente aufgelöst. Das Subjekt wird im wahrsten Sinne des Wortes als gespalten visualisiert. Vgl. hierzu Norbert Haas (Hrsg.), *Das Werk von Jacques Lacan. Das Seminar: Buch 1,* Wien u. a. 1990. Siehe auch Peter Widmer, *Subversion des Begehrens. Eine Einführung in Jacques Lacans Werk,* Wien 2009. Zu einer Analyse der Werke von Coplans anhand psychoanalytischer Überlegungen von Jacques Lacan siehe Melody D. Davis, *The Male Nude in Contemporary Photography,* Philadelphia 1991, S. 63. Zu einer lacanschen Analyse der Werke von Hannah Villiger siehe Griselda Pollock, »Der Körper, mein Körper, ihr Körper«, in: Jolanda Bucher & Eric Hattan (Hrsg.), *Hannah Villiger,* Zürich 2001, S. 200–202.

33 Zum Verhältnis von Skulptur und Coplans' Fotografien siehe Jean-François Chevrier, »Archaism in Times of Reproduction«, in: *John Coplans, Self Portrait Hand / Foot,* Ausst.-Kat. Museum Boijmans Van Beuningen, Rotterdam, Rotterdam 1990. Zwei Bücher behandeln hingegen Hannah Villigers Werke im Kontext der Skulptur: *Hannah Villiger, Skulptural,* Ausst.-Kat. Museum für Gegenwartskunst, Basel, Basel 1989; siehe außerdem Herta Wolf (Hrsg.), *Skulpturen. Fragmente,* Ausst.-Kat. Wiener Secession 1992, Zürich 1992.

34 Vgl. Chevrier 1990 (wie Anm. 33), S. 6. Siehe auch Christina Natlacen, *Am Beispiel Dieter Appelt, John Coplans und Arno Rafael Minkkinen: Zur Komplexität männlicher Selbstdarstellung in der zeitgenössischen Fotografie,* Diplomarbeit Universität Wien, 2001, S. 57–61.

35 Vgl. Coplans 2002 (wie Anm. 1), S. 175.

36 Die Darstellung afroamerikanischer Modelle als explizit sexuelle Körper, die durch die visuelle Fragmentierung des Körpers oftmals anonymisiert wiedergegeben werden, hat Mapplethorpe den Vorwurf eingebracht, kolonial-rassistische Stereotype zu bedienen. Kobena Mercer hat zu diesem Thema die nach wie vor differenziertesten Aufsätze geschrieben: Kobena Mercer, »Just Looking for Trouble: Robert Mapplethorpe and Fantasies of Race«, in: Lynne Segal und Mary McIntosh (Hrsg.), *Sex Exposed. Sexuality and the Pornography Debate,* New Jersey 1992. Kobena Mercer, »Skin Head Sex Thing: Racial Difference and the Homoerotic Imaginary«, in: *How Do I Look? – Queer Film and Video,* Seattle 1991. Siehe dazu auch Gen Doy, *Black Visual Culture. Modernity and Postmodernity,* New York 2000, S. 156–203.

37 Coplans 2002 (wie Anm. 1), S. 175.

38 Hannah Wilke stellt hier eine Ausnahme dar. In *Portrait of the Artist with Her Mother, Selma Butter,* aus der Serie *So Help Me Hannah* zeigt die Künstlerin ihre ältere, an Krebs erkrankte Mutter. Die Fotografin Melanie Manchot fotografierte in den 1990er-Jahren ebenfalls den Körper ihrer alternden Mutter. Zu einem Vergleich der Fotos von Manchot und Coplans siehe Chris Townsend, *Vile Bodies. Photography and the Crisis of Looking,* New York 1998, S. 97–104.

39 Vgl. Coplans 2002 (wie Anm. 1), S. 175.

40 Vgl. Claudia Benthien, *Haut – Literaturgeschichte – Körperbilder – Grenzdiskurse,* Hamburg 1999. Zur künstlerischen Auseinandersetzung mit Haut, beispielsweise bei VALIE EXPORT oder Jenny Holzer, siehe *Auf den Leib geschrieben,* Ausst.-Kat. Kunsthalle Wien, Wien 1995.

41 Roland Barthes, *Die helle Kammer,* Frankfurt am Main 1989.

Christina Natlacen # Body—Medium—Image: Viennese Actionism and Body Art

This body looks back at you like few others: John Coplans's photographic staging of his own body (fig. 2, p. 13) leaves no doubt as to the directness and immediacy of its address to the observer. He positions himself frontally before the camera in his studio, trains the camera on selected parts of his aging body—always truncated, in close-up, and in a well-calculated pose. Nothing distracts the gaze from these limp masses of skin and flesh in which Coplans forcibly intervenes with his hands and which he presents to the camera with a focus on his sex and shows in all its monumentality. As a textbook case of postmodern staged photography, Coplans interrogates his body in a manner that is rich in quotations and affords multiple ways of giving expression to the ugly and beautiful, humorous and serious, culturally established and new, male and female, provocative and restrained.

John Coplans, whose work as an artist began in the nineteen-eighties, belongs to a generation of artists that arrived on the scene in the wake of the historical avant-gardes of the twentieth century, including Viennese Actionism and the Body Art of the nineteen-seventies. For an artistic position such as that of John Coplans to be possible at all, art first needed to pass through a number of stages from the actionist painterly gesture to actionist works and finally to staged photographic actions. Viennese Actionism made a crucial contribution to these developments. In the course of the nineteen-sixties Otto Muehl, Günter Brus, Hermann Nitsch, and Rudolf Schwarzkogler, who make up the inner core of the group, developed an actionist oeuvre that, for the first time and with a previously unknown radicalism, placed the body at the center of the work, and thus, formally and thematically, prepared the ground for Body Art. The Viennese Actionists played a pioneering role not only in their use of the body as material, but also in the way, more than other performance artists of the time, they allowed photography to enter the conceptual framework of their artistic practice.[1] Even if the "artistic priority of the action is preserved in relation to the photographic reproduction," and it was not until the Body Art of the seventies that "the difference between artistic and photographic action [would] level out,"[2] from today's point of view Viennese Actionism represents a crucial contribution to the development of staged photography.

In the following essay, Viennese Actionism will be placed in relation to positions in the exhibition *The Body as Protest,* which should then lead to a discussion of its anticipations of, parallels with, and continued relevance in Body Art.[3] Such comparisons are exemplary attempts to grasp the body as medium and image, and to investigate these in relation to their structural similarities. Three superordinate categories serve as a guideline for the investigation of the relationship between the body and photography, or between the body and film: "the body as material," "the body as gesture," and "the body as fragment," which should provide a link between the action

Christina Natlacen Körper – Medium – Bild: Wiener Aktionismus und Body Art

Dieser Körper blickt uns wie kaum ein anderer an: John Coplans' fotografische Inszenierungen des eigenen Körpers (Abb. 2, S. 13) lassen an Direktheit und Unmittelbarkeit in der Betrachteradressierung keine Zweifel aufkommen. Frontal positioniert er sich in seinem Atelier vor der Kamera, bringt ausgewählte Partien seines alternden Körpers ins Bild – immer angeschnitten, in Nahsicht und wohlkalkulierter Pose. Nichts lenkt den Blick ab von dieser welken Haut- und Körpermasse, in die Coplans mit seinen Händen gewaltsam eingreift, sie mit Fokus auf sein Geschlecht der Kamera darbietet und jenes in seiner Monumentalität ausstellt. Als Paradefall der postmodernen inszenierten Fotografie praktiziert Coplans einen zitatreichen Umgang mit dem eigenen Körper: Dieser bietet eine Vielzahl an Möglichkeiten, Hässliches und Schönes, Humorvolles und Ernstes, kulturhistorisch Bekanntes und Neues, Männliches und Weibliches, Provokantes und Zurückhaltendes zum Ausdruck zu bringen.

John Coplans, dessen künstlerisches Werk in den 1980er-Jahren ansetzt, gehört jener Künstlergeneration an, die nach den historischen Avantgarden des 20. Jahrhunderts, zu denen auch der Wiener Aktionismus und die Body Art der 1970er-Jahre gehören, auf den Plan tritt. Bevor eine künstlerische Position wie John Coplans' überhaupt möglich wird, durchläuft die Kunst mehrere Etappen, die sie von der aktionistischen Malgeste über die Aktion hin zur inszenierten Fotoaktion führt. Der Wiener Aktionismus stellt einen wesentlichen Beitrag zu diesen Entwicklungen dar. Im Laufe der 1960er-Jahre entwickeln Otto Muehl, Günter Brus, Hermann Nitsch und Rudolf Schwarzkogler als innerer Kern der Gruppe ein aktionistisches Œuvre, das erstmals den Körper in bisher ungekannter Radikalität künstlerisch in den Mittelpunkt stellt und damit inhaltlich und formal den Boden für die Body Art bereitet. Die Wiener Aktionisten nehmen nicht nur eine Vorreiterrolle in der Verwendung des Körpers als Material ein, sondern zeichnen sich auch dadurch aus, dass sie mehr als andere Performance-Künstler dieser Zeit die Fotografie in den konzeptuellen Rahmen ihrer künstlerischen Praxis einfließen lassen.[1] Auch wenn die »künstlerische Priorität der Aktion gegenüber ihrer fotografischen Abbildung […] gewahrt [bleibt]« und erst die Body Art der 1970er-Jahre »die Differenz zwischen künstlerischem und fotografischem Handeln einebnen [wird]«,[2] so stellt der Wiener Aktionismus aus heutiger Sicht einen wesentlichen Beitrag für die weitere Entwicklung der inszenierten Fotografie dar.

Im Folgenden soll der Wiener Aktionismus mit Positionen der Ausstellung *Körper als Protest* in Beziehung gesetzt werden, um auf Vorwegnahmen, Parallelen und Nachwirkungen in der Body Art zu sprechen zu kommen.[3] Die Vergleiche sind exemplarische Versuche, den Körper als Medium und Bild zu fassen und im Hinblick auf strukturelle Ähnlichkeiten zu untersuchen. Als Leitlinie für die Untersuchung der Relation zwischen Körper und Fotografie beziehungsweise Körper und Film dienen die drei übergeordneten Kategorien »Körper als Material«, »Körper als Geste« und »Körper als Fragment«, die den Bogen von der Aktion mit dem Körper als Material hin zu einer stärker konzeptuell und

with the body as material and a stronger conceptual and media-art-based encounter with the body. However, to think about Viennese Actionism from the perspective of Body Art should not mean being limited to isolated thematic analogies; rather, it should sharpen our awareness for a multidimensional contextualization.

The Body as Material: (De)Formations

What was revolutionary in Viennese Actionism was the way in which, for the first time, the human body was rigorously deployed as artistic material. The body no longer served solely as the basis of a pictorial transformation in the form of a painting or a photograph, but was now simultaneously "medium and constituent of the action."[4] Although various other materials are used in the actions of Otto Muehl, Günter Brus, Hermann Nitsch, and Rudolf Schwarzkogler, these only have the character of aids that are there to provide support for the body as the actual and central bearer of information. The artistic act occurs through the body. The use of the body as material extends in Viennese Actionism from piling-up and covering-over to violent deformations of the body's surface as well as dangerous interventions and cuts in its substance. Forming and deforming should therefore be understood as crucial strategies for reinterpreting the body in relation to dominant social conventions, and for putting it to use as a tool of protest.

The choice of the body as basic material results from the search for a direct access to reality. In a revolutionary act of liberation, the Viennese Actionists abandon painting's representational function, instead treating art and nature in equal terms by replacing canvas and paint with body and reality. Analogous to the sound poetry of the Vienna Group of the nineteen-fifties, in which language's acoustic value is made autonomous as a means of expression, in Viennese Actionism the body itself in its entire expressive spectrum becomes the artwork. Viennese Actionism, which is essentially based on an explicit notion of material, is less interested in the form, function, and meaning of the material body than in the physical qualities of its materiality and tactility.

Of all the Viennese Actionists, it was Otto Muehl who most fundamentally shaped and developed this notion of material. He uses the term *Materialaktion* (Material action) to describe numerous actions taking place in the sixties in which the human body is variously plied with paint, foodstuffs, and a broad range of altered objects used as props. In his *Materialaktion Nr. 30* with the title *Nahrungsmitteltest* (Food test) from 1966 (fig. 1), the transition from paint to body as artistic material—a process that is of general significance for the development of Actionism—can be clearly observed. A large sheet of paper lying horizontally on the floor acts as a canvas from which various body parts and objects project in three dimen-

medienkünstlerisch orientierten Auseinandersetzung mit dem Körper spannen. Den Wiener Aktionismus von der Body Art aus zu denken soll dabei nicht heißen, sich auf punktuelle inhaltliche Analogien zu beschränken, sondern soll vielmehr das Bewusstsein für eine mehrdimensionale Kontextualisierung schärfen.

Körper als Material: (Ver)Formungen

Das Revolutionäre des Wiener Aktionismus besteht darin, dass der menschliche Körper erstmals konsequent als künstlerisches Material verwendet wird. Der Körper dient nicht mehr lediglich als Vorlage für eine bildnerische Transformation in Form eines Gemäldes oder einer Fotografie, sondern ist gleichzeitig »Medium und Konstituens der Aktion«.[4] Obwohl verschiedene andere Materialien in den Aktionen von Otto Muehl, Günter Brus, Hermann Nitsch und Rudolf Schwarzkogler verwendet werden, so haben diese doch nur den Charakter von Hilfsmitteln, die den Körper als eigentlichen zentralen Informationsträger unterstützend bearbeiten. Durch den Körper vollzieht sich der künstlerische Akt. Die Verwendung des Körpers als Material reicht im Wiener Aktionismus von Anhäufungen und Überschüttungen über gewaltsame Deformationen der Oberfläche bis hin zu gefährlichen Eingriffen und Einschnitten in das Körperganze. Formen und Verformen ist damit als wesentliche Strategie zu verstehen, den Körper entgegen der herrschenden gesellschaftlichen Konventionen umzudeuten und als Werkzeug des Protests einzusetzen.

Die Wahl des Körpers als zentrales Material resultiert aus der Suche nach einem direkten Zugriff auf die Wirklichkeit. In einem revolutionären Befreiungsschlag lösen sich die Wiener Aktionisten von der abbildenden Funktion der Malerei und setzen stattdessen Kunst und Natur gleich, indem sie Leinwand und Farbe durch Körper und Wirklichkeit ersetzen. Analog zur Lautpoesie der Wiener Gruppe in den 1950er-Jahren, bei der sich der akustische Wert der Sprache zu einem eigenständigen Ausdrucksmittel verselbstständigt, wird im Wiener Aktionismus der Körper selbst in seinem ganzen Ausdrucksspektrum zum Kunstwerk. Der Wiener Aktionismus, der sich maßgeblich auf einen expliziten Materialbegriff stützt, interessiert sich weniger für die Form, Funktion und Bedeutung des Materials Körper als vielmehr für seine physischen Eigenschaften der Materialität und Taktilität.

Von den Wiener Aktionisten hat Otto Muehl am wesentlichsten den Materialbegriff geprägt und entwickelt. Er verwendet die Bezeichnung *Materialaktion* für zahlreiche Aktionen der 1960er-Jahre, in denen der menschliche Körper mit Farbe, Lebensmitteln und einer Vielzahl an zweckentfremdeten Objekten als Requisiten traktiert wird. In seiner *Materialaktion Nr. 30* mit dem Titel *Nahrungsmitteltest* von 1966 (Abb. 1) ist der Übergang von der Farbe zum Körper als künstlerischem Material – ein für die Entwicklung des Aktionismus allgemein bedeutsamer Prozess – deutlich nachzuvollziehen. Eine horizontal auf dem Boden liegende Papierplane fungiert als Leinwand, von welcher sich verschie-

sions, either poking through from below or applied to the surface. This heterogeneous jumble of forms is unified and simultaneously abstracted by a gestural application of multicolored paint. In this material action the step from canvas to body as surface is exemplified particularly clearly. In a second step, the body is given a spatial articulation in the form of an action.

Not only with the Viennese Actionists, but also with other Austrian artists whose work involves actions, work on the body stands essentially under the sign of formation and deformation. The artist's own and the foreign body are grasped as a sculptural mass that can be moved and modeled and in which one can intervene up to and beyond the pain threshold. In such instances, the use of the living body as material often shows "iconoclastic"[5] traits. Two works produced almost simultaneously—*Face Farces* by Arnulf Rainer[6] (fig. 2) and *Studies for Holograms* by Bruce Nauman (cat. 13)—begin with the face as malleable material. Through the grimaces, which in Nauman's and Rainer's works should be understood less as a playful than as a violent "derailing and exaggeration of facial expression,"[7] destruction takes place on three different levels: on the level of the traditional portrait genre, on that of the legibility of facial expression, and finally on that of the individual's capacity for socialization. Both Rainer and Nauman aim with their photographs at a critique of the social body's normalization. While in the distorted faces for his first hologram series, with the descriptive title *Making Faces*, Nauman attempts this via a negation of the subject,[8] Rainer's photo-booth pictures are instead characterized by their strong individual charge. Arnulf Rainer's intense, eight-year exploration of the expressive potential of his own body can be understood as an artistic action of the appropriation and development of a repertoire of gestures and poses that was fundamentally influenced by the body language of the mentally ill.

On one crucial point, Arnulf Rainer's approach conforms to the program of the Viennese Actionists: he does his utmost to overcome the body's social limitations. The Viennese Actionists, especially Otto Muehl and Günter Brus, use the body to carry out, via the performative act, a critique and protest vis-à-vis the dominant conditions of the conservative Austria of the sixties. Kerstin Braun speaks of an "environmentally- or socially-related material analysis"[9] in which the body as the most important social signifier is placed in the foreground. It was Günter Brus whose actions were derived most strongly from his own body, and whose body actions took the body as their primary material. In relation to the status the body assumes as material, the body actions find their climax in Brus's *Körperanalyse* (Body analysis) works. In 1967 the first of the actions took place that essentially dealt with the sexual codification of the body (such as the *Transvestiten-Aktion* [Transvestite action] from 1967). In 1970, away from

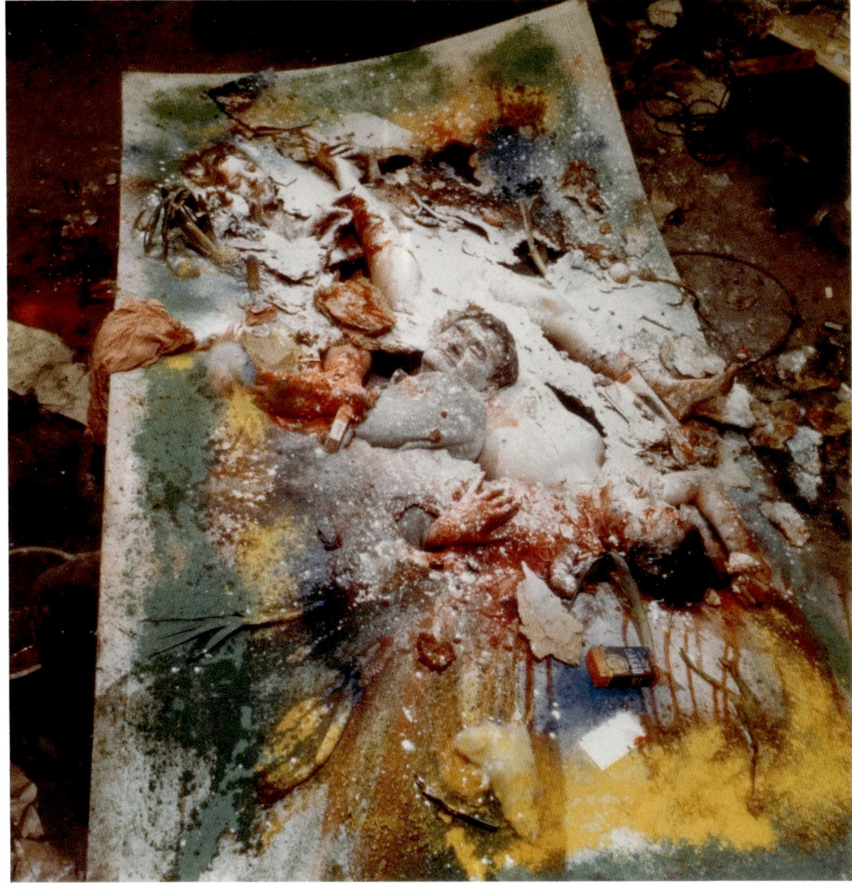

Abb. Fig. 1 Otto Muehl, *Materialaktion Nr. 30: Nahrungsmitteltest* (Material action no. 30: food test), 1966, mit with Anni Brus und and Ziemi Schieb, Fotografie photograph: Ludwig Hoffenreich

dene Körperteile und Objekte plastisch abheben, die entweder die Unterseite durchstoßen oder auf ihrer Oberfläche appliziert sind. Dieses heterogene Formgefüge wird durch einen gestischen Auftrag von bunten Farben vereinheitlicht und gleichzeitig abstrahiert. Der Schritt vom Tafelbild hin zum Körper als Oberfläche wird in dieser Materialaktion besonders klar versinnbildlicht. In einem nächsten Schritt wird es zu einem Raumgreifen des Körpers in der Aktion kommen.

Nicht nur bei den Wiener Aktionisten, sondern auch bei anderen österreichischen Künstlern, die aktionistisch arbeiten, steht die Auseinandersetzung mit dem Körper maßgeblich unter dem Zeichen der Formung und Verformung. Der eigene und fremde Körper wird als plastische Masse begriffen, die man bewegen, modellieren und in die man bis über die Schmerzgrenze hinaus eingreifen kann. Die Verwendung des lebendigen Körpers als Material trägt dabei oft »ikonoklastische«[5] Züge. Zwei beinahe zeitgleich entstandene Arbeiten – die *Face Farces* von Arnulf Rainer[6] (Abb. 2) und die *Studies for Holograms* von Bruce Nauman (Kat. 13) – setzen beim Gesicht als formbarem Material an. Über die Grimasse, die bei Nauman und Rainer weniger als spielerische, denn als gewalttätige »Entgleisung und Übertreibung der Mimik«[7] zu verstehen ist, findet Destruktion auf drei verschiedenen Ebenen statt: Zerstört wird das traditionelle Porträtbildnis, die Lesbarkeit des mimischen Ausdrucks und schließlich die Gesellschaftsfähigkeit des Individuums an sich. Sowohl Rainer als auch Nauman zielen mit ihren Fotografien auf eine Kritik an der Normierung des Gesellschaftskörpers ab. Während Nauman mit den Gesichtsverzerrungen

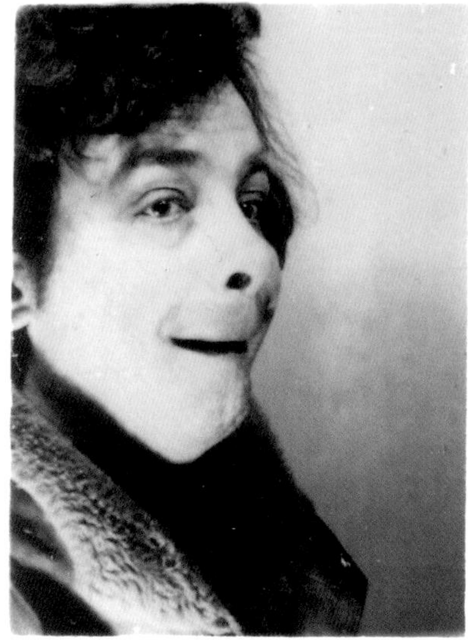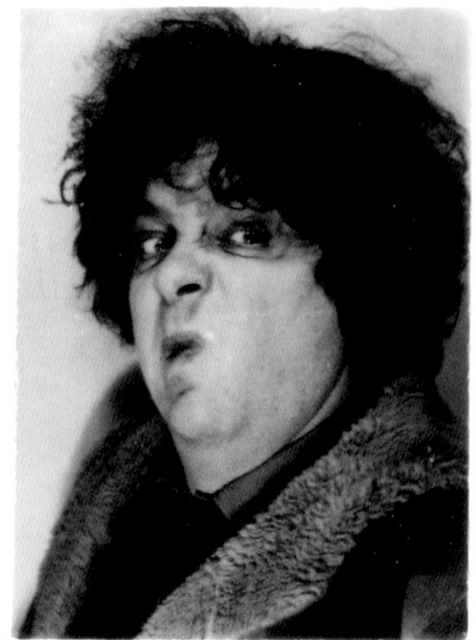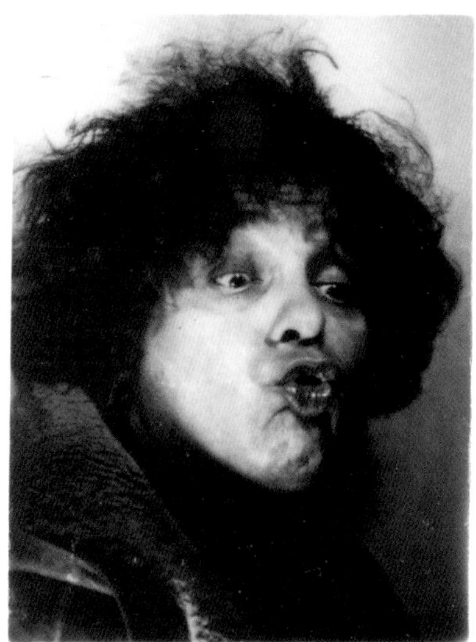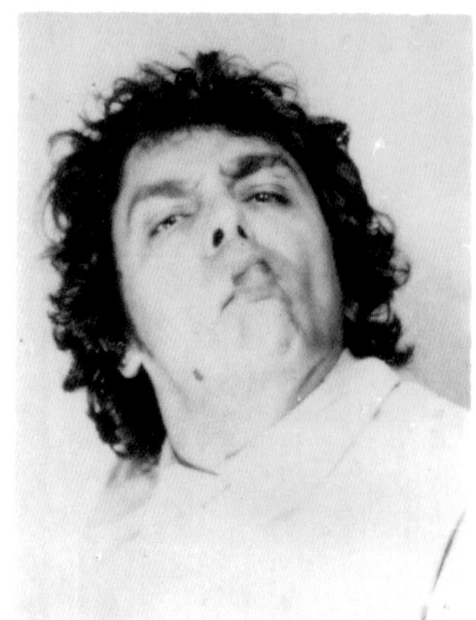

Abb. Fig. 2 Arnulf Rainer, Tableau mit Aufnahmen aus der *Automatenserie* tableau with prints from the *Automatenserie* (Photo-booth series), 1969/70

the public gaze in his Berlin studio, Günter Brus staged a further action with the title *Körperanalyse* (fig. 3). Here, the artist's body with a focus on the sex appears in all its ambivalence: the fully shaved torso and the extremely feminine pose evoke a body image that is clearly connoted as female. In addition, the still-visible, but folded sex does not suggest a classical male attitude, but is shown through its female-connoted softness and flexibility. At the same time, however, the male parts of the body image are not masked by a costume, but remain visible in the juxtaposition of male and female, "sex" and "gender." In view of the increased interest in "queer" body images over the last few years, Brus's *Körperanalyse,* in its singularity, appears almost prophetic.

In the context of the thematic focus on the reinterpretation of the male, Brus's *Körperanalyse* works can be profitably compared with the photographic and film works of Vito Acconci.[10] In Acconci's *Openings,* made around the same time, the viewer observes the artist extracting hair after hair from his conspicuously male stomach (cat. 3). In a fourteen-minute static shot, the underside of the dark tangle of hair is gradually made vis-

für die erste Hologramm-Serie, die den bezeichnenden Titel *Making Faces* trägt, dies über eine Negation des Subjekts[8] versucht, zeichnen sich Rainers in der Automatenkabine entstandene Fotografien im Gegenteil durch eine starke individuelle Aufladung aus. Arnulf Rainers acht Jahre dauernde intensive Auseinandersetzung mit den Ausdruckspotenzialen des eigenen Körpers versteht sich als künstlerische Aktion der Aneignung und Entwicklung eines Posen- und Gestenrepertoires, das maßgeblich von der Körpersprache psychisch Kranker beeinflusst ist.

Arnulf Rainer geht in einem wesentlichen Punkt mit dem Programm der Wiener Aktionisten konform: Er setzt alles daran, die sozialen Einschränkungen des Körpers zu überwinden. Die Wiener Aktionisten, insbesondere Otto Muehl und Günter Brus, setzen den Körper dazu ein, um über den performativen Akt Kritik und Protest an den herrschenden Zuständen des konservativen Österreichs der 1960er-Jahre zu üben. Kerstin Braun spricht von einer »umwelt- bzw. gesellschaftsbezogenen Materialanalyse«,[9] bei welcher der Körper als wichtigster sozialer Zeichenträger im Fokus steht. Am stärksten geht Günter Brus in seinen Aktionen von seinem eigenen Körper aus und setzt diesen in seinen Körperaktionen als primäres Material ein. Die Körperaktionen finden in Bezug auf den Stellenwert, den der Körper als Material einnimmt, ihren Höhepunkt in seinen *Körperanalyse*-Arbeiten. 1967 finden dazu erste Aktionen statt, die sich maßgeblich mit der sexuellen Codierung des Körpers auseinandersetzen (etwa die *Transvestiten-Aktion* von 1967). 1970 inszeniert Günter Brus in seinem Berliner Atelier unter Ausschluss der Öffentlichkeit eine weitere Aktion mit dem Titel *Körperanalyse* (Abb. 3). Der Körper des Künstlers mit dem Fokus auf das Geschlecht erscheint hier in all seiner zwitterhaften Existenz: Mit der glattrasierten Rumpfpartie und der äußerst femininen Standpose wird ein eindeutig weiblich konnotiertes Körperbild evoziert. Auch das noch sichtbare, aber zusammengekrümmte Geschlecht vermittelt keinen klassisch-männlichen Gestus, sondern zeigt sich vielmehr über seine als weiblich verstandene Weichheit und Anpassungsfähigkeit. Gleichzeitig werden die männlichen Anteile des Körperbildes nicht durch Kostümierung maskiert, sondern bleiben im Nebeneinander von männlich und weiblich, »sex« und »gender«, sichtbar. In Anbetracht des erst vor wenigen Jahren erstarkten Interesses für »queere« Körperbilder erscheint Brus' *Körperanalyse* in seiner Singularität geradezu prophetisch.

Brus' *Körperanalyse*-Arbeiten lassen sich vom inhaltlichen Fokus einer Umdeutung des Männlichen her gut mit dem fotografischen und filmischen Werk von Vito Acconci vergleichen.[10] Zeitgleich entstanden, kann der Betrachter in Acconcis *Openings* mitverfolgen, wie sich der Künstler Haar um Haar von seinem männlichen Bauch ausreißt (Kat. 3). Mit fixer Kameraeinstellung wird in 14 Minuten sukzessive das Darunter des dunklen Haargewirrs sichtbar – eine epilierte Hautregion, die Assoziationen zum Jungfräulichen hervorruft. Das bewusst weibliche Gebaren eines Mannes – Amelia Jones spricht in ihrer

ible—an epilated area of skin that suggests associations with the virginal. The deliberately feminine pose by a man—Amelia Jones speaks in her analysis of "effeminization"[11]—is given expression in a simple body gesture that does without any additional material. In this work, Acconci intervenes more directly in the surface of the body than in the performances subsumed under the title *Conversions,* in which, in a sequence of images, he clamps his member between his legs, thereby simulating the female pubic region. The film *Openings,* in contrast, deals with a painful opening process that can be equated on a symbolic level with an act of defloration.

The Body as Gesture: Traces

Beside the body's fundamental use as material, in both Viennese Actionism and Body Art the body also becomes a "speaking" material.[12] Here the focus is on the body in relation to its legibility, expressiveness, and interpretation—in short, to its capacity to speak. The full range of possibilities of analyzing the body on political, aesthetic, and moral levels vis-à-vis its semantic meaning finds its most concrete expression in the concept of the gesture. As Sigrid Adorf has written:

> The concept of the gesture serves to name a relationship of body, language, and mediality, within which actions are to be located. Unlike the movements of a marionette, these are no longer actions that raise questions about the center of power that holds all the strings, but rather, allow for the recognition of the driving forces that now correlate more . . . with images of the self-organization of matter and systems.[13]

In Viennese Actionism the earliest use of gesture was still linked to painting and clearly shows the genesis of action art from the earlier abstract works of Art Informel. The formerly Tachist gesture of mark-making is subsequently transformed into a body trace, which is generally recorded photographically. The work of Günter Brus can be considered as paradigmatic for this performative turn, in which the pictorial limits are opened up to include a space of action in which the artist operates as an actor. According to Peter Weibel, Günter Brus "was the first to clearly recognize the growing autonomy of the body that resulted from the growing autonomy of the painterly elements introduced by Art Informel."[14] In his first action *Ana* (fig. 4) from 1964, Brus makes the step to the direct representation of the painting act as a process. Drawing the necessary conclusions from his earlier efforts to push forward into space and to overcome the limits of painting, Brus now includes the body in the creative process by using its surface as a direct painterly support. Even in this first body painting the expressive activity of the artist-subject is given its full range with the focus on the expressive potential of the body. In his actions, Brus works succes-

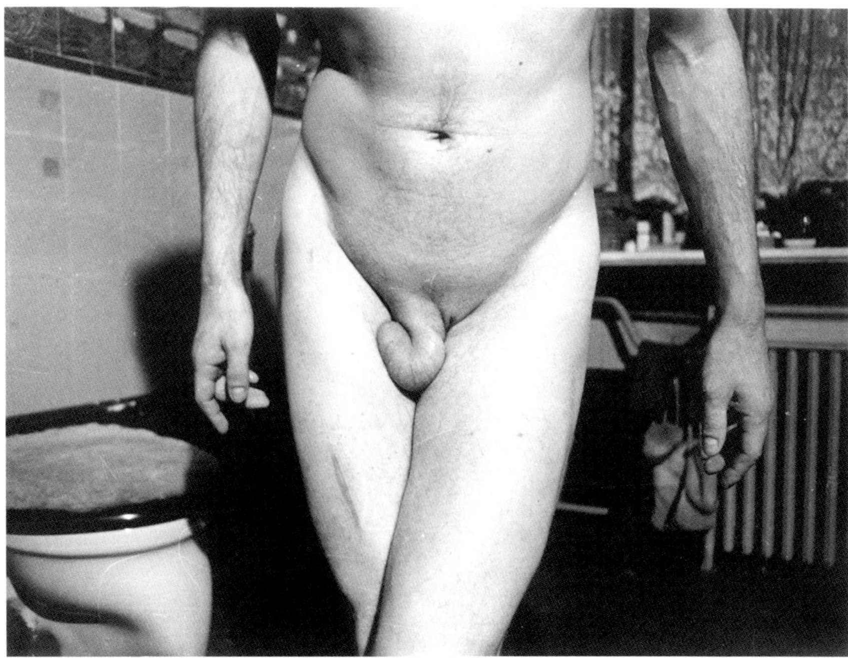

Analyse von »effeminization«[11] – findet hier in einer einfachen Körpergeste ihren
Ausdruck, die ohne zusätzliches Material auskommt. Acconci greift hier noch
direkter in die Körperoberfläche ein als in seinen unter dem Titel *Conversions*
subsummierten Performances, in denen er sich in einer Sequenz sein Glied
zwischen die Beine klemmt und so eine weibliche Schampartie mimt. Im Gegensatz dazu handelt es sich bei dem Film *Openings* um einen schmerzhaften
Öffnungsprozess, der auf symbolischer Ebene mit einem Deflorationsakt gleichgesetzt werden kann.

Körper als Geste: Spuren

Neben der grundsätzlichen Verwendung des Körpers als Material kristallisiert
sich sowohl im Wiener Aktionismus als auch in der Body Art die Verwendung
des Körpers als »sprechendes« Material heraus.[12] Der Körper steht hier bezüg-
lich seiner Lesbarkeit, Aussagekraft und Deutung im Fokus, kurz: in seiner
Sprachlichkeit. Die gesamte Breite an Möglichkeiten, den Körper auf politischer,
ästhetischer und moralischer Ebene auf seine semantische Bedeutung hin zu
analysieren, findet im Begriff der Geste seinen konkretesten Ausdruck. Denn
dieser

> dient der Benennung eines Verhältnisses von Körper, Sprache und Media-
> lität, innerhalb dessen Handlungen verortet werden sollen, die im Unter-
> schied zu den Bewegungen der Marionette nicht mehr nach dem Zentrum
> der Macht fragen lassen, die alle Fäden in der Hand hält, sondern die
> strukturellen Triebkräfte erkennen ließen, die […] nun eher mit Bildern der
> Selbstorganisation von Materie und Systemen korrelieren.[13]

Die früheste Bedeutung der Geste im Wiener Aktionismus knüpft noch an die
Malerei an und verdeutlicht die Genese der Aktionskunst aus dem vorange-
henden abstrakten Informel. Die ehemals tachistische Zeichengeste wandelt

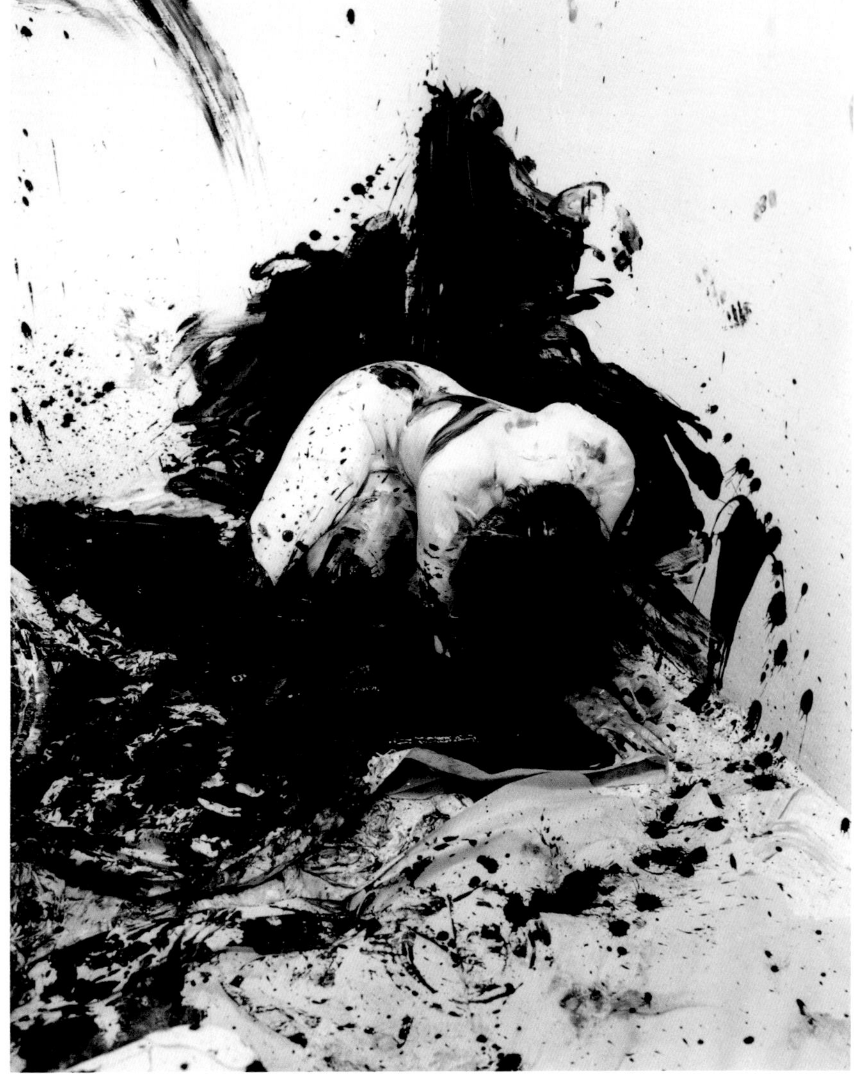

Abb. Fig. 4   Günter Brus, Aktion *Ana (Ana* action), 1964, mit with Anni Brus, Fotografie photograph: Siegfried Klein (Kasaq)

sively on the power of "pantomime and gesture as a substitute for expressive pictorial structures,"[15] while also reflecting on the legacy of Austrian Expressionism, which around fifty years earlier saw body language as a way of dramatically heightening artistic expression. *Ana* marks the transition in Brus's work from Tachist painting to body action in which paint, as the connecting element, is spattered over both the white-primed space and the naked bodies within. The body frees itself from the abstraction of the expressive Art Informel and acquires ever-greater autonomy.

Once the body has been established as an autonomous expressive support, it enters into a broad field of expressive and gestural body language. Now, gesture no longer represents a stage in the process of the production of a picture, as was the case in Art Informel, but becomes the actual artistic action. It is significant that body-language works often draw attention to their processual nature, and thereby have recourse to the medium of film. Although a gesture can be caught in a photograph, it is determined and fixed based on a single expressive moment. Therefore, if artists want to show a gesture's development from its beginning to its end, they tend to use film as a means of documentation. In his essay "Notes on Gesture," Giorgio Agamben has pointed out precisely this difference

sich in Folge in eine Körperspur, die meist fotografisch aufgezeichnet wird. Das Werk von Günter Brus kann als paradigmatisch für diese performative Wende angesehen werden, bei der die Erweiterung der Bildgrenzen in einen Aktionsraum, in dem der Künstler als Akteur wirkt, vollzogen wird. Nach Peter Weibel hat Günter Brus »als erster und am deutlichsten die Verselbständigung des Körpers als Konsequenz der vom Informel eingeleiteten Kette von Verselb- ständigungen der malerischen Elemente erkannt«.[14] 1964 vollzieht Brus in seiner ersten Aktion *Ana* (Abb. 4) den Schritt zur direkten Abbildung des Malakts als Prozess. Brus zieht aus seinen vorhergehenden Bestrebungen, in den Raum vorzustoßen und die Grenzen des Tafelbildes zu überwinden, die Konsequenz und bezieht den Körper nun in den Schaffensprozess ein, indem er die Ober- fläche als direkten Farbträger verwendet. Schon in dieser ersten Körperbema- lung kann sich der expressive Handlungsspielraum des Künstlersubjekts voll entfalten und das Ausdruckspotenzial des Körpers in den Vordergrund treten. Brus arbeitet in seinen Aktionen sukzessiv an der Kraft von »Pantomime und Geste als Ersatz für expressive Bildstrukturen«[15] und besinnt sich dabei auf das Erbe des österreichischen Expressionismus, der rund 50 Jahre früher die Körpersprache als dramatische Steigerung des künstlerischen Ausdrucks er- kannt hat. *Ana* markiert den Übergang in Brus' Werk von der tachistischen Malerei zur Körperaktion, indem Farbe als verbindendes Element sowohl auf den weiß grundierten Raum als auch auf die sich darin befindenden nackten Körper gespritzt wird. Der Körper löst sich förmlich aus der Abstraktion des expressiven Informels heraus und erlangt immer größere Autonomie.

Ist der Körper einmal als autonomer Ausdrucksträger etabliert, tritt er in das weite Feld der mimischen und gestischen Körpersprache ein. Die Geste stellt nun nicht mehr eine Etappe im Prozess des Generierens eines Bildes dar, wie es im Informel der Fall gewesen ist, sondern wird zur eigentlichen künstleri- schen Aktion. Es ist bezeichnend, dass körpersprachliche Arbeiten oft ihre Prozesshaftigkeit selbst ausstellen und dabei auf das Medium Film zurück- greifen. Eine Geste kann zwar auch momenthaft durch die Fotografie dargestellt werden, allerdings wird sie hier auf einen einzigen Ausdruckshöhepunkt fest- gelegt und fixiert. Daher greifen die Künstler in jenen Fällen, in denen sie das Hervorbringen einer Geste von Anfang bis Ende ausstellen möchten, auf den Film als Dokumentationsmittel zurück. Giorgio Agamben hat in seinem Essay »Noten zur Geste« genau auf diese Differenz zwischen Bild und Geste hinge- wiesen und folgerichtig den Film als Medium der Geste definiert.[16]

Das differenzierteste Ausdrucksspektrum des Körpers bietet das Gesicht mit seinen mimischen Variationsmöglichkeiten. Seit dem 18. Jahrhundert wer- den die pathognomischen Leidenschaftsdarstellungen in Kunst und Wissen- schaft verstärkt diskutiert. Auf der Suche nach dem richtigen Gesichtsausdruck und seiner eindeutigen Entzifferung werden von bildenden Künstlern, Schau- spielern und Medizinern Bildkompendien angelegt, die sich der Klassifizierung von verschiedenen Gefühlszuständen widmen. In der Kunst der späten 1960er-

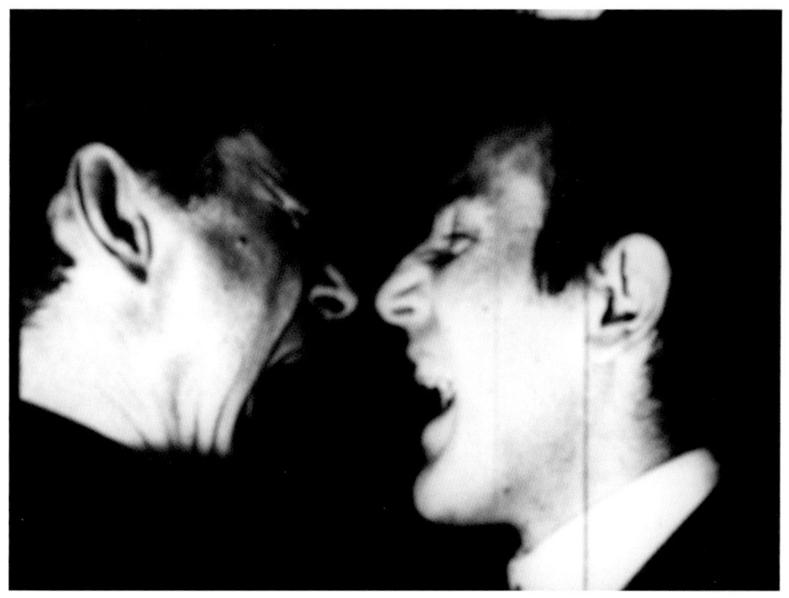

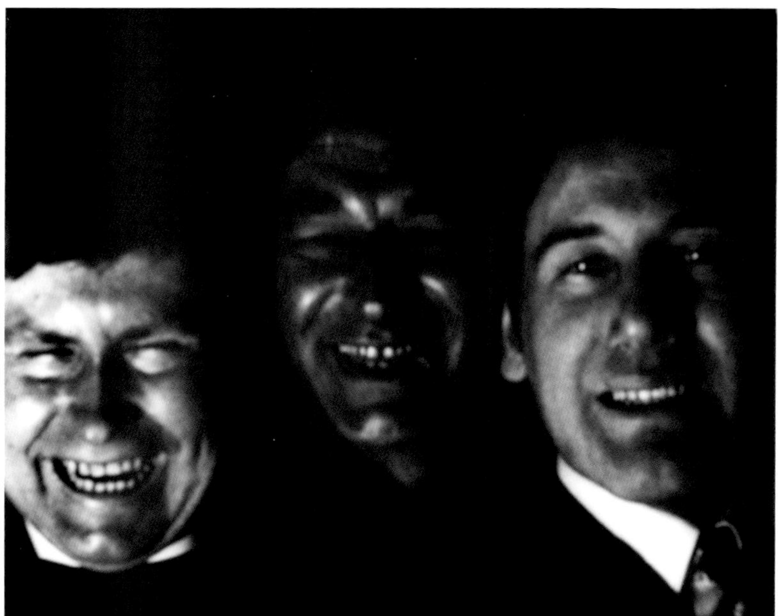

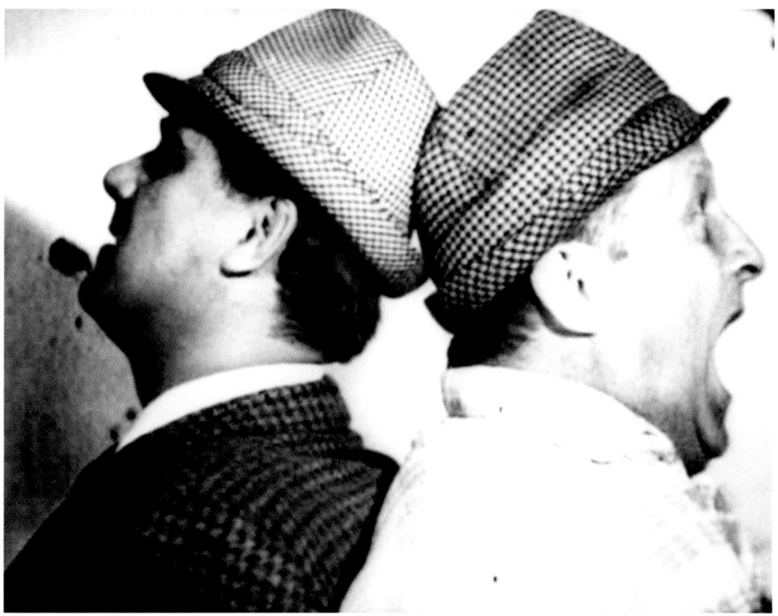

Abb. Fig. 5   Otto Muehl, *Grimuid,* 1967 (Kadervergrößerungen frame enlargements)

und frühen 1970er-Jahre lebt dieses Interesse für die Mimik wieder auf. Der Wiener Aktionismus zeichnet sich ganz allgemein durch seinen Fokus auf alles Körpersprachliche aus, in Reinform setzt er sich damit jedoch dort auseinander, wo nicht die Aktion als öffentliches Ereignis im Vordergrund steht, sondern eine Performance vor und für die Kamera. 1967 entsteht unter der Federführung von Otto Muehl der Film *Grimuid* (Abb. 5). Otto Muehl, Peter Weibel, Hermann Nitsch, Oswald Wiener und andere treten als Akteure auf, indem sie frontal zur Kamera Gesichter und Grimassen schneiden. Anfangs richtet sich die Kamera in statischer Einstellung auf Gesichter, die in einem befremdlichen Lachen erstarren, bevor in schneller Abfolge unterschiedliche Gesichtsteile und Gesichtsausdrücke aneinander montiert werden. Der Fokus liegt wiederholt auf der Mundpartie, zwischen schiefe Lippen zwängt sich die Zunge wie bei Debilen. Die Assoziation mit dem pathologischen Gesichtsausdruck liegt auf der Hand, es geht nicht um eine reziproke Kommunikation mit einem Gegenüber, sondern um die Präsentation eines jenseits der Norm angesiedelten Mimikrepertoires.

Eine ähnliche Anordnung zwischen Performer beziehungsweise Performerin und Kamera weist das Video *Gestures* von Hannah Wilke (1974) auf, das auf den Begriff der Geste buchstäblich Bezug nimmt (Kat. 2). Während der Dauer von 30 Minuten richtet sich der Kamerafokus maßgeblich auf das Gesicht der Künstlerin, das mithilfe der ins Bild ragenden Hände verschiedene faziale Bewegungsmuster mimt. Im Gegensatz zum Interesse der Wiener Aktionisten an den Extremen der Mimik in Form der psychopathologischen Grimasse geht es Wilke vielmehr um eine poetische und intime Befragung von Alltagsgesten, die um die Darstellung von Weiblichkeit kreisen. Wie in einem Atlas mit Vorlagenzeichnungen für Mimikstudien wird das Gesicht als plastische Masse zu verschiedenen Ausdruckszuständen verformt – nicht ohne Grund wurde *Gestures* mit einem skulpturalen Bildhauerwerk verglichen.[17]

Eine weitere Dimension der Geste betrifft deren Zeichenhaftigkeit. Eine Geste beschränkt sich nie auf den Akt ihres Vollzugs selbst, sondern stellt immer auch gleichzeitig einen Verweis dar. Codierte Gesten beinhalten immer auch ein Vorher und ein Nachher: ein Vorher, da sie sich auf ein kulturelles Verständnis beziehen, ein Nachher, da sie von jeder beliebigen Person erneut reproduziert werden können. Als Spur eines vorangegangenen Ereignisses sind sie mit der medialen Verfasstheit der Fotografie vergleichbar: So wie sich hier die Lichtstrahlen eines einzigen Moments auf der fotosensiblen Oberfläche abdrücken, so vermittelt sich das Resultat einer Geste ebenfalls in verschiedenen Formen der Einschreibungen. In der Körperkunst ist es vorzugsweise die Haut, die als Trägermedium von Spuren fungiert. In ihrer Arbeit *Body Sign Action* von 1970/1972 (Abb. 6) thematisiert VALIE EXPORT auf drei Ebenen die Zeichenhaftigkeit einer Geste, die als eminent feministisches Statement verstanden werden möchte. Als Offenlegung von sexistischen Strukturen lässt sich die Künstlerin einen täuschend echten Strumpfhalter auf die entsprechen-

between image and gesture and, accordingly, defined film as the medium of the gesture.[16]

It is the face with its range of possible expressions that provides the body with its most differentiated expressive spectrum. At the beginning of the eighteenth century, there was a growing interest in the pathognomic depictions of emotion in art and science. In search of correct facial expressions and their clear deciphering, artists, actors, and medics compiled visual compendia dedicated to the classification of various affective states. With the art of the late nineteen-sixties and early seventies there has been a revival of interest in facial expression. What characterizes Viennese Actionism in very general terms is its focus on everything related to body language. In a pure form, however, this occurs in a place in which the focus is not on an action as a public event, but on a performance for and in front of the camera. In 1967 the film *Grimuid* (fig. 5) was made under the direction of Otto Muehl. Otto Muehl, Peter Weibel, Hermann Nitsch, Oswald Wiener, and others appear as actors making various faces and grimaces toward the camera. The film starts with a static shot showing faces set in a disconcerting laugh, before a variety of facial details and expressions are edited together in quick succession. The focus is repeatedly placed on the mouth area; as with the mentally retarded, a tongue forces its way between crooked lips. There is a clear association with the pathological facial expressions: this is not about reciprocal communication, but the presentation of a repertory of facial distortions situated outside the norm.

A similar arrangement between performer and camera can be seen in the video *Gestures* by Hannah Wilke (1974), which makes literal reference to the concept of gesture (cat. 2). For the duration of thirty minutes the camera focuses on the artist's face, which, with the help of hands that jut into the image, executes various facial expressions. Compared to the Viennese Actionists' interest in extreme expressions in the form of psychopathological grimaces, Wilke is primarily concerned with a poetic and intimate inquiry into everyday gestures circling around the representation of femininity. As in an atlas with studies for different expressions, the face as sculptural mass is formed into different expressive states; not without reason, *Gestures* has been compared with a work of sculpture.[17]

A further dimension of the gesture relates to its semiotic character. A gesture is never limited to the act of its execution, but always also refers beyond itself. Encoded gestures always comprise a before and an after: a before, since they draw on a cultural understanding; an after, since they are constantly and freely reproduced. As a trace of a preceding event they can be compared with photography in its role as a medium. Just as the light rays of a single moment are registered on a photosensitive surface, the result of a gesture is conveyed in the various forms of its registration. In Body Art it is especially the skin that acts as the bearer of traces. In her

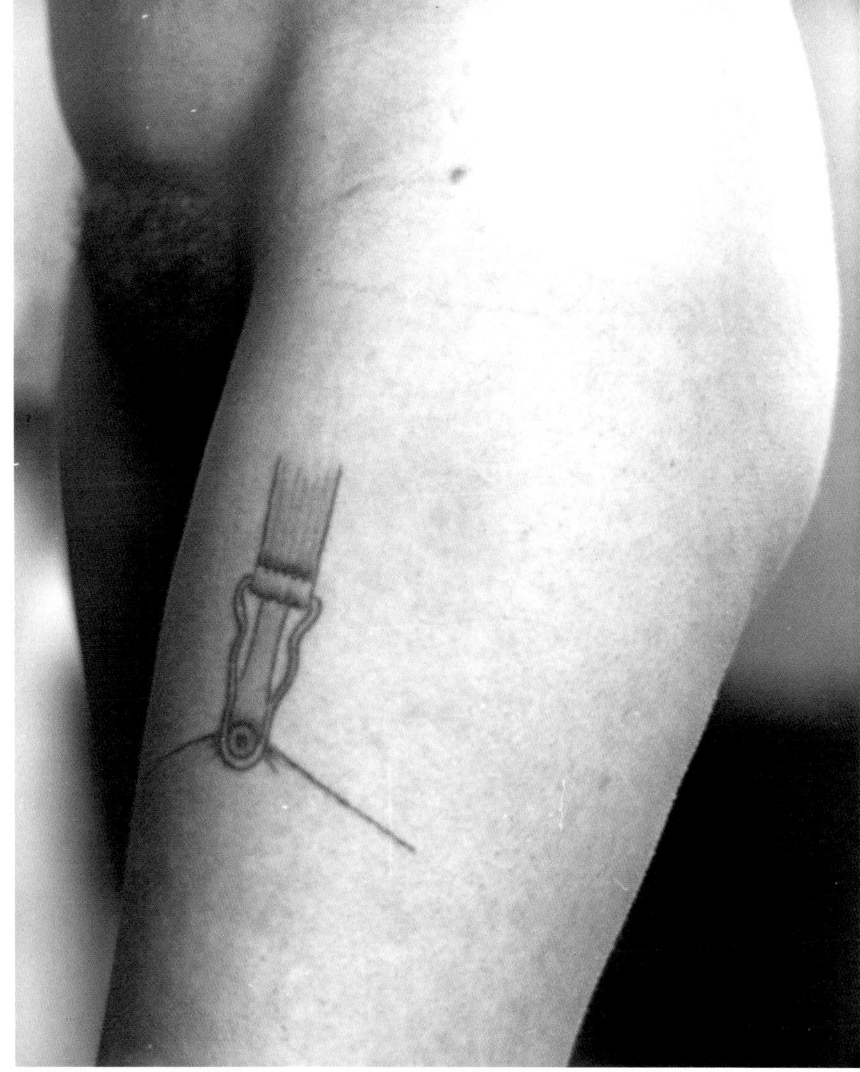

Abb. Fig. 6 VALIE EXPORT, *Body Sign Action,* tätowiert am 2. Juli 1970 tattooed July 2, 1970, Frankfurt am Main, Abzug photographic print 1972

de Stelle ihres Oberschenkels tätowieren. Diese eindrucksvolle Geste streut ihren Sinngehalt auf allen drei Ebenen der peirceschen Zeichentheorie aus.[18] Erstens offenbart sich im Akt des Tätowierens die Haut als Träger einer Spur der Einschreibung. Diese Form der Körperzeichnung zollt mit ihrer Endgültigkeit dem Indexikalischen besonders eindrücklich Tribut. Zweitens operiert EXPORT mit der Wahl des Strumpfbandes als »Zeichen einer vergangenen Versklavung, als Symbol verdrängter Sexualität, [...] als Zeichen der Zugehörigkeit zu einer Klasse, die ein bedingtes Verhalten fordert« auf einer symbolischen Ebene.[19] Drittens schließlich mündet das Ergebnis dieser Geste des Protests gegen patriarchale Unterdrückungsmechanismen in ein ikonisches Bild, das über das Medium Fotografie vermittelt wird. Während VALIE EXPORT mit der Geste des Tätowierens auf eine außerbildliche Wirklichkeit hinweisen möchte, erhebt Ketty La Rocca in ihrer Arbeit *You You* den Zeigegestus selbst zum Bild (Kat. 17).[20] Beide Arbeiten sind explizite Kommentare zu einer aus feministischer Sicht revidierten Körperpolitik, bei der Sprache, Geste und deren Zeichenhaftigkeit die Grundelemente darstellen.

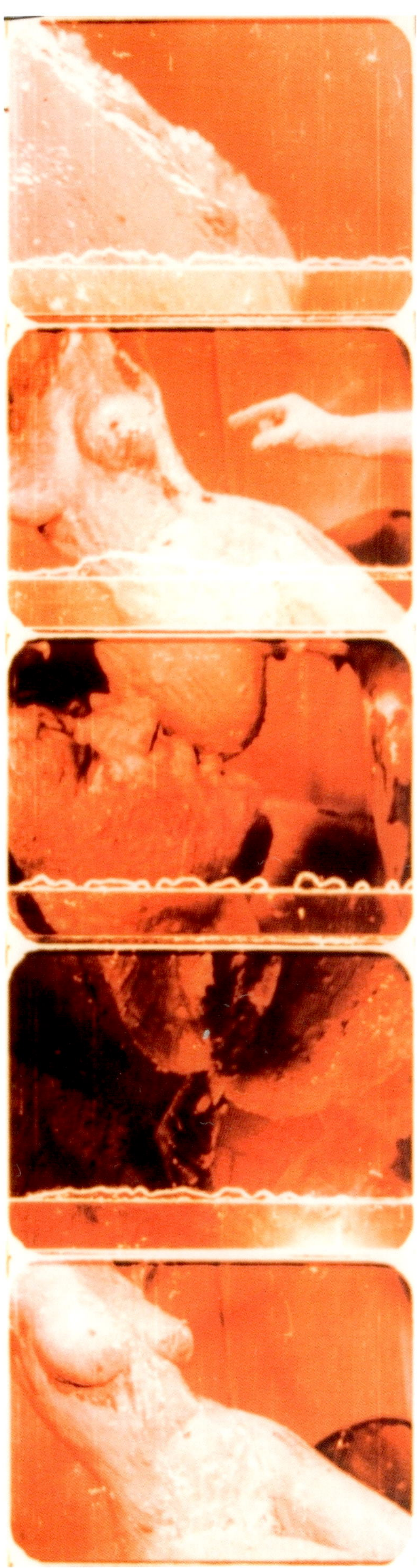

Abb. Fig. 7   Kurt Kren, *6/64 Mama und Papa*, 1964
(Kadervergrößerungen frame enlargements)

Körper als Fragment: Schnitte

Vorbereitet insbesondere durch den Surrealismus erscheint der menschliche Körper in der Kunst des voranschreitenden 20. Jahrhunderts immer seltener in seiner Integrität, sondern wird zerstückelt, fragmentiert und seiner Ganzheit beraubt. Einen wesentlichen Anteil an diesen Prozessen hat die mediale Vermittlung des Körperbildes. Es ist nun nicht mehr der Künstler allein, der (seinen) Körper als Material verwendet, sondern die Aktion erhält ihre eigentliche Bedeutung durch die mediale Form ihrer Bearbeitung. Auch wenn jede Fotografie an sich als Schnitt durch die Zeit und den Raum zu verstehen ist,[21] bekommt in den folgenden Arbeiten der Schnitt eine explizite und weitreichende Bedeutung. Der Schnitt zerstückelt den Körper – sowohl real als auch virtuell.

Kurt Krens Aktionsfilme sind das beste Beispiel, um den Wechsel von der Bearbeitung des Körpers selbst hin zur Bearbeitung des Körpers über das visuelle Material aufzuzeigen. Der Avantgarde-Filmemacher Kren kommt 1963 durch Otto Muehl mit den Wiener Aktionisten in Kontakt und bedingt sich aus, für seine Zusammenarbeit mit Muehl und Brus völlig frei über das von ihm gedrehte Filmmaterial der Aktionen verfügen zu können. 1964 filmt Kren erstmals anlässlich von Muehls Aktion *Mama und Papa*. Aus dem Material schneidet er nach einem präzisen Plan seinen knapp vierminütigen sechsten Film (Abb. 7). Kren löst sich komplett von jeder dokumentierenden Funktion, die Aktion wird nicht mehr in ihrem chronologischen Verlauf gezeigt, sondern in Einzelbildern, die aufgrund ihrer radikalen Montage mit einer bislang nicht gekannten Wucht auf den Betrachter einstürzen. Es wird gleichermaßen die Aktion selbst wie auch der Blick auf das Geschehen zerstückelt. Kren überwindet sowohl bereits beim Filmen ein ganzheitliches Körperbild, indem er Details in den Blick nimmt, als auch bei der Montage, die einzelne Körperansichten so schnell aneinanderreiht, dass jeder Holismus verloren geht. Sein serielles Kurzschnittverfahren ist dem Ansinnen der Wiener Aktionisten, eine »möglichst einfach[e]« Aufnahme »ohne Mätzchen«[22] im Stile einer distanzierten Fotoreportage zu erlangen, diametral entgegengesetzt. Dennoch schließt er konzeptionell an den Aktionismus an, indem er deren »Gestus des Bearbeitens des Körpers/Dinges-als-Material auf den Film [überträgt]«.[23]

Der einzige Künstler unter den Wiener Aktionisten, der den Schritt von der Aktion und ihrer einfachen Dokumentation hin zu einer Bildinszenierung vollzieht, ist Rudolf Schwarzkogler. Mit seinen sechs Aktionen aus den Jahren 1965/66 schafft er einen »Modellfall ›inszenierter Fotografie‹«,[24] der aufgrund seines konzeptuellen Ansatzes internationale Vorbildwirkung hat. Die Aktion dient ausschließlich als Mittel zur Inszenierung und wird »nach dem Gesichtspunkt ihrer fotografischen Eignung [konzipiert]. Die Aktion verwandelte sich in eine Fotoseance«.[25] Peter Weibel positioniert Schwarzkoglers aktionsfotografisches Werk, das durch eine Rückkehr zum Bild gekennzeichnet ist und daher auch konsequenterweise unter Ausschluss der Öffentlichkeit im eigenen Atelier stattfindet, am Ende einer Reihe unterschiedlicher Gebrauchsweisen der Fotografie im

work *Body Sign Action* from 1970/1972 (fig. 6), VALIE EXPORT treats on three levels the semiotic character of a gesture, which is intended as an eminent feminist statement. As a disclosure of sexist structures, the artist had a deceptively real-looking suspender strap tattooed over the corresponding area of her thigh. This striking gesture scatters its meaning over all three levels of the Peircean theory of signs:[18] First, in the act of tattooing, the skin reveals itself as bearer of a trace of inscription. Due to its definitiveness, this form of body marking pays particularly remarkable tribute to the indexical. Second, EXPORT, with the choice of the suspender as a "sign of former enslavement, as symbol of repressed sexuality . . . as sign of the membership in a cast that demands conditioned behavior"[19] operates on a symbolic level. Third, this gesture of protest against patriarchal methods of oppression results in an iconic image that is conveyed via the medium of photography. Whereas with the gesture of tattooing VALIE EXPORT intends a reference to an extra-pictorial reality, in her work *You You* Ketty La Rocca raises the pointing gesture itself to the level of the image (cat. 17).[20] Both works are explicit commentaries on a body politics revised from a feminist point of view, in which the key elements are language, gesture, and their semiotic character.

The Body as Fragment: Cuts

As prepared for especially by Surrealism, the human body appears less and less in its integrity in the art of the advancing twentieth century. Instead, it is cut up, fragmented, and deprived of any sense of wholeness. A crucial part in this process is played by the mediation of the body image. From now on it would no longer be the artist alone who uses (his) body as material; rather, the action acquires its actual meaning through the media form of its reproduction. Even if each photograph as such should be understood as a cut through time and space,[21] in subsequent works the cut itself is given an explicit and far-reaching significance. The cut fragments the body—both in reality and virtually.

The actionist films of Kurt Kren provide the best example to cast light on the shift from the treatment of the body itself to the treatment of the body via the visual material. The avant-garde filmmaker Kren came into contact with the Viennese Actionists in 1963 through Otto Muehl. His stipulation for the collaboration with Muehl and Brus, however, was total freedom in the use of the film material he produced of the actions. Kren filmed the Actionists for the first time in 1964, on the occasion of Muehl's action *Mama und Papa*. He edited from the material, according to a precise plan, his approximately four-minute sixth film (fig. 7). Here, Kren entirely abandons any documentary function; the action is no longer shown in its chronological development, but in single images, which, on the basis of their radical montage, assail the viewer with a previously unknown force.

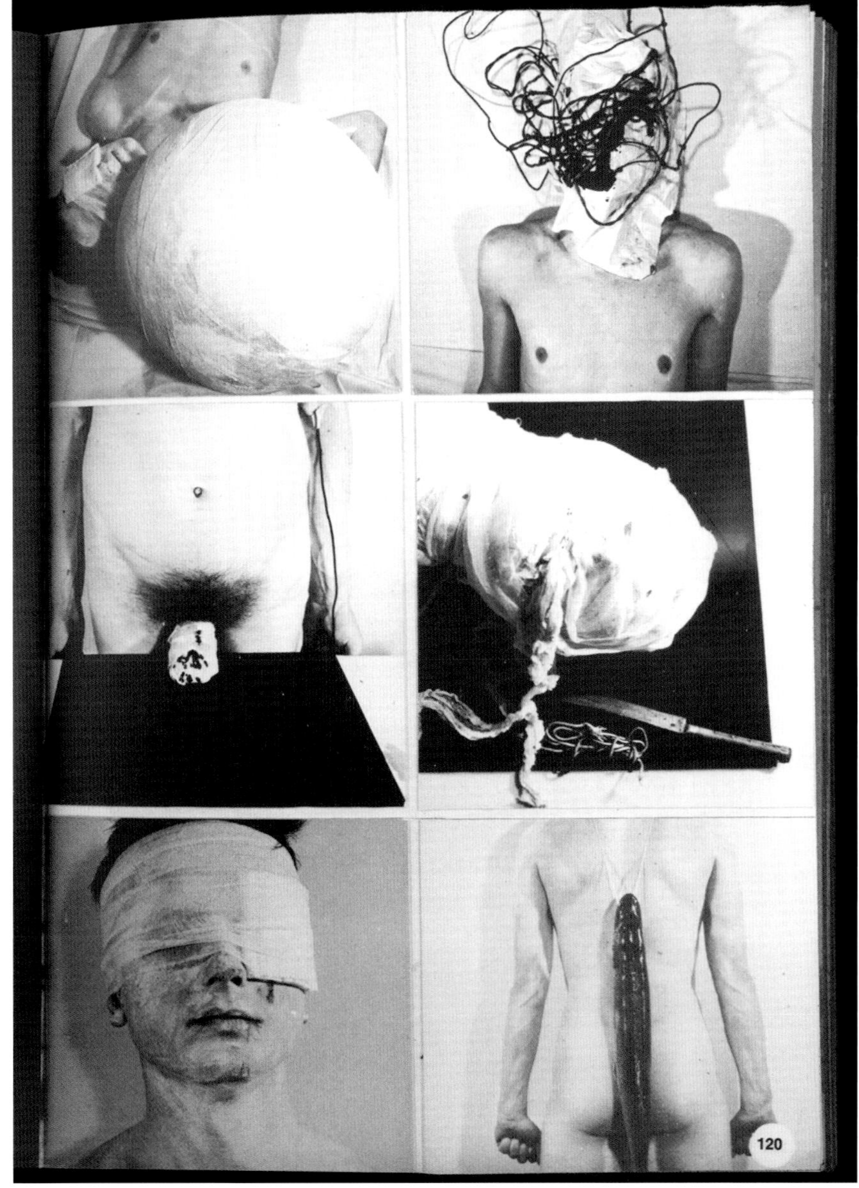

Abb. Fig. 8 Rudolf Schwarzkogler, Montage mit Aufnahmen aus verschiedenen Aktionen
montage with photographs from various actions, 1965/66, aus from: Peter Weibel und and
VALIE EXPORT (Hrsg. eds.), *Wien. Bildkompendium Wiener Aktionismus und Film,* Frankfurt
am Main 1970

Wiener Aktionismus, die mit der dokumentarischen Funktion ansetzen.[26] Statt
Aktionen erzeugt Schwarzkogler Bildarrangements, die sich durch eine hohe
visuelle Präzision auszeichnen. Entsprechend der Bedeutung des Bildes arbeitet Schwarzkogler dann auch an dem Fotomaterial selbst weiter, gruppiert, arrangiert und montiert es neu wie auf einer Collage, die in den Band *Wien.
Bildkompendium Wiener Aktionismus und Film* von Peter Weibel und VALIE
EXPORT aufgenommen wurde (Abb. 8).[27] Der Schnitt wird hier auf mehreren
Ebenen explizit: Zunächst aufgrund der Wahl der inszenierten Fotografie, die
wohlkomponierte Schnitte durch Raum und Zeit darstellt, genauso aber auf der
motivischen Ebene, indem Körper bedingungslos nur im Anschnitt gezeigt
werden. Schließlich hat der Schnitt eine hohe symbolische Bedeutung: Das
Messer und der bandagierte Penis evozieren Kastrationsfantasien. Zuletzt wird
das Phänomen des Schnittes in die Form der Montage überführt, die sich durch
das Zusammenfügen von zerstückelten Elementen auszeichnet.

In equal measure, the action itself and the view of the events are cut up. In both the filming—by showing only details—as well as in the editing—which combines individual views of the body in such quick succession that any sense of a whole is lost—Kren abandons an integral image of the body. His procedure of rapid serial cuts is diametrically opposed to the idea of the Viennese Actionists, who wanted the "simplest possible" document "without gimmicks,"[22] in the style of an objective photo reportage. However, as a result of his translations of their "gesture of the processing of the body/thing-as-material to film," he is still linked to Actionism on a conceptual level.[23]

The only artist among the Viennese Actionists who made the step from the action and its simple documentation to a pictorial staging is Rudolf Schwarzkogler. With his six actions from 1965–66 he created a "model case of 'staged photography,'"[24] which, due to Schwarzkogler's conceptual approach, has had an international influence. Here, the action served exclusively as a means of staging and was conceived "with regard to its photographic suitability. The action was transformed into a photo session."[25] Peter Weibel positions Schwarzkogler's action-photography, which is characterized by a return to the image and accordingly took place away from the public gaze in his own studio, at the end of a series of ways of using photography in Viennese Actionism that began with its documentary function.[26] Instead of actions, Schwarzkogler produced pictorial arrangements with extreme visual precision. According to the meaning of the image, Schwarzkogler then continued to work on the photographic material itself, grouping, arranging, and mounting it anew, as in a collage that was included in the book *Wien: Bildkompendium Wiener Aktionismus und Film* (Vienna: Pictorial compendium of Viennese Actionism and film) by Peter Weibel and VALIE EXPORT (fig. 8).[27] Here, the cut becomes explicit on a number of levels: initially on the basis of the choice of staged photography, which represents well-composed cuts through space and time; but equally on the level of the motif, in the sense that bodies are shown without qualification as a series of details; the cut also has a strong symbolic meaning, as the knife and the bandaged penis evoke castration fantasies; finally, the phenomenon of the cut is carried over into the form of montage, which is characterized by an assemblage of cut-up elements.

In Polaroid tableaus showing scarcely identifiable fragments of her own body, Hannah Villiger draws on the principle of the cut already tested in the work of Kurt Kren and Rudolf Schwarzkogler (cat. 14, 15). At the center of these photographs is the artist's own body, which is first recorded snapshot-like in individual details with a Polaroid camera. What is decisive, however, is the work that she carries out afterward. Through selection, enlargement, and arrangement, Villiger assembles together various "blocks," which she puts together from a group of single images. The square format

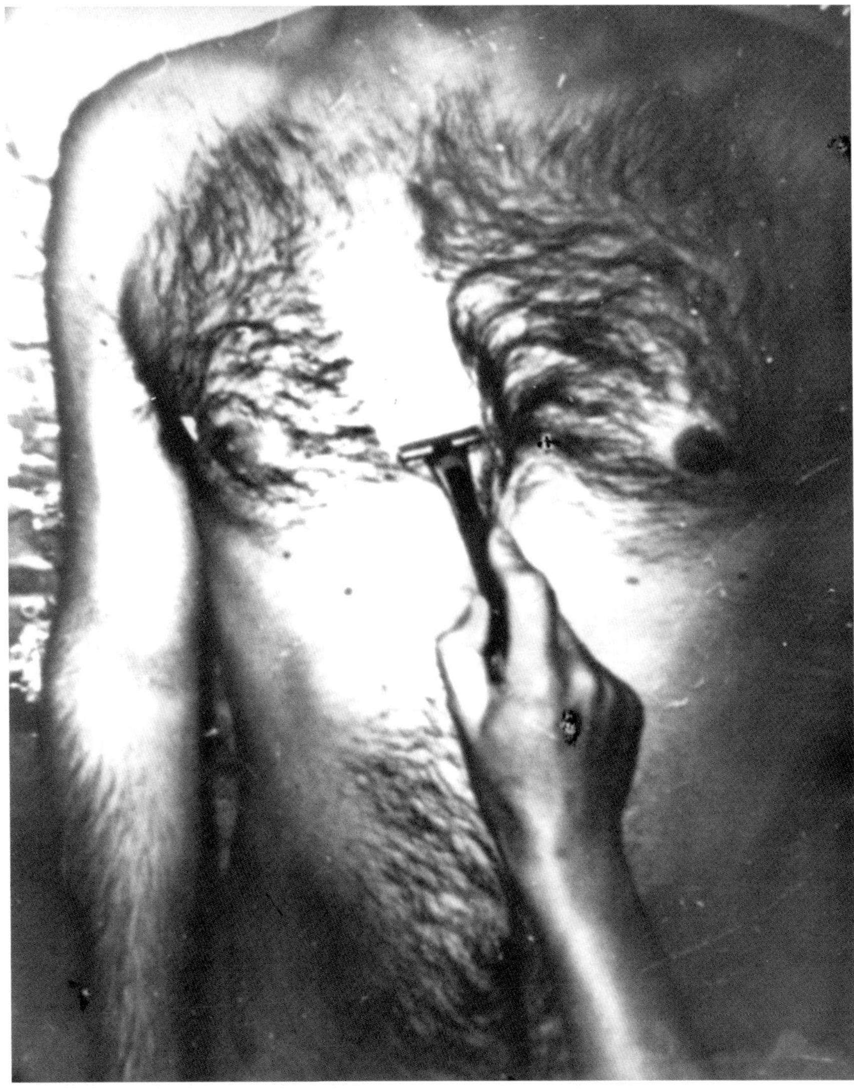

Abb. Fig. 9   VALIE EXPORT, *Cutting, Part IV: A Silent Movie,* Aktion action 1967/68, Abzug
photographic print 1972

Hannah Villiger knüpft mit ihren Polaroidtableaus, die schwer lesbare Fragmente ihres eigenen Körpers zeigen, an jene Prinzipien des Schnitts an, die
bereits bei Kurt Kren und Rudolf Schwarzkogler erprobt werden (Kat. 14, 15).
Im Mittelpunkt der Fotografien der Künstlerin steht ihr eigener Körper, der
zuerst schnappschussartig in einzelnen Teilen mit der Polaroidkamera aufgenommen wird. Entscheidend ist dann die weitere Arbeit: Durch Auswahl, Ver-
größerung und Arrangement stellt Villiger verschiedene »Blöcke« zusammen,
die sich aus mehreren Einzelbildern zusammensetzen. Das quadratische Format des Polaroids erlaubt es ihr, die Nahblicke auf den Körper zu drehen, nach
vier Richtungen hin zusammenzusetzen und damit das Abgebildete zu ver-
fremden und abstrahieren. Spontaneität und Kalkül treffen hier auf kongeniale
Weise aufeinander, neue fragmentarische An- und Ausschnitte des Körpers
sind die Folge. Ziel der Künstlerin ist die Transformation des Körpers zum Bild:
»An die Stelle des Körpers tritt ein Bildkörper, die Haut wird zur Bildhaut.«[28]
Der eigentliche Schnitt findet bei Villigers Blöcken nicht mehr auf der Ebene
des Körpers, sondern des Bildes statt: Die weißen Linien zwischen den Einzelbildern zerteilen, trennen und fragmentieren.
    Eine medientheoretische Auseinandersetzung mit dem Schnitt stellt auch
VALIE EXPORTS Expanded-Cinema-Aktion *Cutting* (Abb. 9) von 1967/68 dar.

of the Polaroids makes it possible to rotate the close-up details of the body and combine them in four different directions, thus defamiliarizing and abstracting the motifs. The result is a congenial encounter between spontaneity and calculation, creating new fragmentary details and sections of the body. The artist's aim is to transform the body into an image: "In place of the body is a pictorial body; the skin becomes a pictorial skin."[28] In Villiger's blocks the actual cut no longer takes place on the level of the body, but on that of the image. The white lines between the single images divide, separate, and fragment.

A work examining the cut from the standpoint of media theory is VALIE EXPORT's Expanded Cinema action *Cutting* (fig. 9) from 1967–68. The aim was to present "the film-based procedure of cutting in an abstraction."[29] Beginning with an analogy between the human body and the film screen, the cutting is presented on a number of levels: first, as a literal opening of windows projected on a paper screen by cutting these out with a pair of scissors, then by cutting out a text so that a sentence by the media theorist Marshall McLuhan becomes visible in the negative space. In the next part of the performance, the screen is replaced by a body. The shape of a bubblegum bubble is cut out from a T-shirt featuring the character Bazooka Joe, exposing actor Peter Weibel's chest, before the latter is itself shaved. The action ends with a fellatio.

EXPORT's Expanded Cinema actions have not only entered art history due to their provocative critical attitude; their seminal importance for the following generation of artists is manifested largely in the paradigm shift from pure body action to a media-reflexive practice. Despite the uncompromising nature of VALIE EXPORT's work on the body, the latter nevertheless remains a tool for analyzing the patriarchal and social power structures underlying film and photography in their form and function as media. As an early representative of media art in Austria, EXPORT makes the step away from the body toward an awareness of the medium's materiality. As a result, the pure action of the Viennese Actionists passes into history, and the path is cleared for a consideration of the body that incorporates an understanding for communicating the body via reproductive visual media. Body Art can begin.

Ziel war es, »das filmtechnische Verfahren des Schneidens in einer Abstraktion« vorzuführen.[29] Ausgehend von einer Analogisierung des menschlichen Körpers mit der Filmleinwand wird das Schneiden auf mehreren Ebenen vorgeführt: zunächst als buchstäbliches Öffnen von auf eine Papierleinwand projizierten Fenstern, indem diese mit einer Schere ausgeschnitten werden, bevor dort durch das Hineinschneiden von Schrift ein Satz des Medientheoretikers Marshall McLuhan als Leerstelle sichtbar wird. Im nächsten Teil der Performance wird von der Leinwand zum Körper gewechselt. Durch ein T-Shirt mit dem Bazooka-Männchen wird die Form des Kaugummiballons auf der Brust des Akteurs Peter Weibel ausgeschnitten, bevor diese selbst rasiert wird. Die Aktion schließt mit einer Fellatio.

EXPORTS Expanded-Cinema-Aktionen sind nicht nur wegen ihrer provokanten systemkritischen Verweise in die Kunstgeschichte eingegangen, sondern sind vor allem wegen ihres Paradigmenwechsels von der reinen Körperaktion hin zu einer medienreflexiven Vorgehensweise für die nachfolgende Künstlergeneration von bahnbrechender Bedeutung. So kompromisslos VALIE EXPORT auch mit dem Körper umgeht, er ist dennoch immer nur das Werkzeug für eine Analyse jener patriarchalen und gesellschaftlichen Machtstrukturen, die hinter den Blick- und Funktionsweisen der Medien Film und Fotografie liegen. Als frühe Vertreterin der Medienkunst in Österreich vollzieht EXPORT den Schritt vom Körper weg zum Bewusstsein für die Materialität des Mediums. Die reine Aktion der Wiener Aktionisten fällt damit der Geschichte anheim; der Weg wird frei für ein In-den-Blick-Nehmen des Körpers unter Miteinbeziehung eines Wissens um die mediale Vermittlung durch reproduzierende Bildmedien. Die Body Art kann beginnen.

1   See Lane Barden, "Wiener Aktionismus," in *Encyclopedia of Twentieth-
Century Photography,* ed. Lynne Warren,
vol. 3 (New York, 2006), pp. 1686–87,
here p. 1686.
2   Peter Gorsen, "Wiener Aktionismus
und Fotografie," in *Das Nachleben des
Wiener Aktionismus: Interpretationen
und Einlassungen seit 1969* (Klagenfurt,
2009), pp. 170–79, here p. 176.
3   In 2010–11, as part of the exhibition *Direct Art: Wiener Aktionismus im internationalen Kontext,* the museum moderne
kunst stiftung ludwig wien undertook
such a situating of Viennese Actionism
in the context of the body-based art of
the nineteen-fifties and sixties.
4   Oliver Jahraus, *Die Aktion des Wiener
Aktionismus: Subversion der Kultur und
Dispositionierung des Bewußtseins* (Munich, 2000); see especially chapter 5:
"Material und Körper," pp. 185ff.
5   Monika Wagner uses this term as a
general description of the body's use
as material in the visual arts from the
mid-nineteen-fifties. Monika Wagner,
*Das Material der Kunst: Eine andere
Geschichte der Moderne* (Munich,
2001), p. 271.
6   This text is partly based on considerations I developed in the context of my
publication on the photographic self-
staging of Arnulf Rainer. See Christina
Natlacen, *Arnulf Rainer und die Fotografie: Inszenierte Gesichter, ausdrucksstarke Posen* (Petersberg, 2010).
7   Petra Löffler, "'Mimische Störungen':
Zum Bild der Grimasse," in *Signale der
Störung,* ed. Albert Kümmel and Erhard
Schüttpelz (Munich, 2003), pp. 173–97,
here pp. 174–75.
8   See Jean-Charles Masséra, "Tanz mit
dem Gesetz," in *Bruce Nauman: Image/
Text 1966–1996,* ed. Christine Van
Assche, exh. cat. Kunstmuseum Wolfsburg (Ostfildern, 1997), pp. 20–33, here
p. 20.
9   Kerstin Braun, *Der Wiener Aktionismus:
Positionen und Prinzipien* (Vienna,
1999), here p. 67.
10 There are further parallels in the form
of their mediation, if one thinks, for example, of the raw documentary form
of the recording of the action *Zerreißprobe* (Acid test) from 1970, of which
there is a fifteen-minute film by Werner
Schulz that consists of a single sequence shot without cuts.
11 Unlike "feminization," "effeminization"
does not merely imply feminine gestures, but more specifically the feminine gestures of a man. See Amelia
Jones, *Body Art: Performing the Subject*
(Minneapolis, 1998), pp. 107–08.
12 See on this Hemma Schmutz and Tanja
Widmann, eds., *That Bodies Speak Has

Been Known for a Long Time,* exh. cat.
Generali Foundation, Vienna (Cologne,
2004).
13 Sigrid Adorf, "A Question of Gesture?
The Act, the Image, Its Language and
Their Movement in Body Art of the Seventies," in Schmutz and Widmann 2004
(see note 12), pp. 89–104, here p. 96.
14 Peter Weibel, "Zur Aktionskunst von
Günter Brus," in *Günter Brus: Der Überblick,* exh. cat. Museum Moderner
Kunst, Vienna (Salzburg and Vienna,
1986), pp. 33–49, here p. 33.
15 Veit Loers, "Als die Bilder laufen lernten," in *Von der Aktionsmalerei zum Aktionismus,* exh. cat. Museum Fridericianum, Kassel (Klagenfurt, 1988), pp. 11–
25, here p. 22.
16 Giorgio Agamben, "Notes on Gesture,"
in Schmutz and Widmann 2004 (see
note 12), pp. 105–14, here pp. 108–09.
17 Tracy Fitzpatrick, "Hannah Wilke: Making Myself into a Monument," in *Hannah Wilke Gestures,* exh. cat. Neuberger
Museum of Art, Purchase College (Purchase and New York, 2009), pp. 8–71,
here p. 40.
18 In his sign theory Peirce distinguishes
between icon, index, and symbol. See
Charles S. Peirce, *Phänomen und Logik
der Zeichen,* ed. Helmut Pape (Frankfurt am Main, 1998), pp. 64ff.
19 VALIE EXPORT, "Body Sign Action," in
*VALIE EXPORT: Dokumentations-Aus-
stellung des österreichischen Beitrags
zur Biennale Venedig 1980* (Vienna,
1980), p. 46.
20 The works of Ketty La Rocca and VALIE
EXPORT have already been compared
in the exhibition *Auf den Leib geschrieben.* On this subject see Brigitte Huck
and Monika Faber, *Auf den Leib geschrieben,* exh. cat. Kunsthalle Wien
(Vienna, 1995).
21 For a detailed description see the
fourth chapter of Philippe Dubois,
L'acte photographique (Brussels, 1983),
pp. 151–202.
22 Hermann Nitsch, *Das Orgien-Mysterien-
Theater: Die Partituren aller aufgeführten Aktionen 1960–1979,* vol. 1 (Naples
and Vienna, 1979), p. 18.
23 Michaela Pöschl, "Die Wahrheit des
Körpers: Aktion und Repräsentation im
Wiener Aktionismus und Post-Aktionismus," in *Wiener Aktionismus,* ed. Julius
Hummel (Milan, 2005), pp. 227–44,
here p. 230.
24 Hubert Klocker, "Der zertrümmerte
Spiegel," in *Der zertrümmerte Spiegel:
Wiener Aktionismus, Wien 1960–1971,*
exh. cat. Albertina, Vienna (Klagenfurt,
1989), pp. 89–112, here p. 93.
25 Peter Weibel, "Die Frage der Fotografie
im Wiener Aktionismus als die Frage
nach Autor und Autonomie in der Foto-

grafie," in *Fotogeschichte* 6, 21 (1986),
pp. 49–58, p. 51.
26 Peter Weibel, "Kunstexpansionen:
Grenzkunst," in *Österreich zum Beispiel:
Literatur, Bildende Kunst, Film und Musik
seit 1968,* ed. Otto Breicha and Reinhard Urbach (Salzburg, 1982), pp. 36–
65, here pp. 42–46.
27 This compendium of visual as well as
textual material such as newspaper
clippings and artist manifestos is a period documentation of all the artistic
statements, primarily from the nineteen-
sixties, that focus on the body in performative actions. The result is an ini-
tial overview of action and film, whose
significance cannot be overestimated.
See Peter Weibel and VALIE EXPORT,
eds., *Wien: Bildkompendium Wiener
Aktionismus und Film* (Frankfurt am
Main, 1970).
28 Claudia Spinelli, "Existential Necessity:
The Life and Work of Hannah Villiger,"
in *Hannah Villiger,* ed. Jolanda Bucher
and Eric Hattan (Zurich et al., 2001),
pp. 31–65, here p. 47.
29 Hans Scheugl and Ernst Schmidt Jr.,
*Eine Subgeschichte des Films: Lexikon
des Avantgarde-, Experimental- und Undergroundfilms* (Frankfurt am Main,
1974), p. 261.

1 Vgl. Lane Barden, »Wiener Aktionismus«, in: Lynne Warren (Hrsg.), *Encyclopedia of Twentieth-Century Photography,* Bd. 3, New York 2006, S. 1686 f., hier S. 1686.

2 Peter Gorsen, »Wiener Aktionismus und Fotografie«, in: ders., *Das Nachleben des Wiener Aktionismus. Interpretationen und Einlassungen seit 1969,* Klagenfurt 2009, S. 170–179, hier S. 176.

3 2010/11 hat das museum moderner kunst stiftung ludwig wien im Rahmen der Ausstellung *Direct Art. Wiener Aktionismus im internationalen Kontext* eine solche Verortung des Wiener Aktionismus im Kontext der körperbezogenen Kunst der 1950er- und 1960er-Jahre unternommen.

4 Oliver Jahraus, *Die Aktion des Wiener Aktionismus. Subversion der Kultur und Dispositionierung des Bewußtseins,* München 2000; siehe insbesondere Kapitel 5: »Material und Körper«, S. 185 ff.

5 Monika Wagner verwendet diesen Begriff allgemein für die Verwendung des Körpers als Material in den Bildkünsten seit Mitte der 1950er-Jahre; Monika Wagner, *Das Material der Kunst. Eine andere Geschichte der Moderne,* München 2001, S. 271.

6 Dieser Text stützt sich ausschnittweise auf Überlegungen, die ich bereits im Rahmen meiner Publikation zu den fotografischen Selbstinszenierungen von Arnulf Rainer angestellt habe (vgl. Christina Natlacen, *Arnulf Rainer und die Fotografie. Inszenierte Gesichter, ausdrucksstarke Posen,* Petersberg 2010).

7 Petra Löffler, »›Mimische Störungen‹. Zum Bild der Grimasse«, in: Albert Kümmel und Erhard Schüttpelz (Hrsg.), *Signale der Störung,* München 2003, S. 173–197, hier S. 174 f.

8 Vgl. Jean-Charles Masséra, »Tanz mit dem Gesetz«, in: Christine Van Assche (Hrsg.), *Bruce Nauman. Image/Text 1966–1996,* Ausst.-Kat. Kunstmuseum Wolfsburg, Ostfildern 1997, S. 20–33, hier S. 20.

9 Kerstin Braun, *Der Wiener Aktionismus. Positionen und Prinzipien,* Wien 1999, hier S. 67.

10 Aber auch hinsichtlich der Form ihrer Vermittlung gibt es Parallelen, denkt man beispielsweise an die rohe dokumentarische Form der Aufzeichnung der Aktion *Zerreißprobe* von 1970, von der ein 15-minütiger Film von Werner Schulz existiert, der als Plansequenz ohne Schnitte auskommt.

11 »Effemination« meint im Unterschied zu »feminization« nicht nur weibliches Gebaren, sondern das weibliche Gebaren eines Mannes. Amelia Jones, *Body Art. Performing the Subject,* Minneapolis 1998, S. 107 f.

12 Vgl. dazu *Dass die Körper sprechen, auch das wissen wir seit langem,* hrsg. von Hemma Schmutz und Tanja Widmann, Ausst.-Kat. Generali Foundation Wien, Köln 2004.

13 Sigrid Adorf, »Eine Frage der Geste? Der Akt, das Bild, seine Sprache und ihre Bewegung in der Body Art der 1970er-Jahre«, in: Wien 2004 (wie Anm. 12), S. 21–37, hier S. 29 f.

14 Peter Weibel, »Zur Aktionskunst von Günter Brus«, in: *Günter Brus. Der Überblick,* Ausst.-Kat. Museum Moderner Kunst Wien, Salzburg und Wien 1986, S. 33–49, hier S. 33.

15 Veit Loers, »Als die Bilder laufen lernten«, in: *Von der Aktionsmalerei zum Aktionismus,* Ausst.-Kat. Museum Fridericianum, Kassel, Klagenfurt 1988, S. 11–25, hier S. 22.

16 Giorgio Agamben, »Noten zur Geste«, in: Wien 2004 (wie Anm. 12), S. 39–48, hier S. 42 f.

17 Tracy Fitzpatrick, »Hannah Wilke: Making Myself into a Monument«, in: *Hannah Wilke Gestures,* Ausst.-Kat. Neuberger Museum of Art Purchase College, Purchase und New York 2009, S. 8–71, hier S. 40.

18 Peirce unterscheidet in seiner Zeichentheorie zwischen Ikon, Index und Symbol; vgl. Charles S. Peirce, *Phänomen und Logik der Zeichen,* hrsg. von Helmut Pape, Frankfurt am Main 1998, S. 64 ff.

19 VALIE EXPORT, »Body Sign Action«, in: *VALIE EXPORT: Dokumentations-Ausstellung des österreichischen Beitrags zur Biennale Venedig 1980,* Wien 1980, S. 46.

20 Die Arbeiten von Ketty La Rocca und VALIE EXPORT wurden bereits in der Ausstellung *Auf den Leib geschrieben* aufeinander bezogen. Vgl. Brigitte Huck und Monika Faber, *Auf den Leib geschrieben,* Ausst.-Kat. Kunsthalle Wien, Wien 1995.

21 Am ausführlichsten dargelegt von Philippe Dubois in seinem vierten Kapitel in *Der fotografische Akt. Versuch über ein theoretisches Dispositiv,* Amsterdam und Dresden 1998, S. 155–213.

22 Hermann Nitsch, *Das Orgien-Mysterien-Theater. Die Partituren aller aufgeführten Aktionen 1960–1979,* Bd. 1, Neapel und Wien 1979, S. 18.

23 Michaela Pöschl, »Die Wahrheit des Körpers. Aktion und Repräsentation im Wiener Aktionismus und Post-Aktionismus«, in: Julius Hummel (Hrsg.), *Wiener Aktionismus,* Mailand 2005, S. 227–244, hier S. 230.

24 Hubert Klocker, »Der zertrümmerte Spiegel«, in: *Der zertrümmerte Spiegel. Wiener Aktionismus. Wien 1960–1971,* Ausst.-Kat. Albertina, Wien, Klagenfurt 1989, S. 89–112, hier S. 93.

25 Peter Weibel, »Die Frage der Fotografie im Wiener Aktionismus als die Frage nach Autor und Autonomie in der Fotografie«, in: *Fotogeschichte,* 6, 21, 1986, S. 49–58, S. 51.

26 Peter Weibel, »Kunstexpansionen: Grenzkunst«, in: Otto Breicha und Reinhard Urbach (Hrsg.), *Österreich zum Beispiel. Literatur, Bildende Kunst, Film und Musik seit 1968,* Salzburg 1982, S. 36–65, hier S. 42–46.

27 Bei diesem Kompendium an Bild-, aber auch Textmaterial wie Zeitungsausschnitten und Künstlermanifesten handelt es sich um eine zeitnahe Dokumentation all jener künstlerischen Äußerungen primär aus den 1960er-Jahren, die den Körper in performativen Handlungen in den Mittelpunkt stellen. Dadurch kann eine erste Zusammenschau von Aktion und Film geleistet werden, deren Bedeutung nicht hoch genug anzurechnen ist. Vgl. Peter Weibel und VALIE EXPORT (Hrsg.), *Wien. Bildkompendium Wiener Aktionismus und Film,* Frankfurt am Main 1970.

28 Claudia Spinelli, »Existentielle Notwendigkeit. Leben und Werk von Hannah Villiger«, in: Jolanda Bucher und Eric Hattan (Hrsg.), *Hannah Villiger,* Zürich u. a. 2001, S. 31–65, hier S. 47.

29 Hans Scheugl und Ernst Schmidt jr., *Eine Subgeschichte des Films. Lexikon des Avantgarde-, Experimental- und Undergroundfilms,* Frankfurt am Main 1974, S. 261.

Bildteil   Plates

4   John Coplans, *Hand, Two Panels, Vertical,* 1988

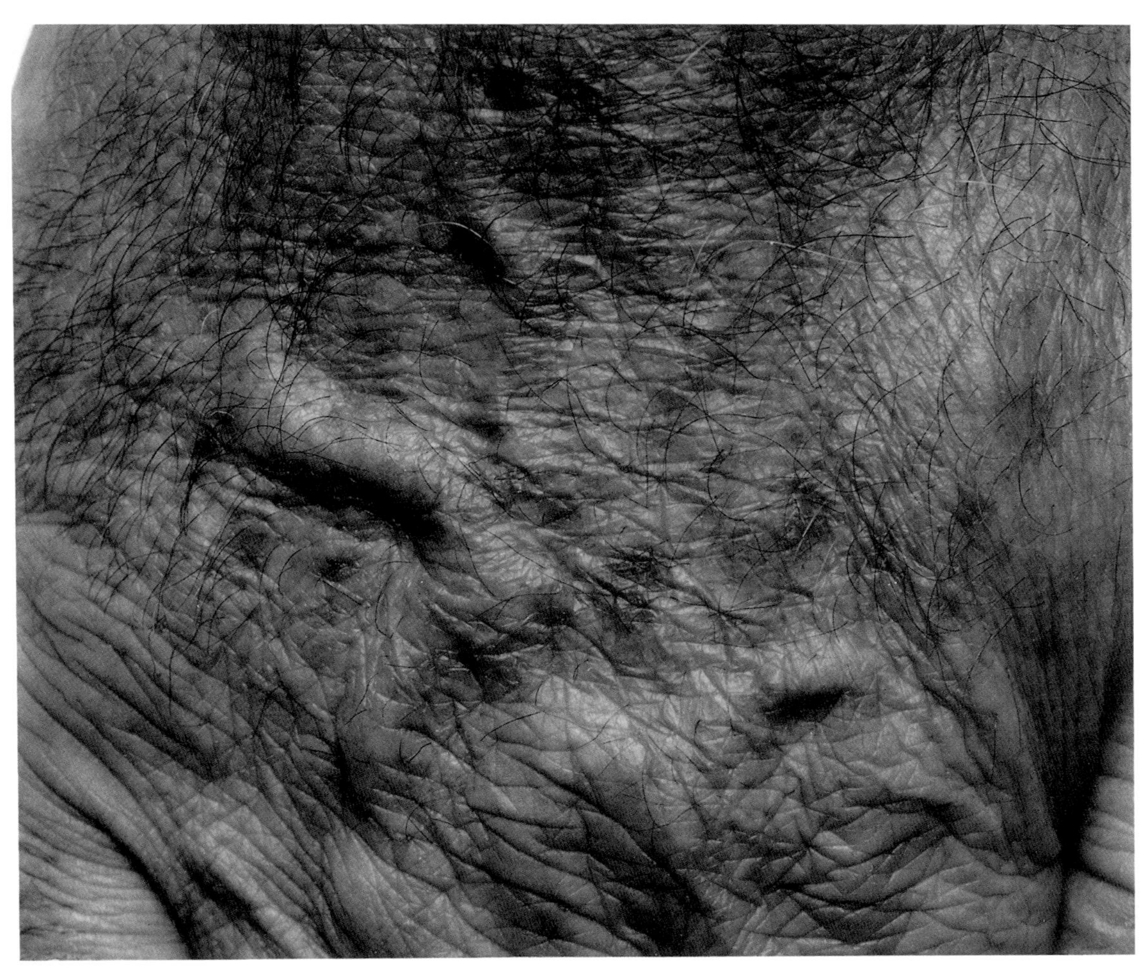

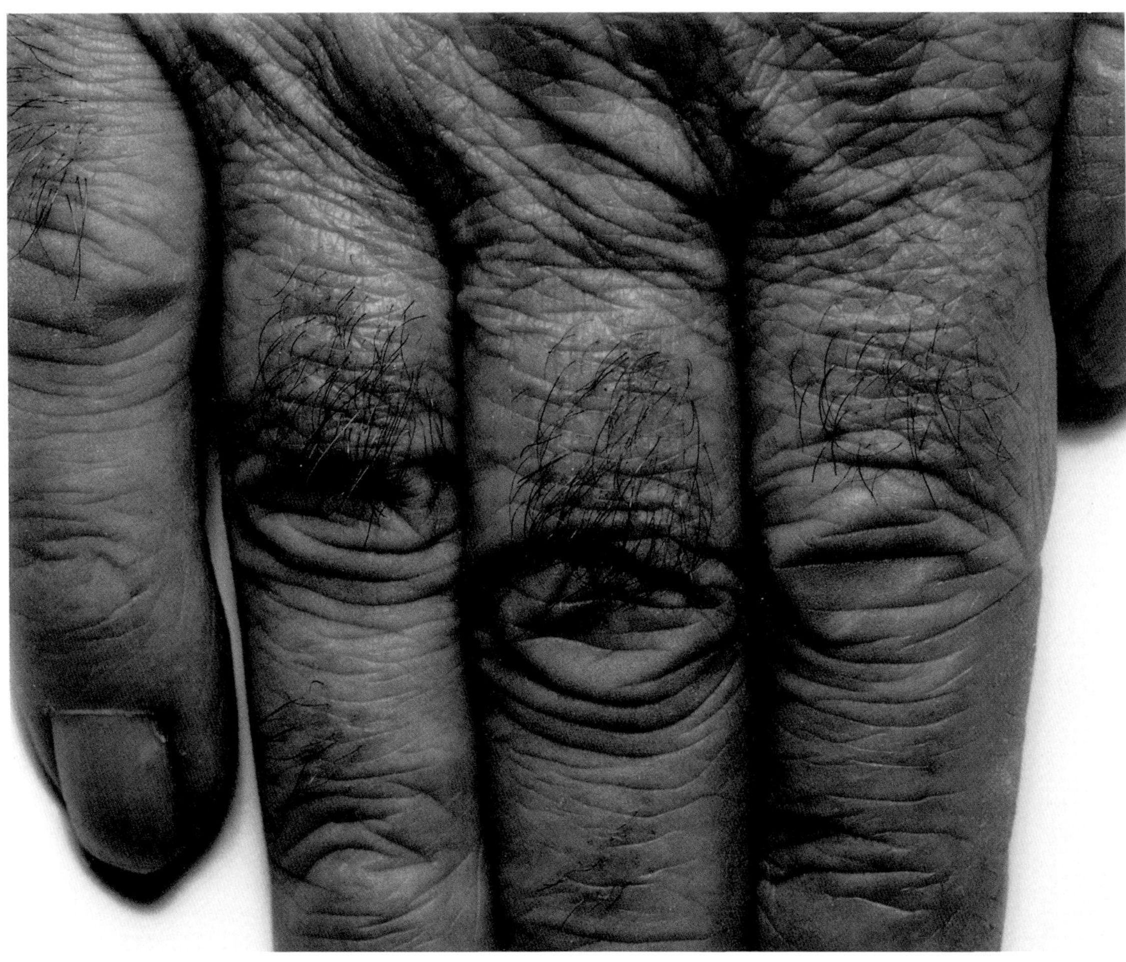

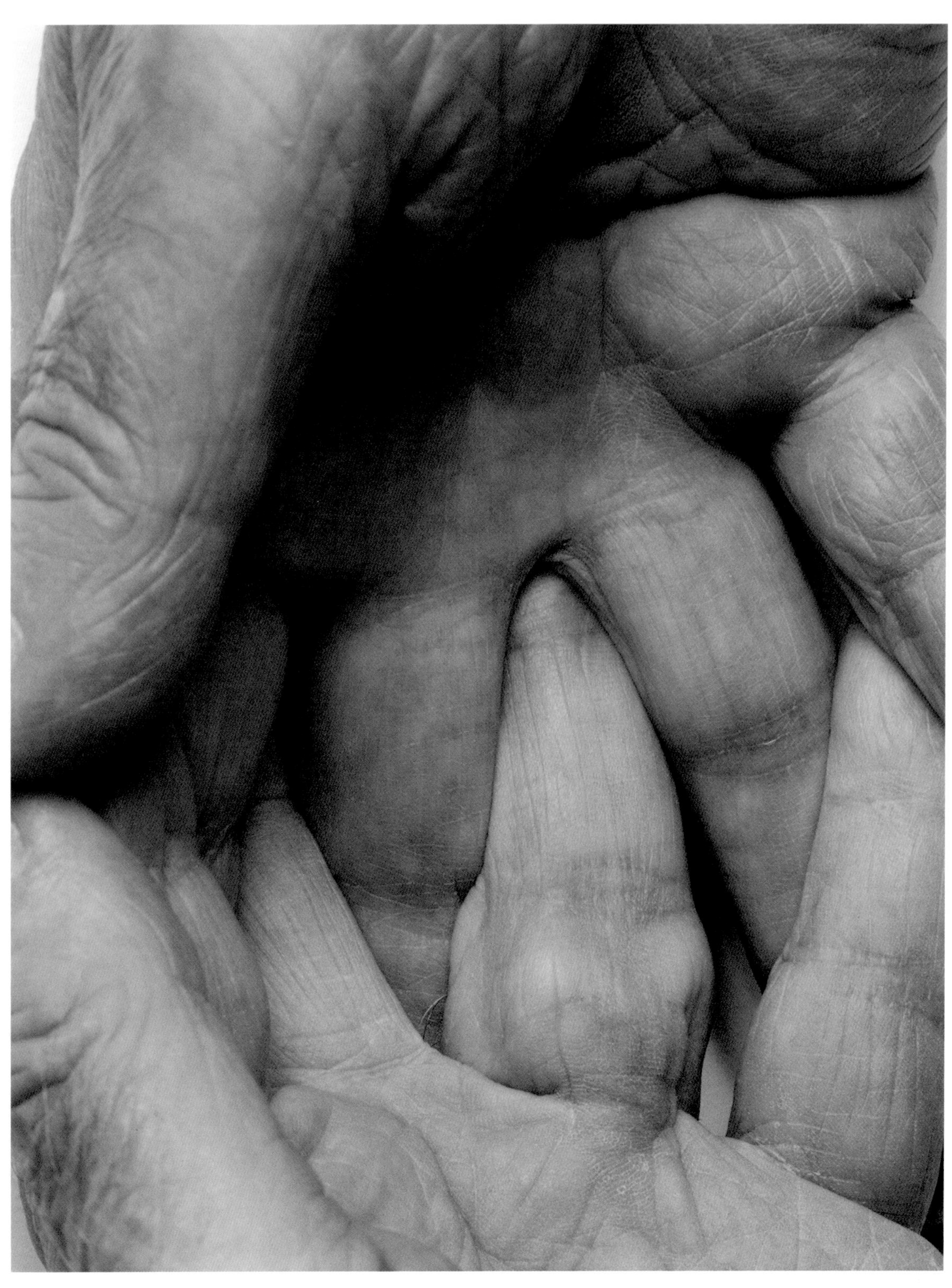

5   John Coplans, *Interlocking Fingers, No. 6,* 1999

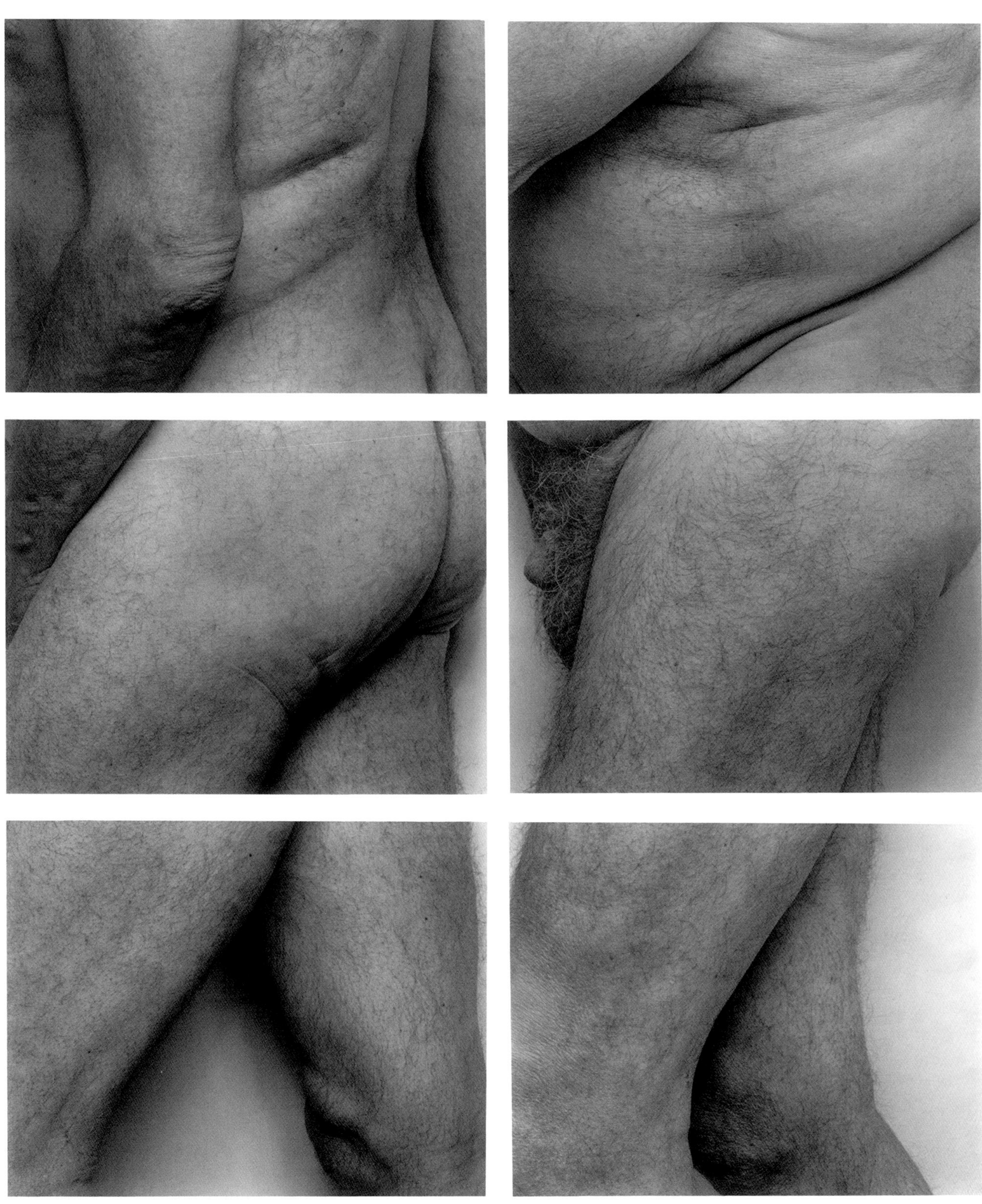

8   John Coplans, *Frieze No. 6,* 1994

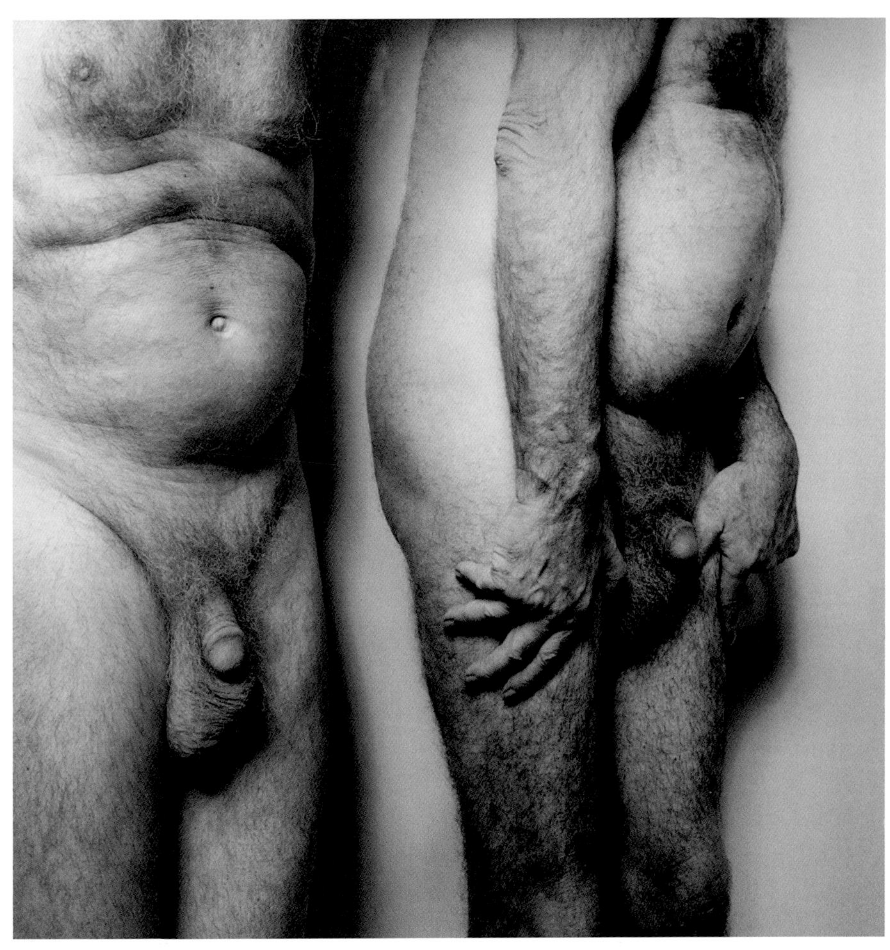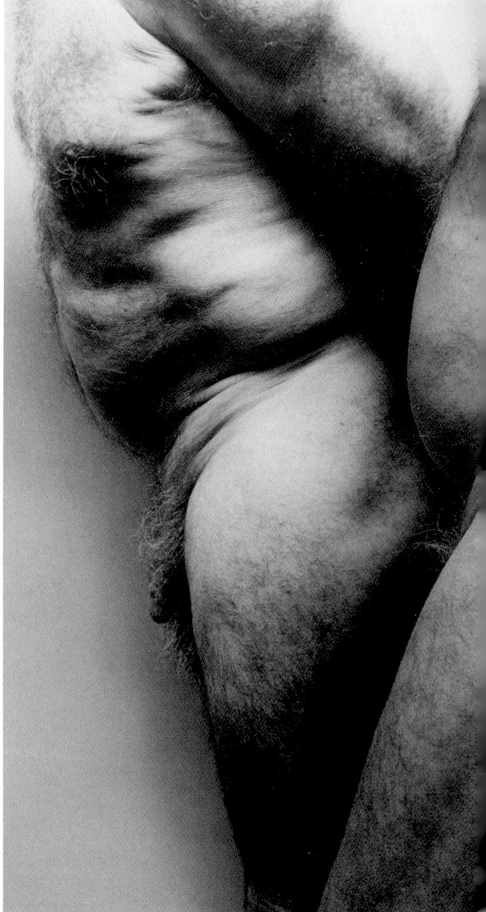

9 John Coplans, *Self-Portrait, Six Times*, 1987

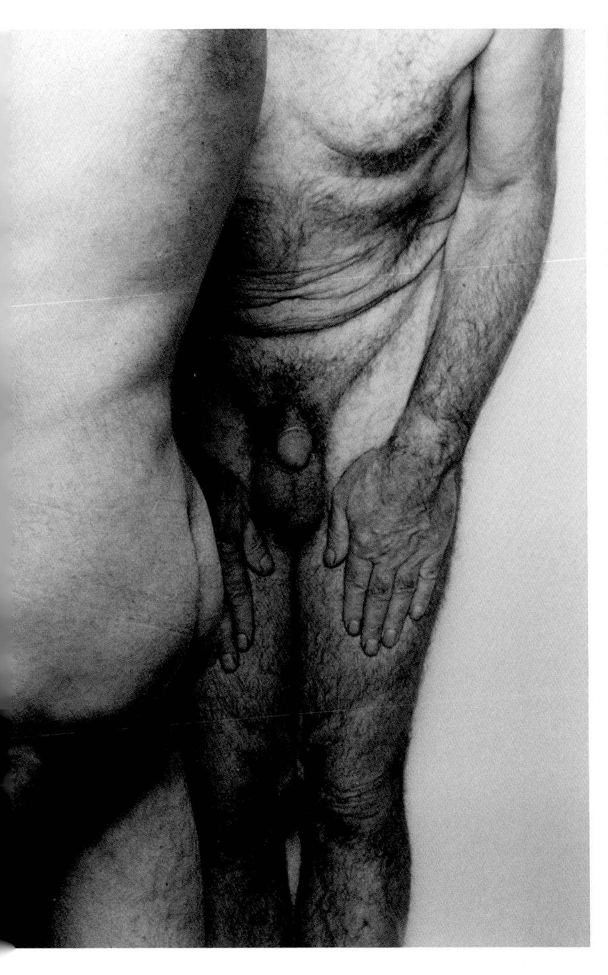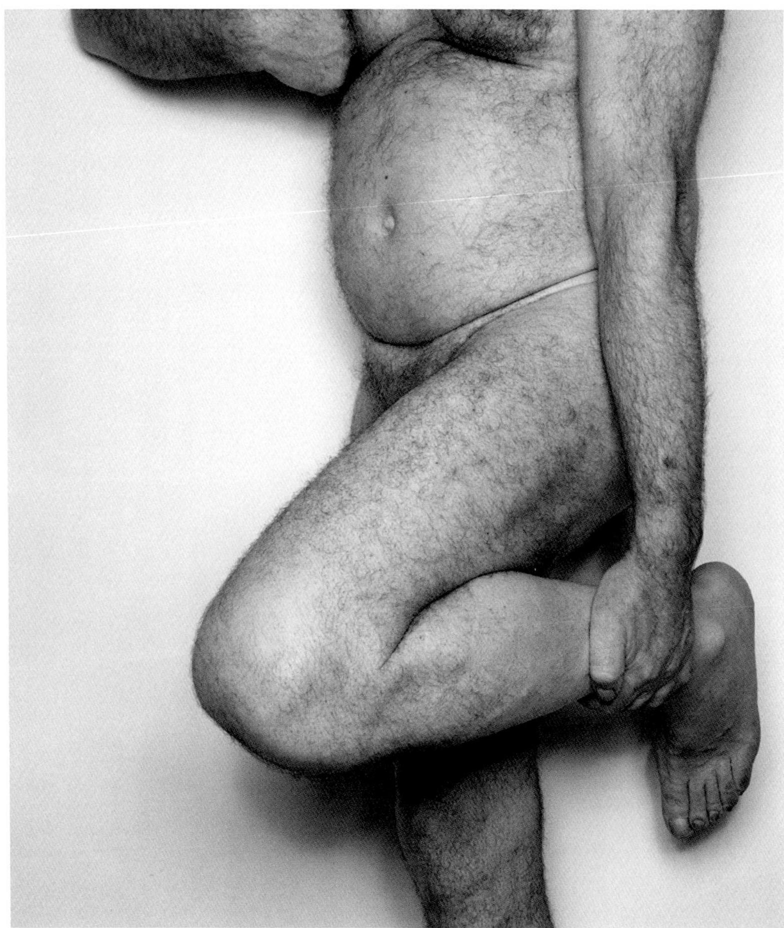

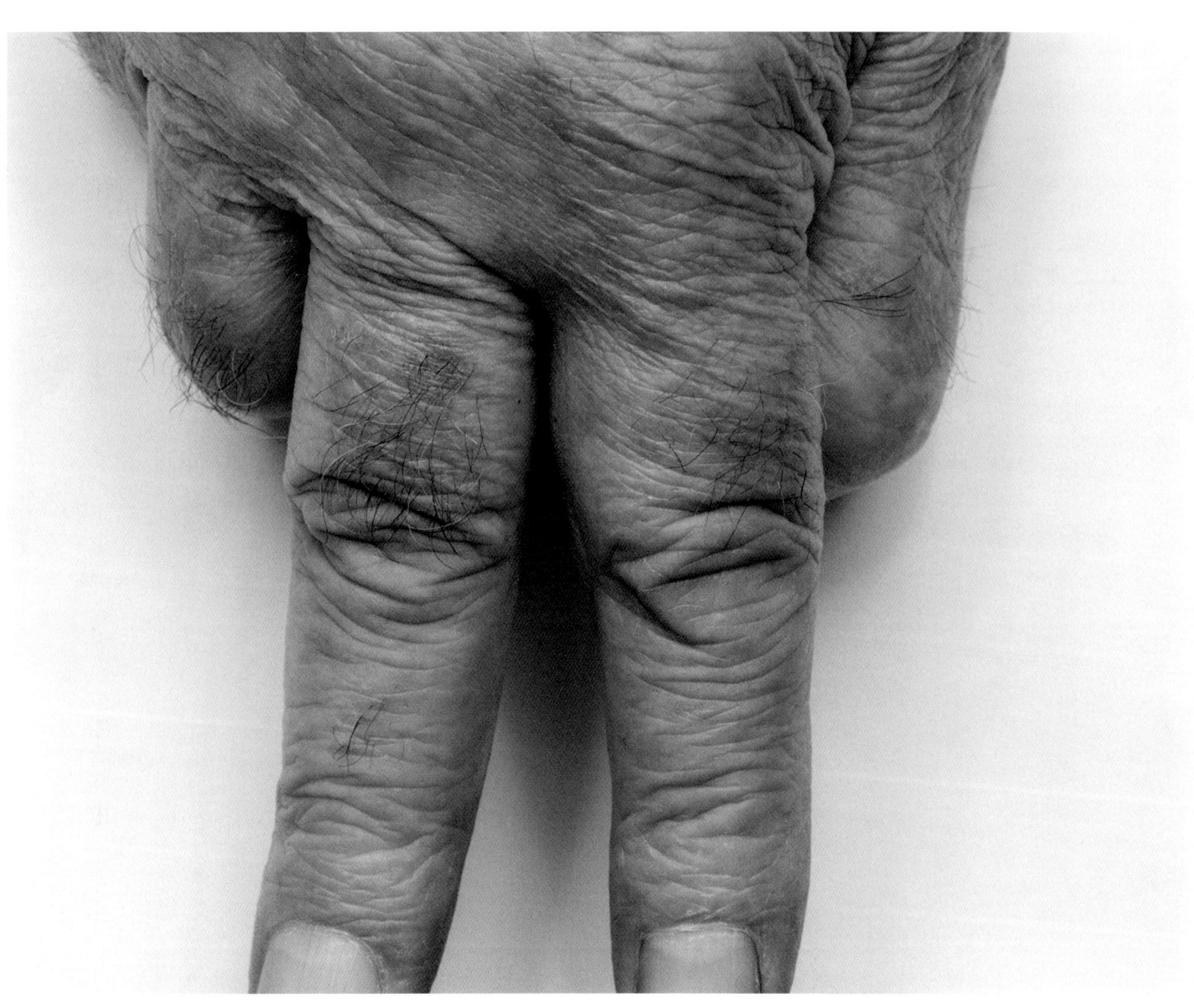

10   John Coplans, *Fingers, Front,* 1999

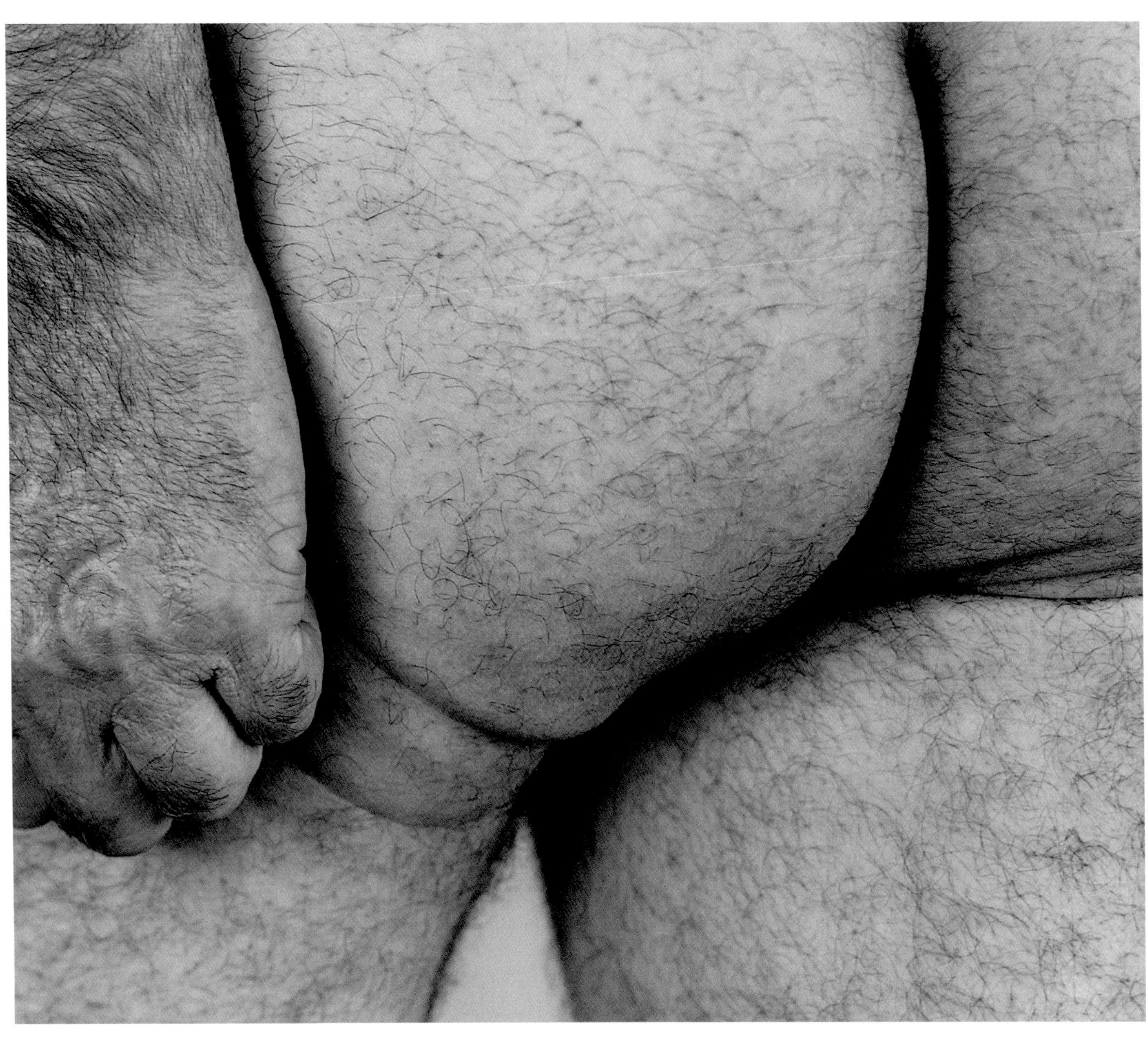

11   John Coplans, *Hand with Buttocks*, 1987

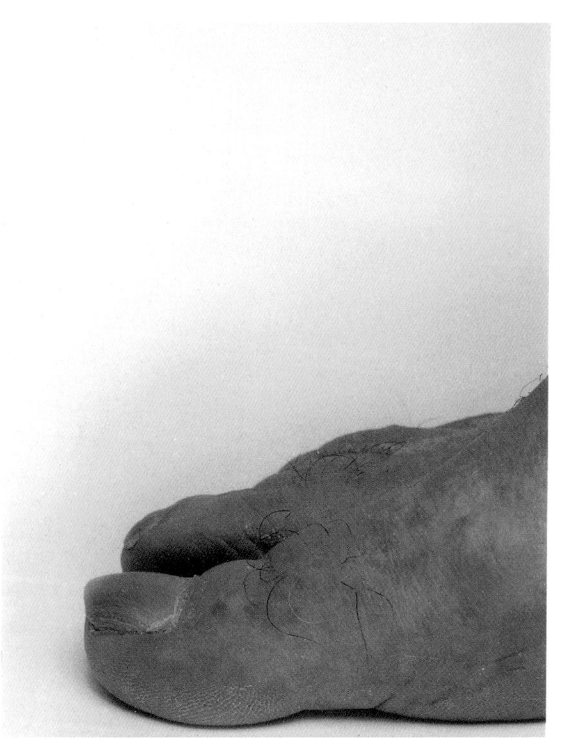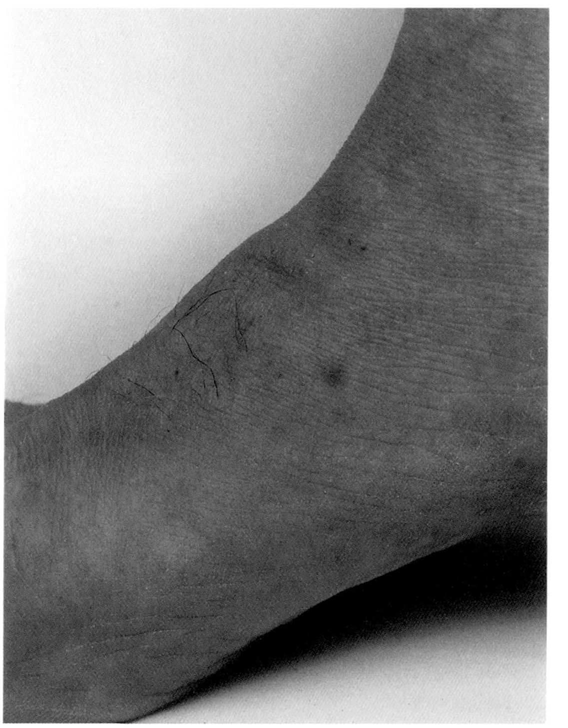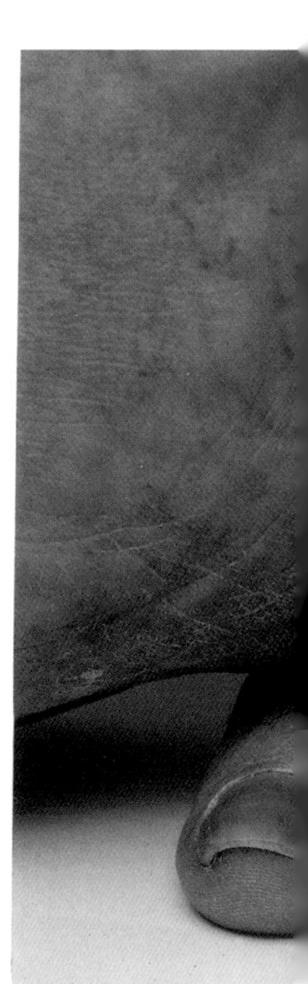

12   John Coplans, *Toes on Foot, Five Panels,* 1989

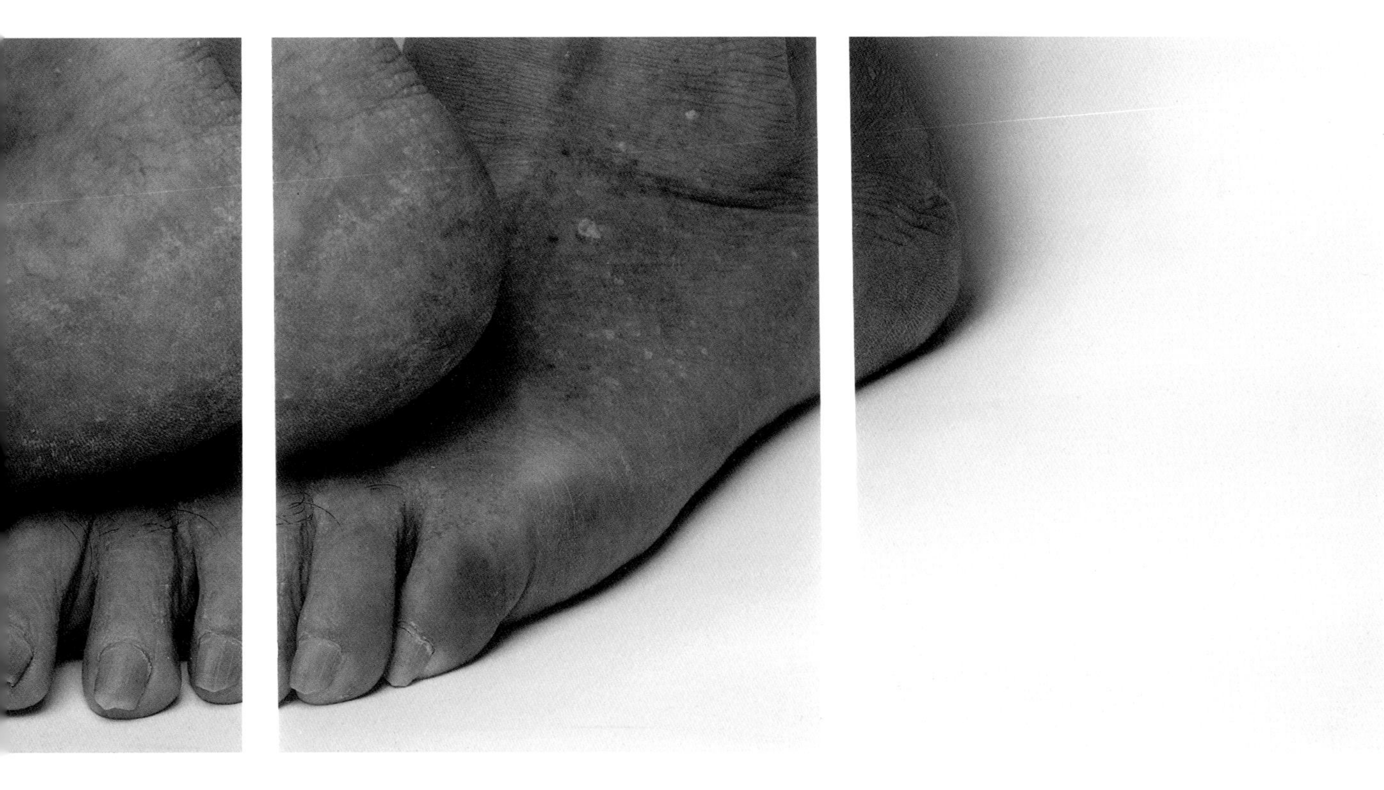

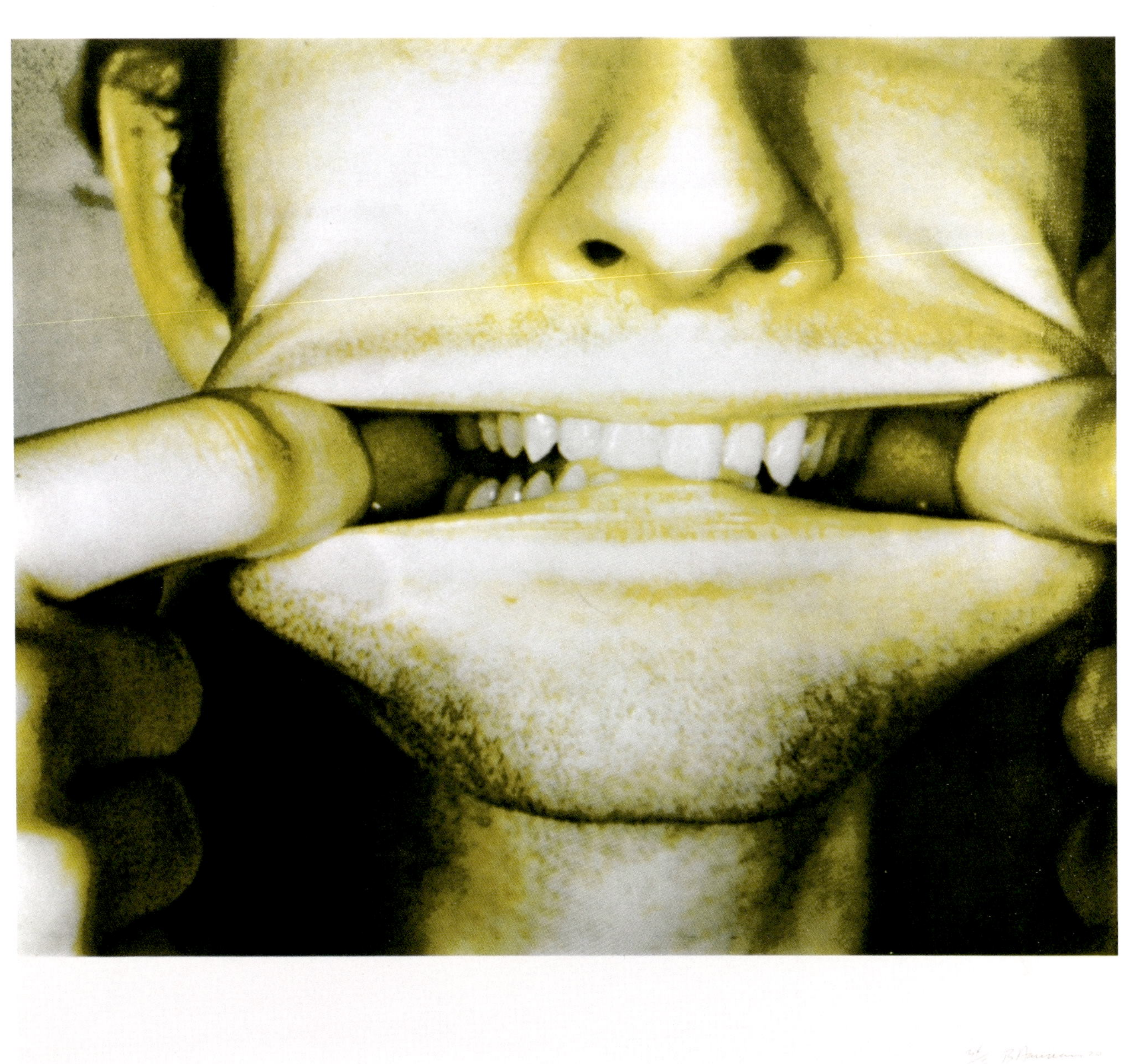

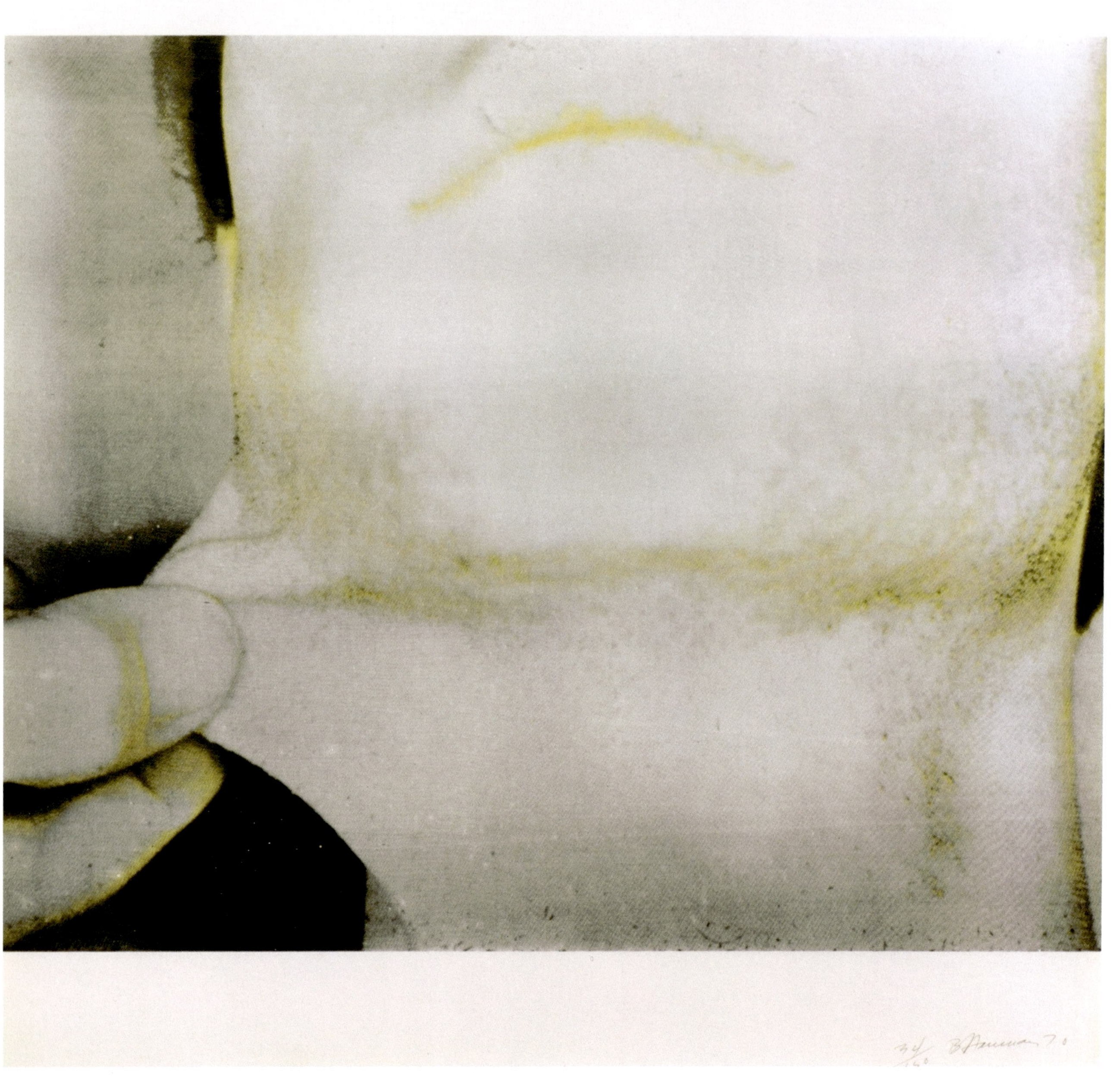

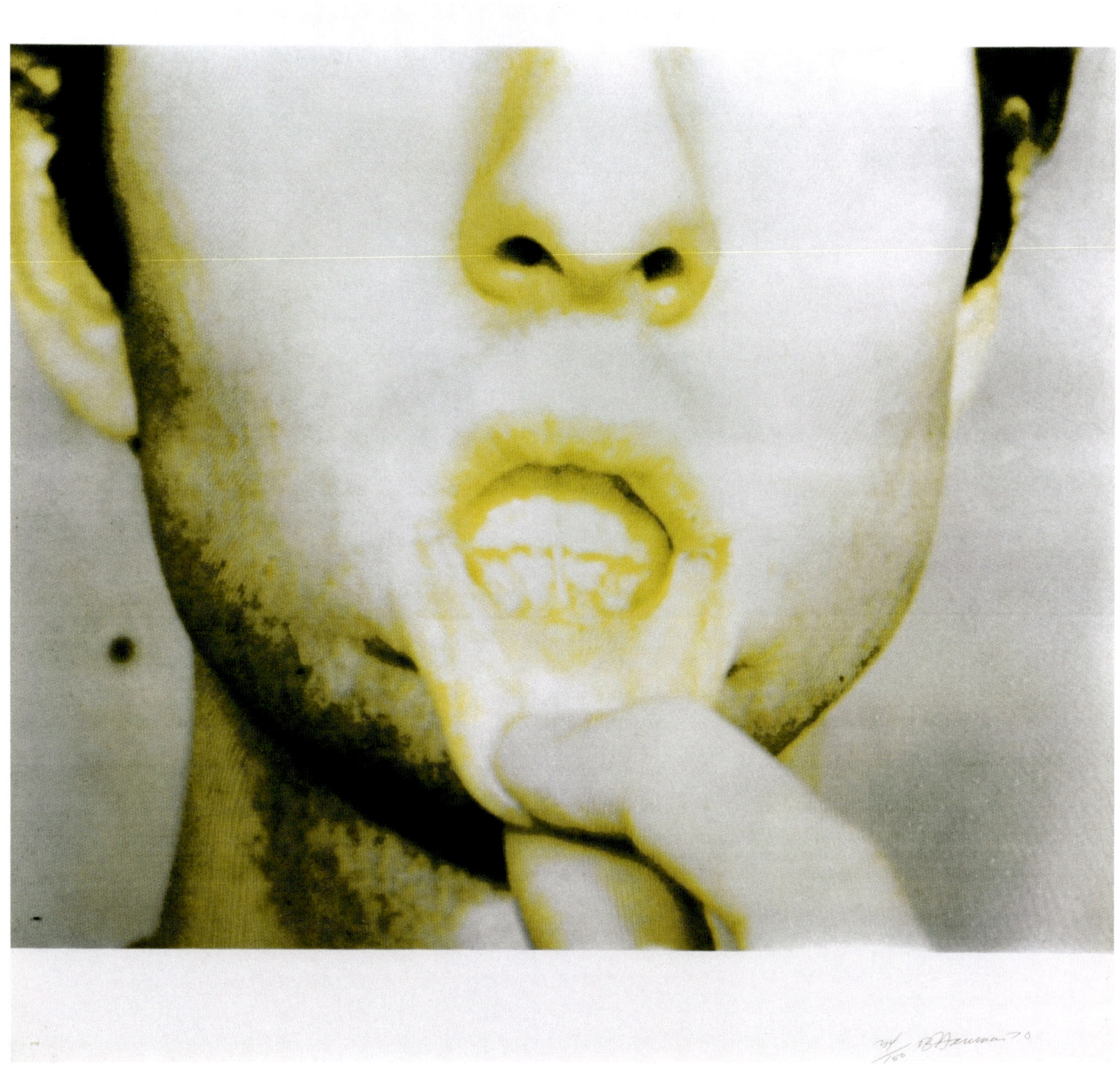

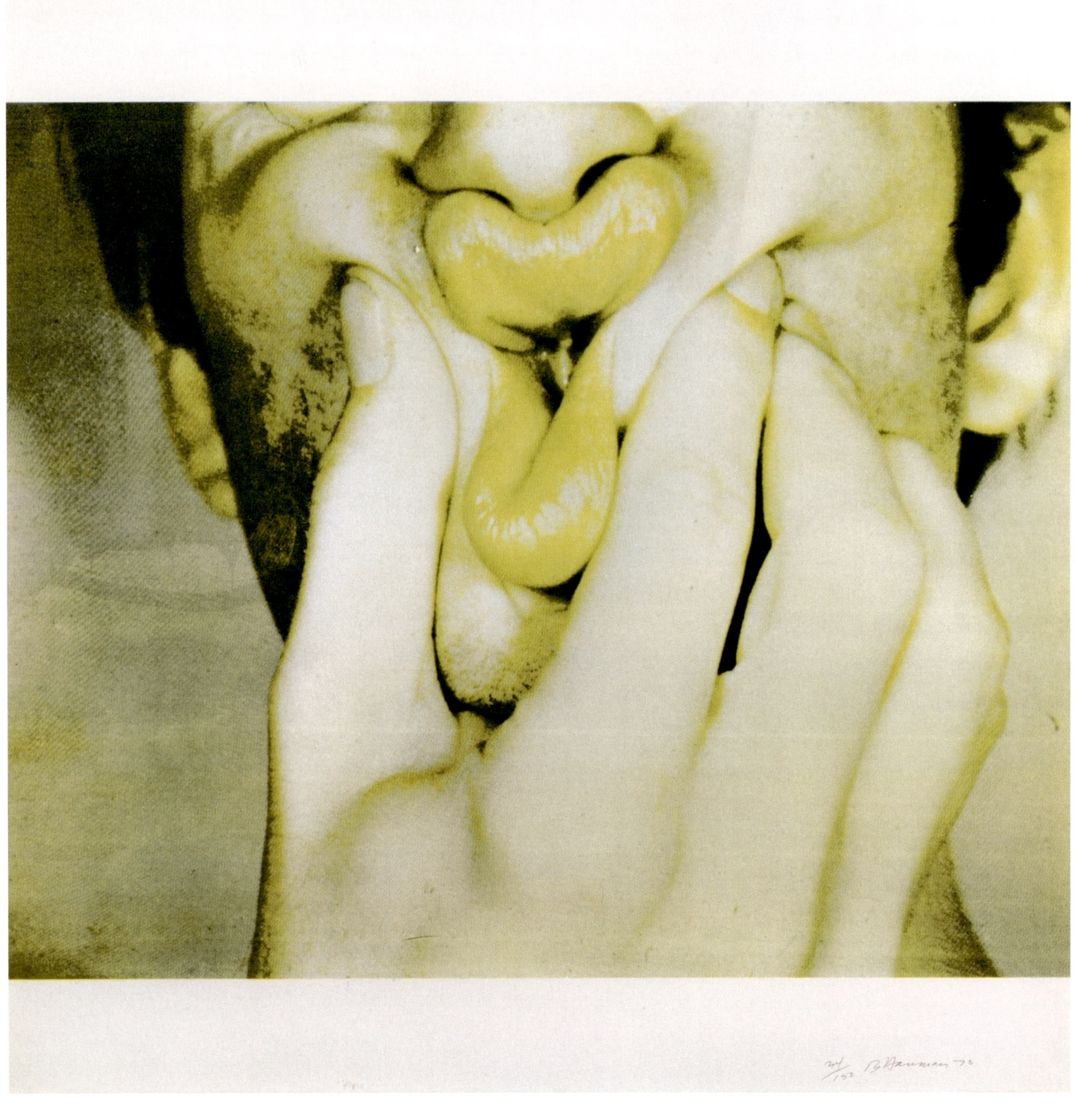

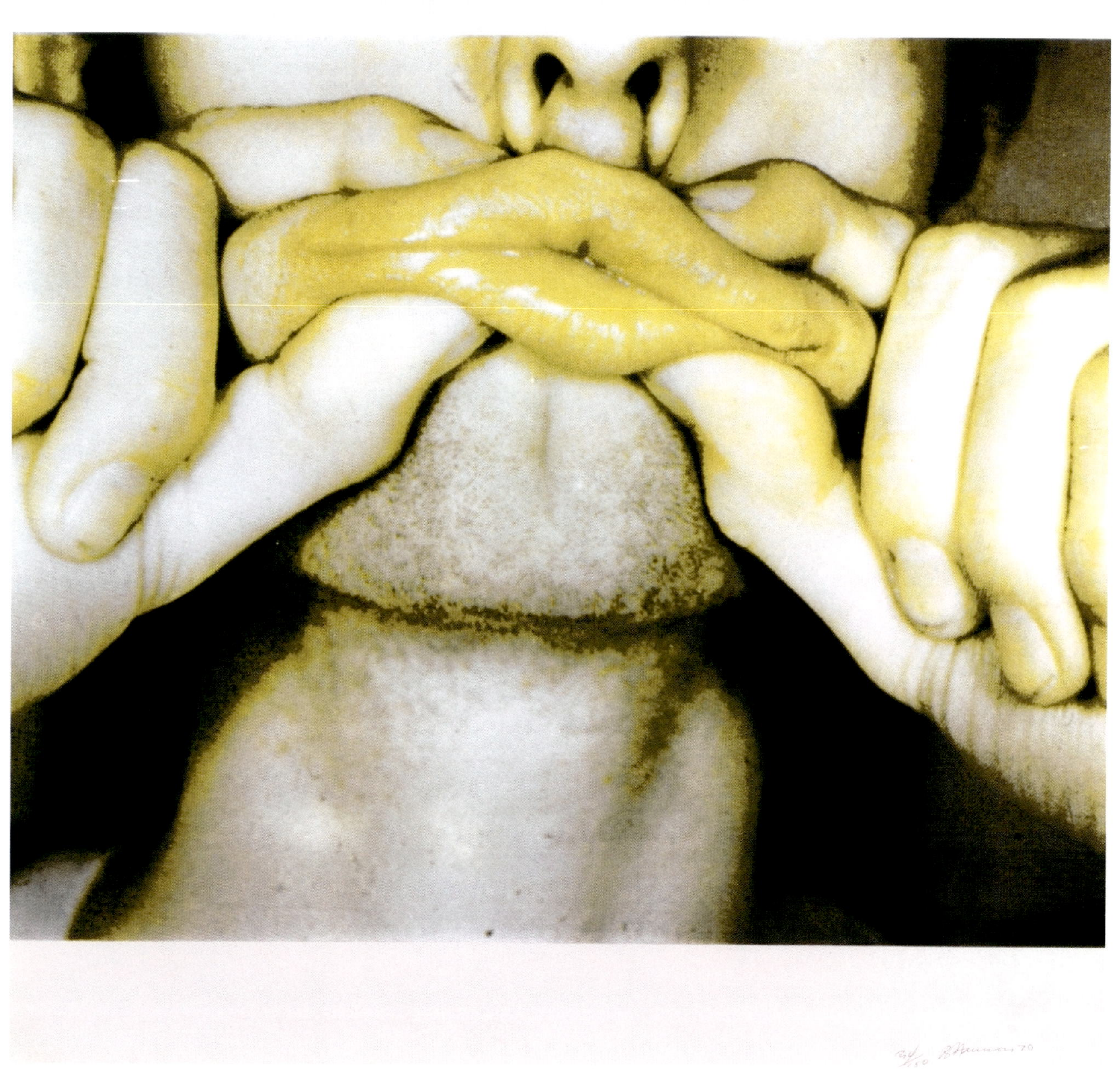

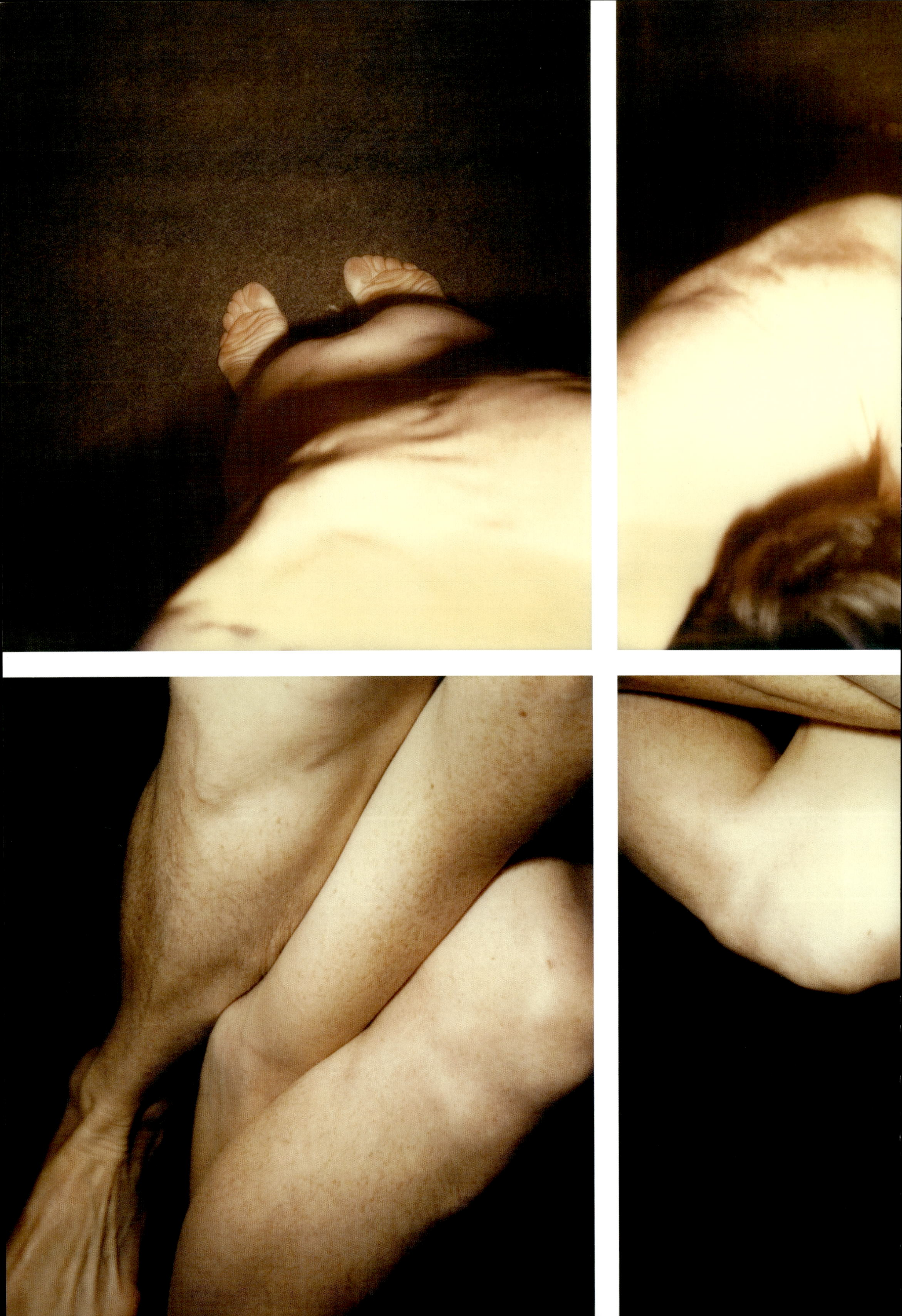

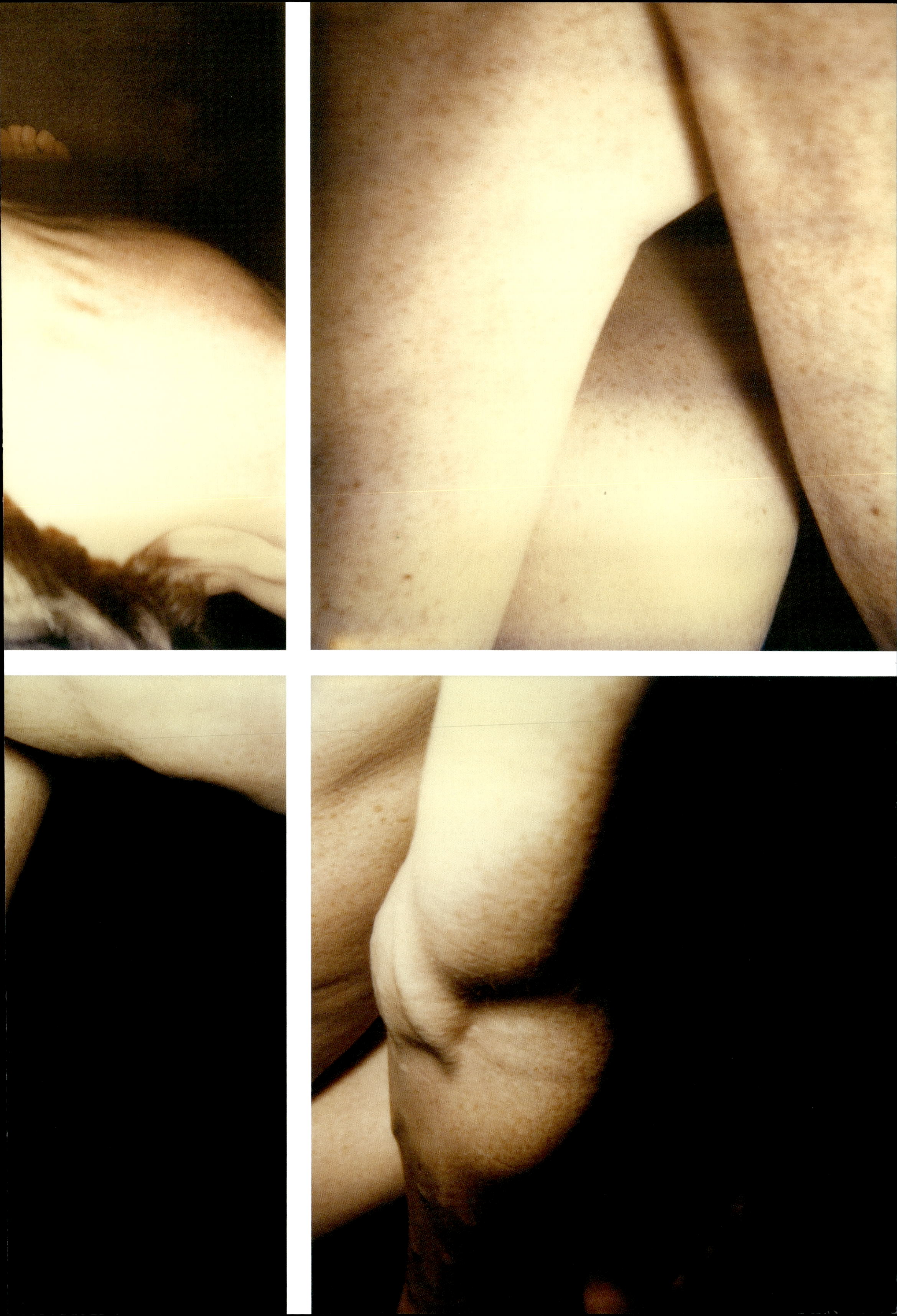

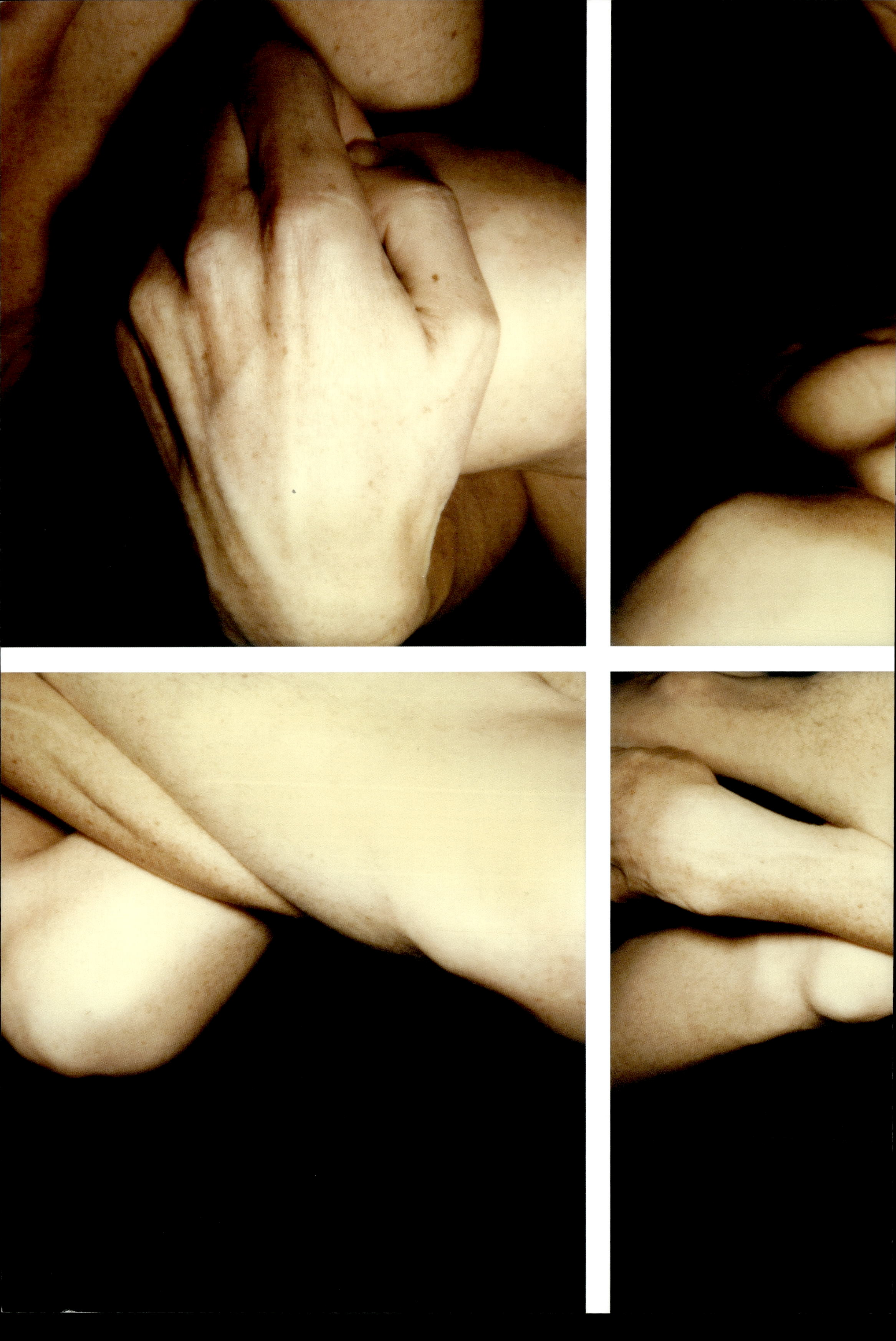

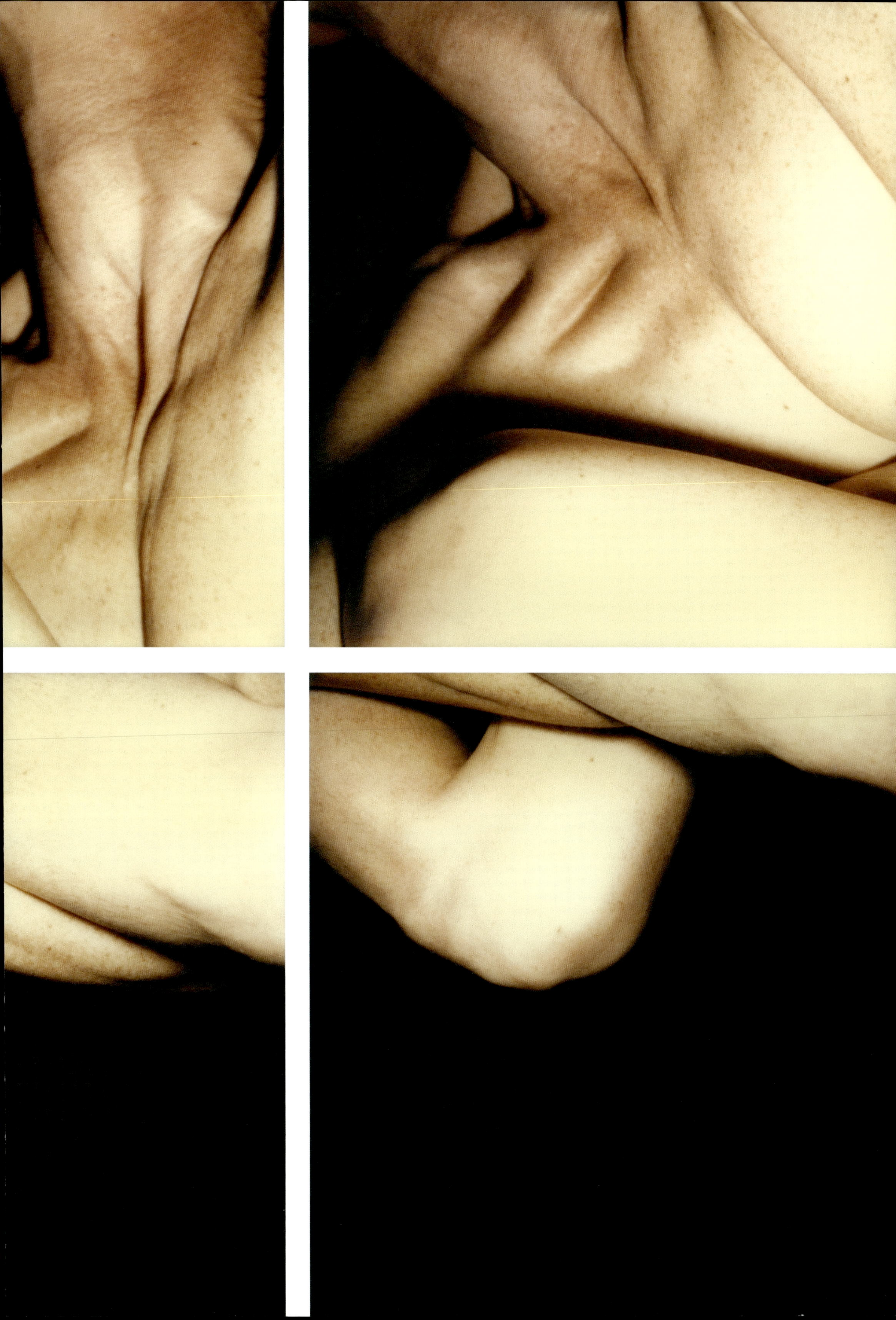

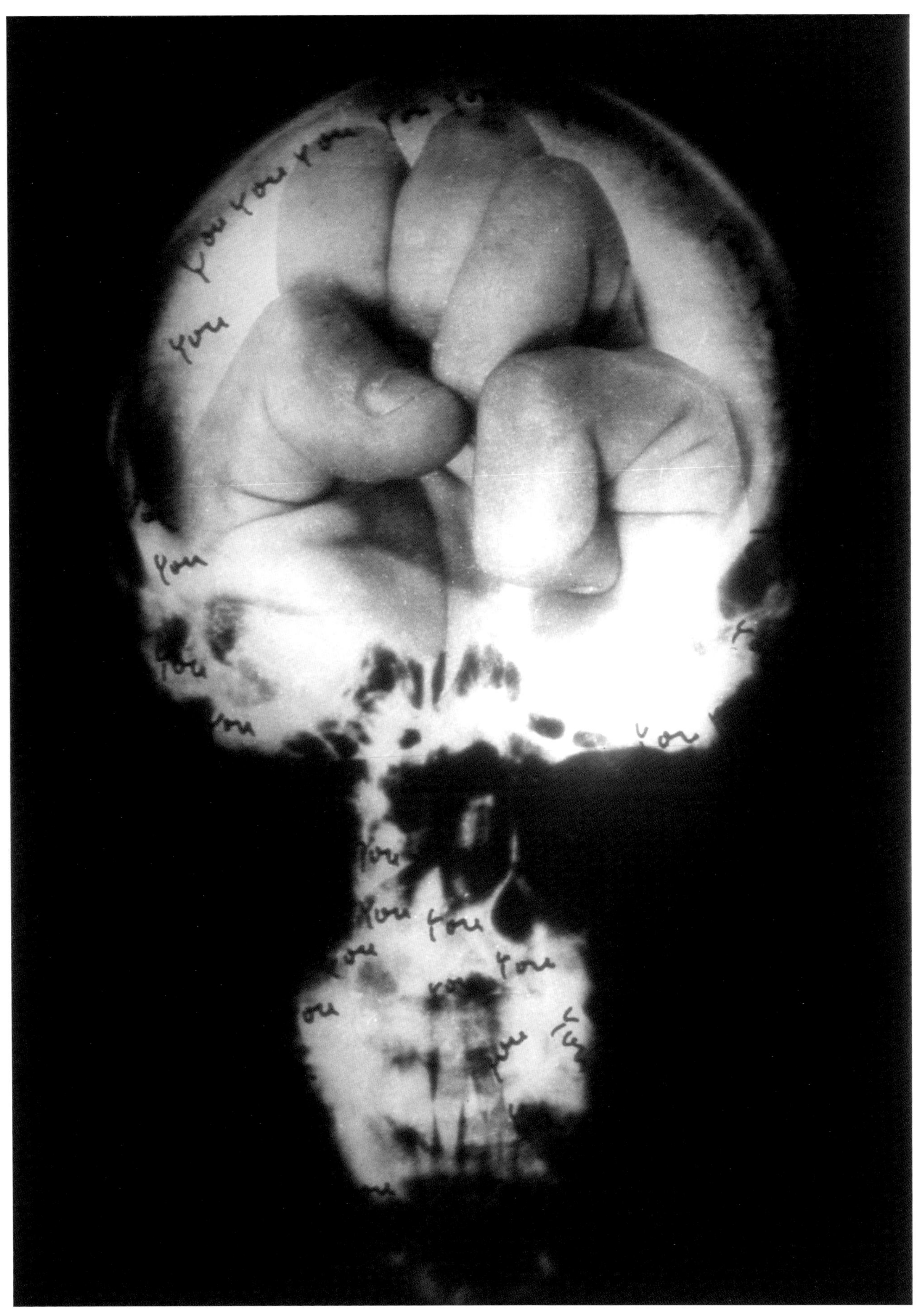

16   Ketty La Rocca, *Untitled (Craniologia)*, 1973

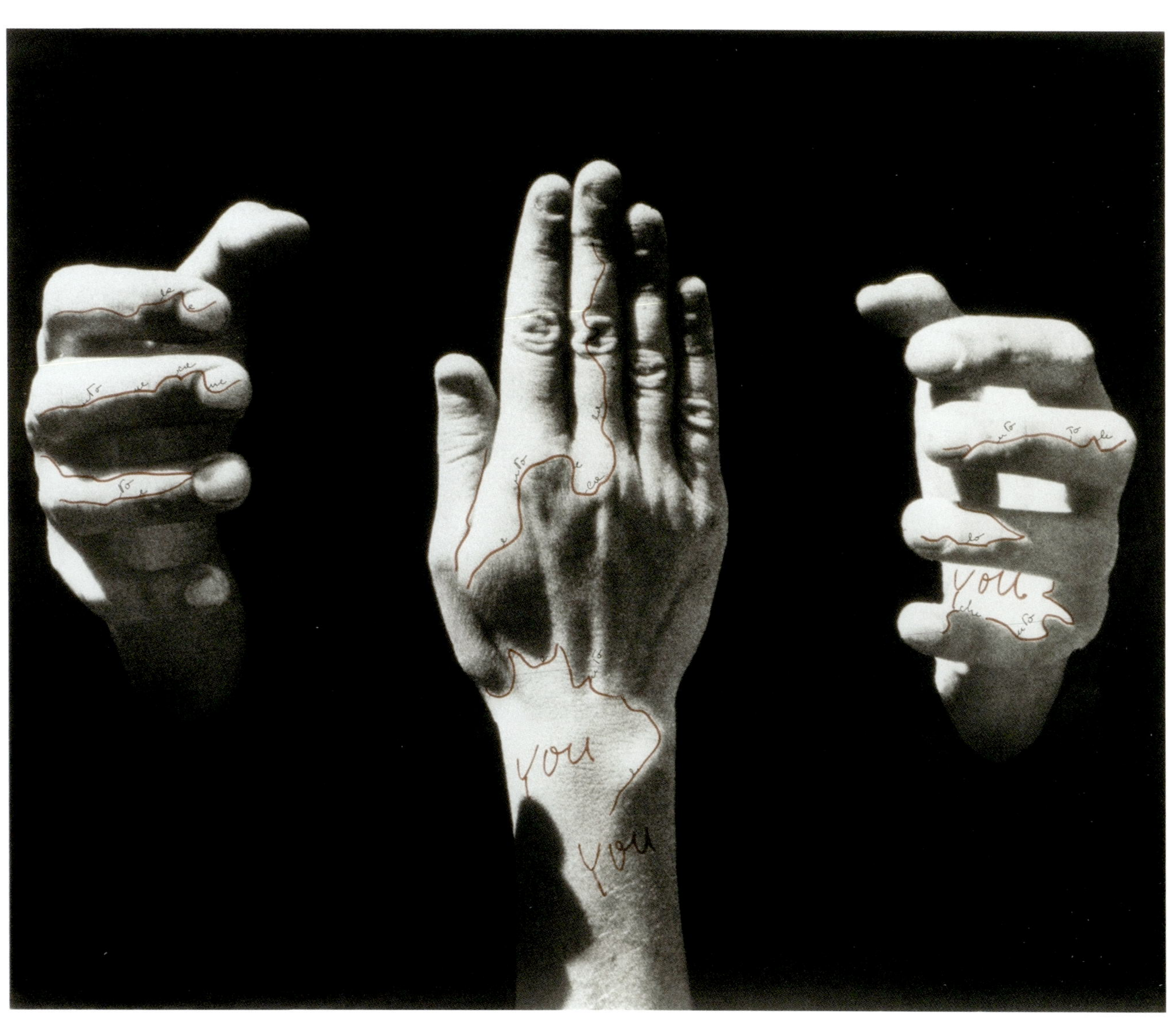

S. Pp. 107–116   17   Ketty La Rocca, *You You,* 1974

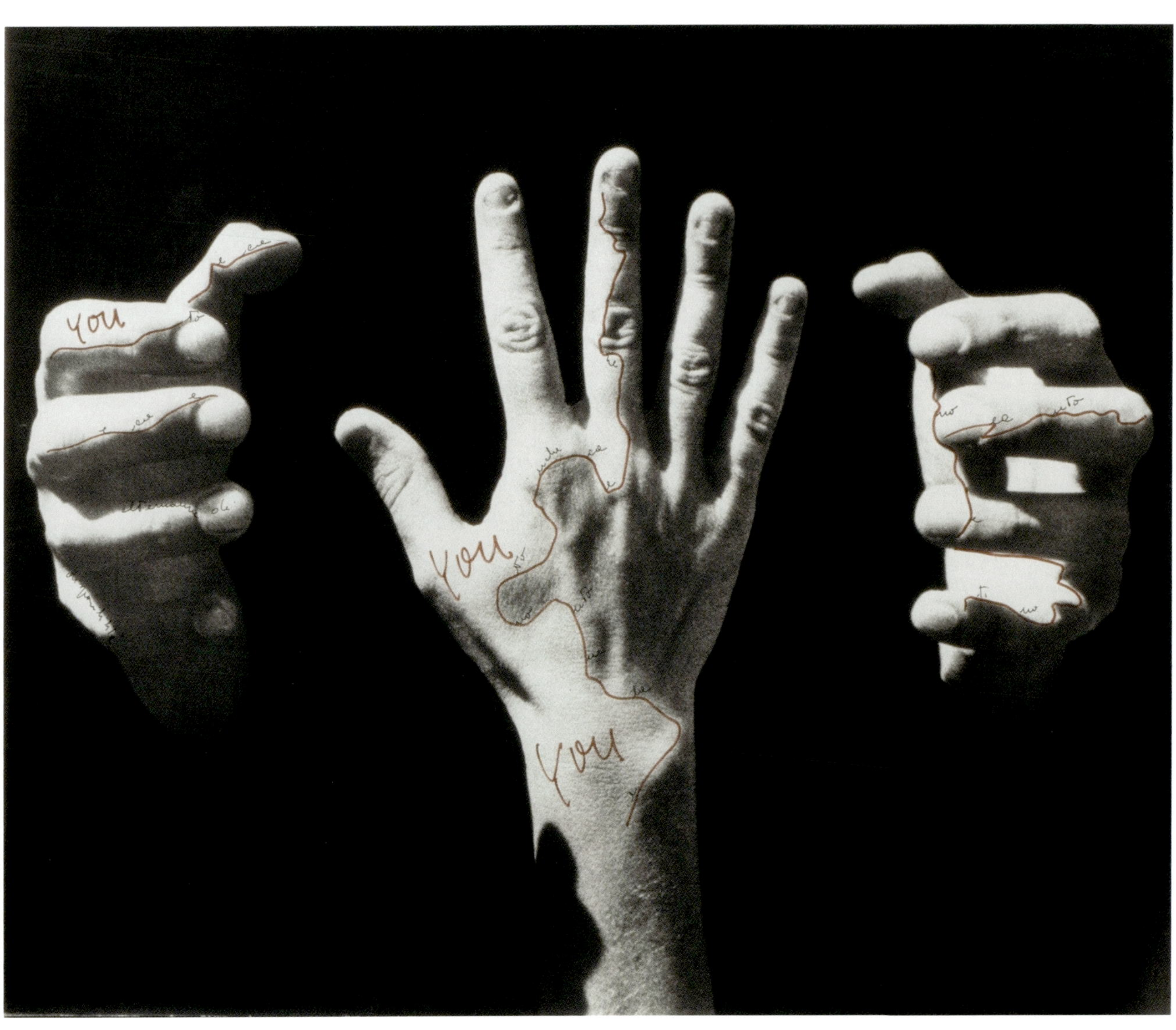
you
you
you

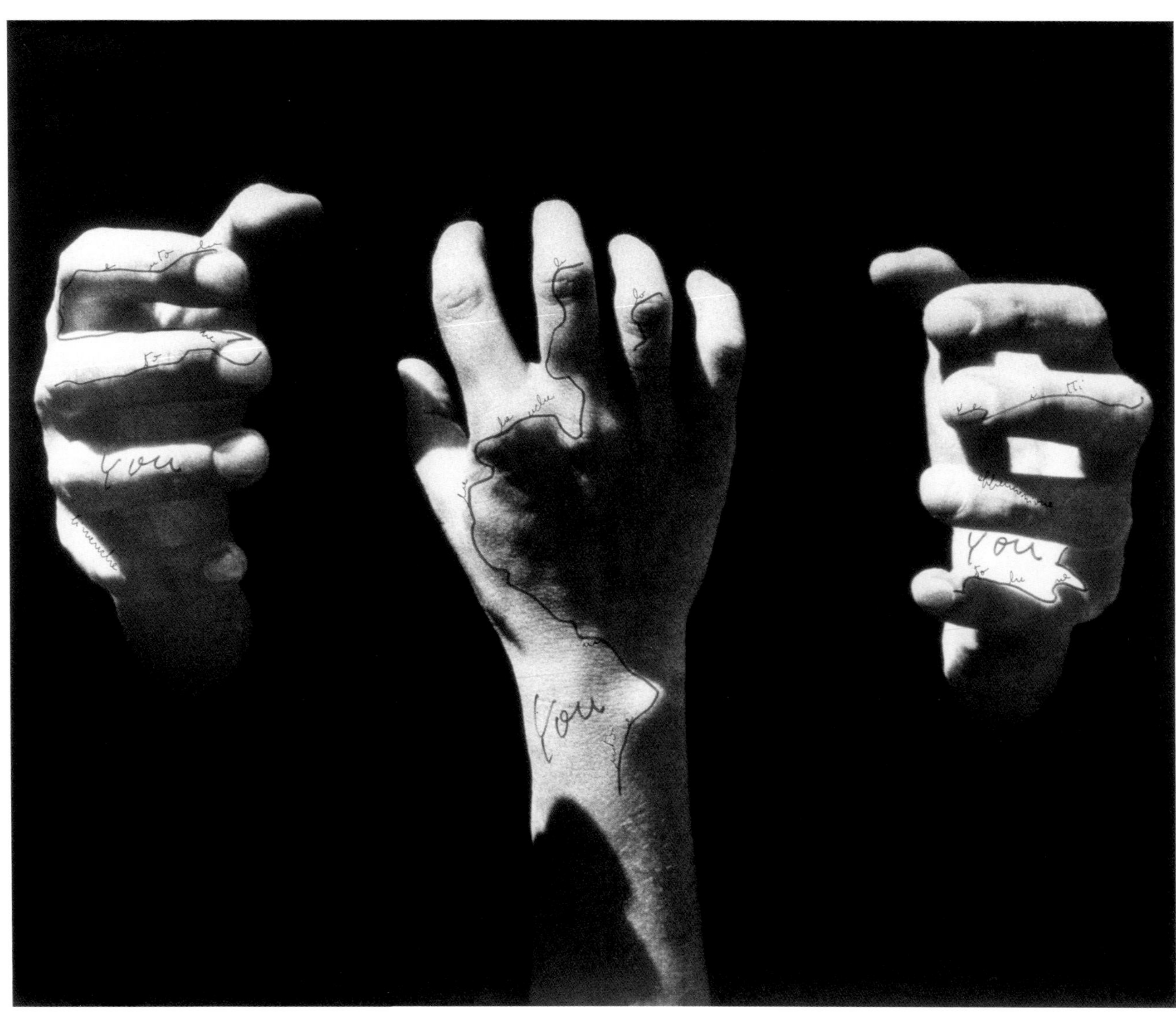

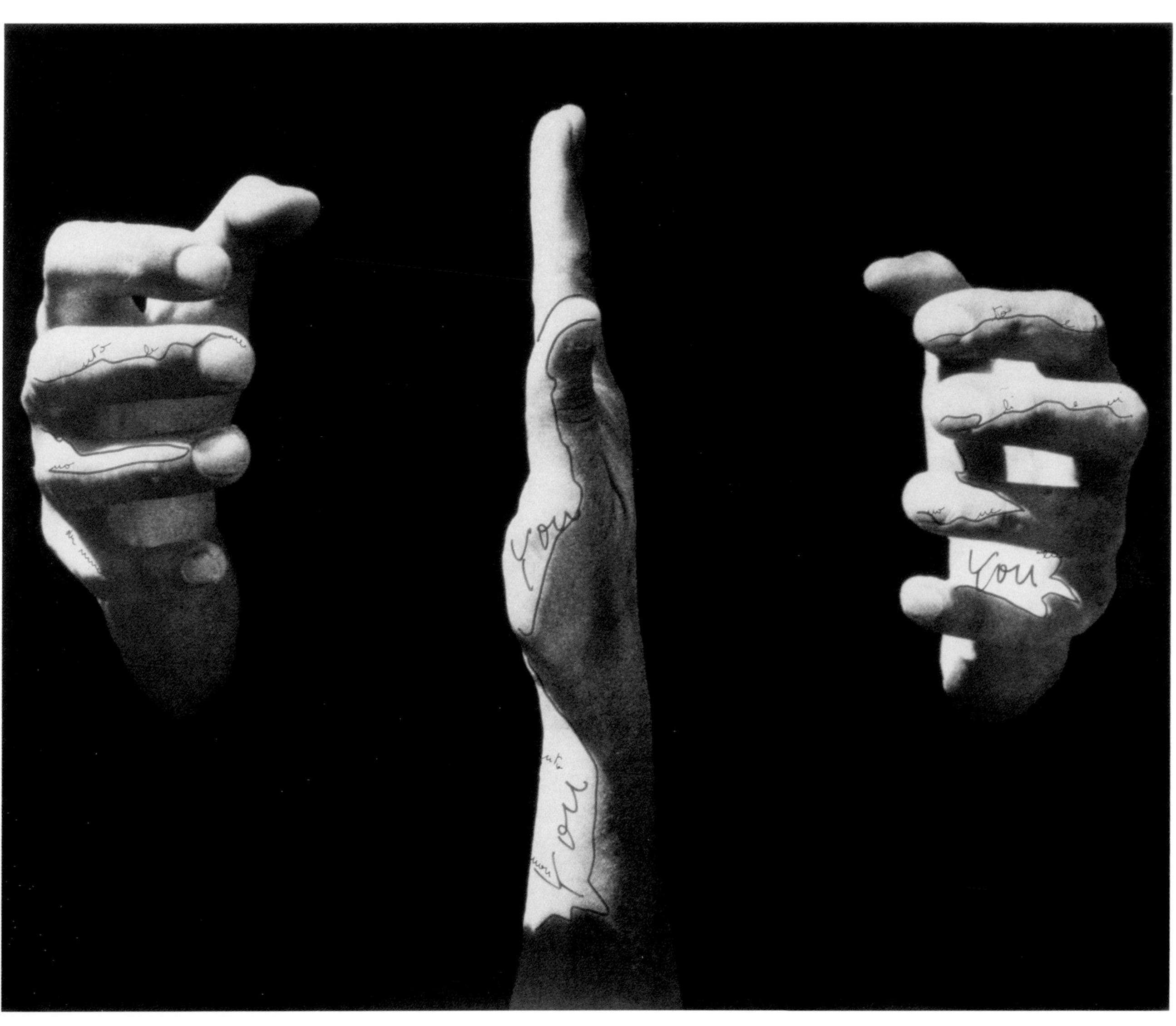
you
you
you

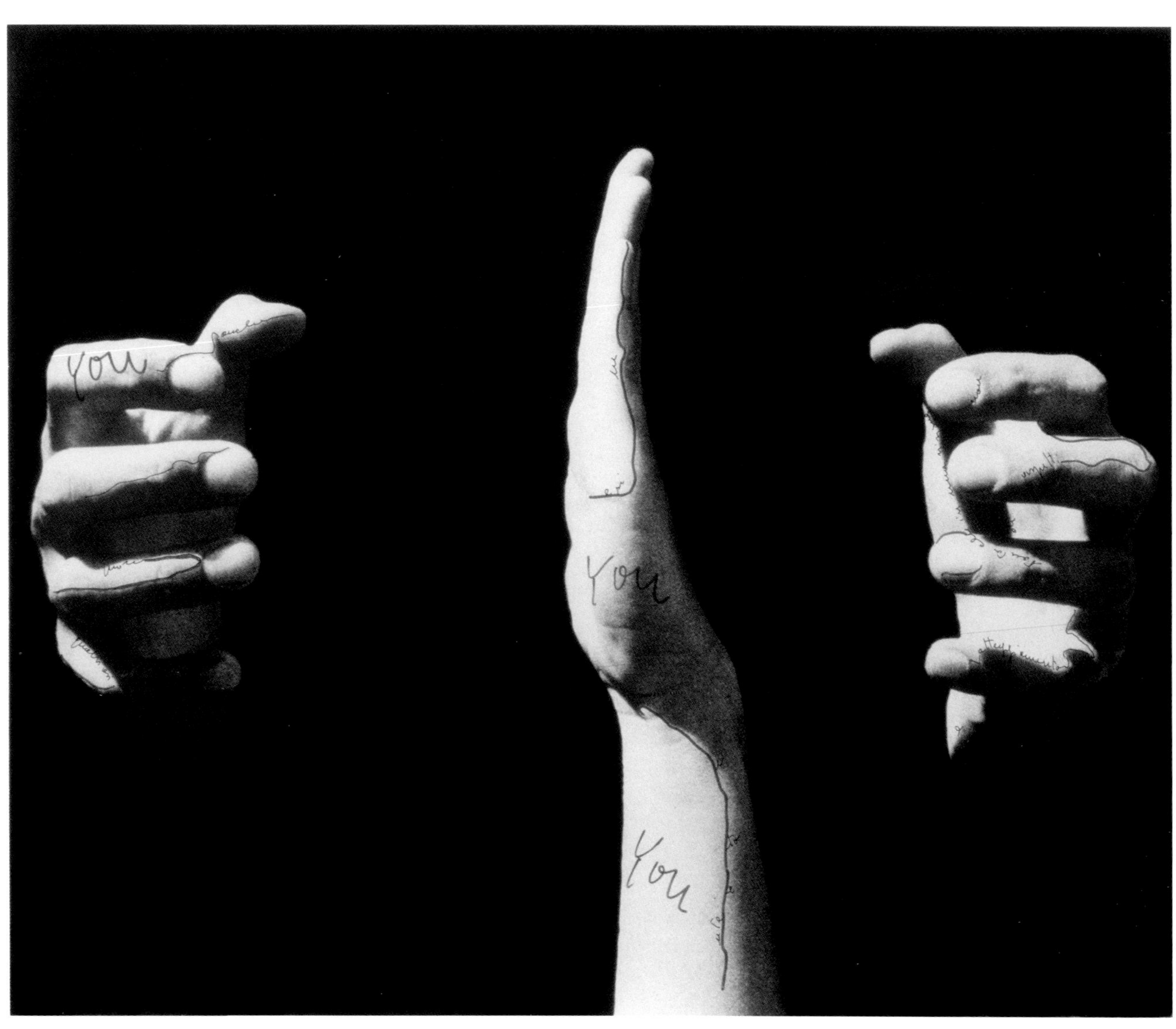
You
You
You

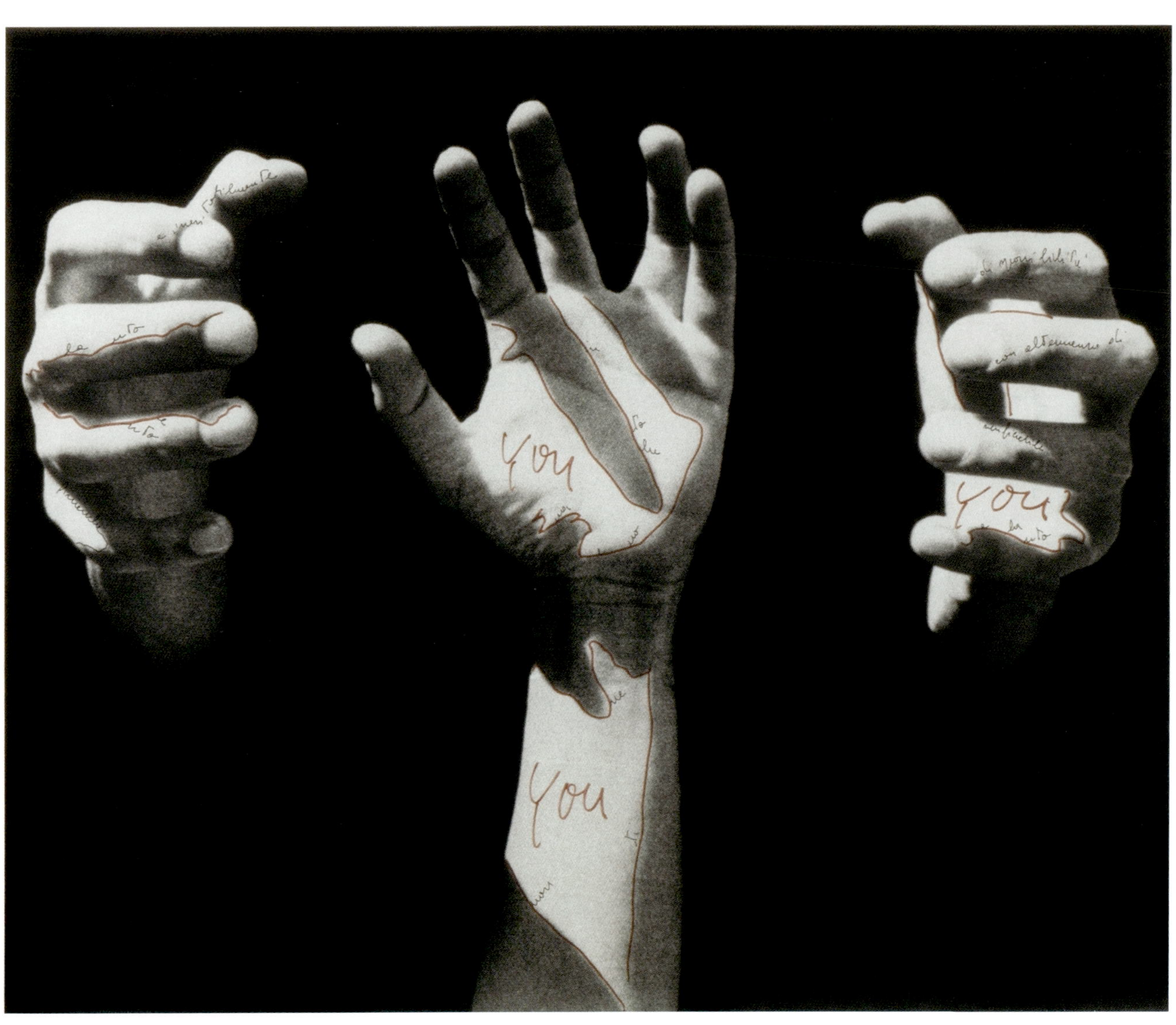

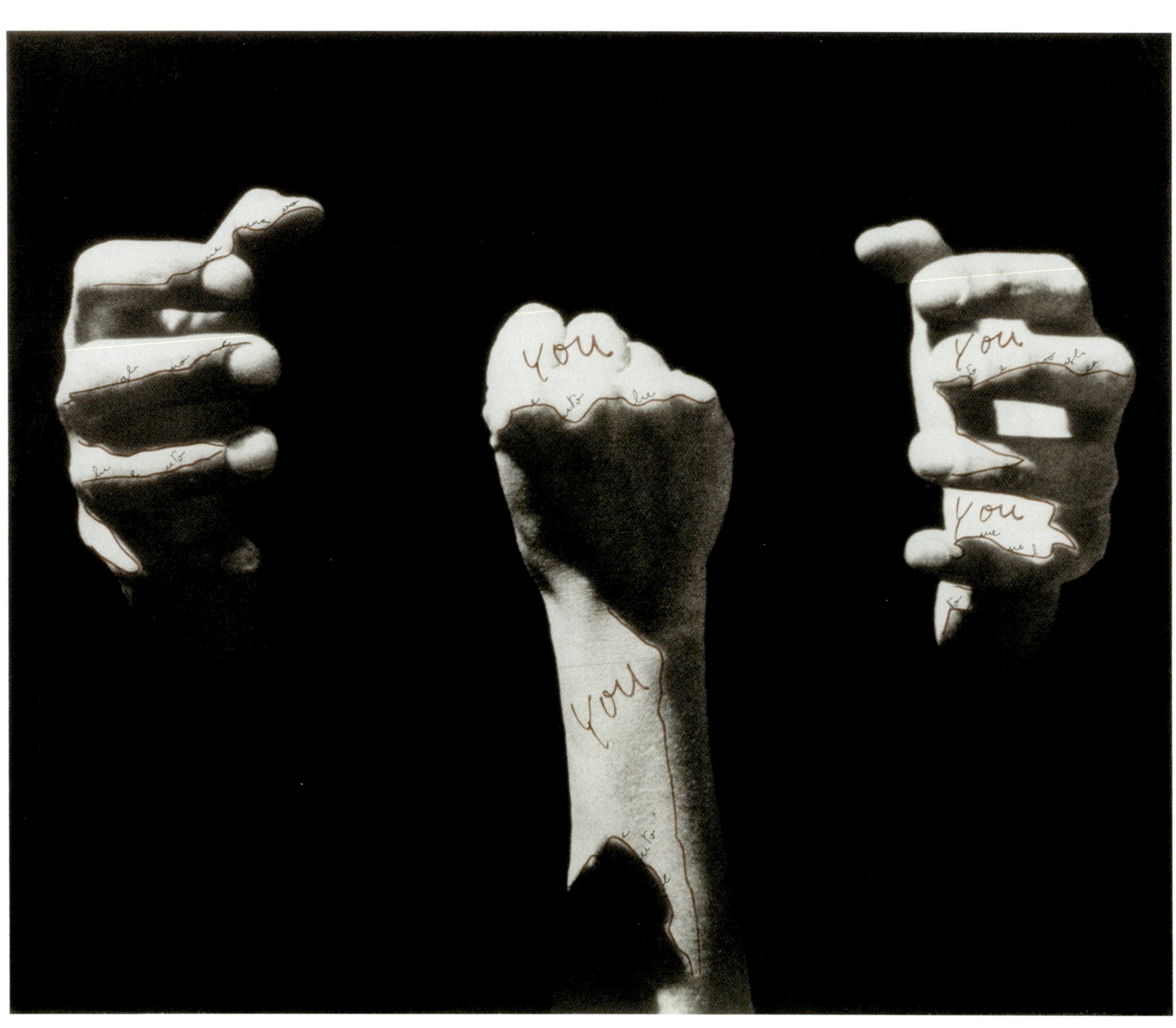
you
you
you
you

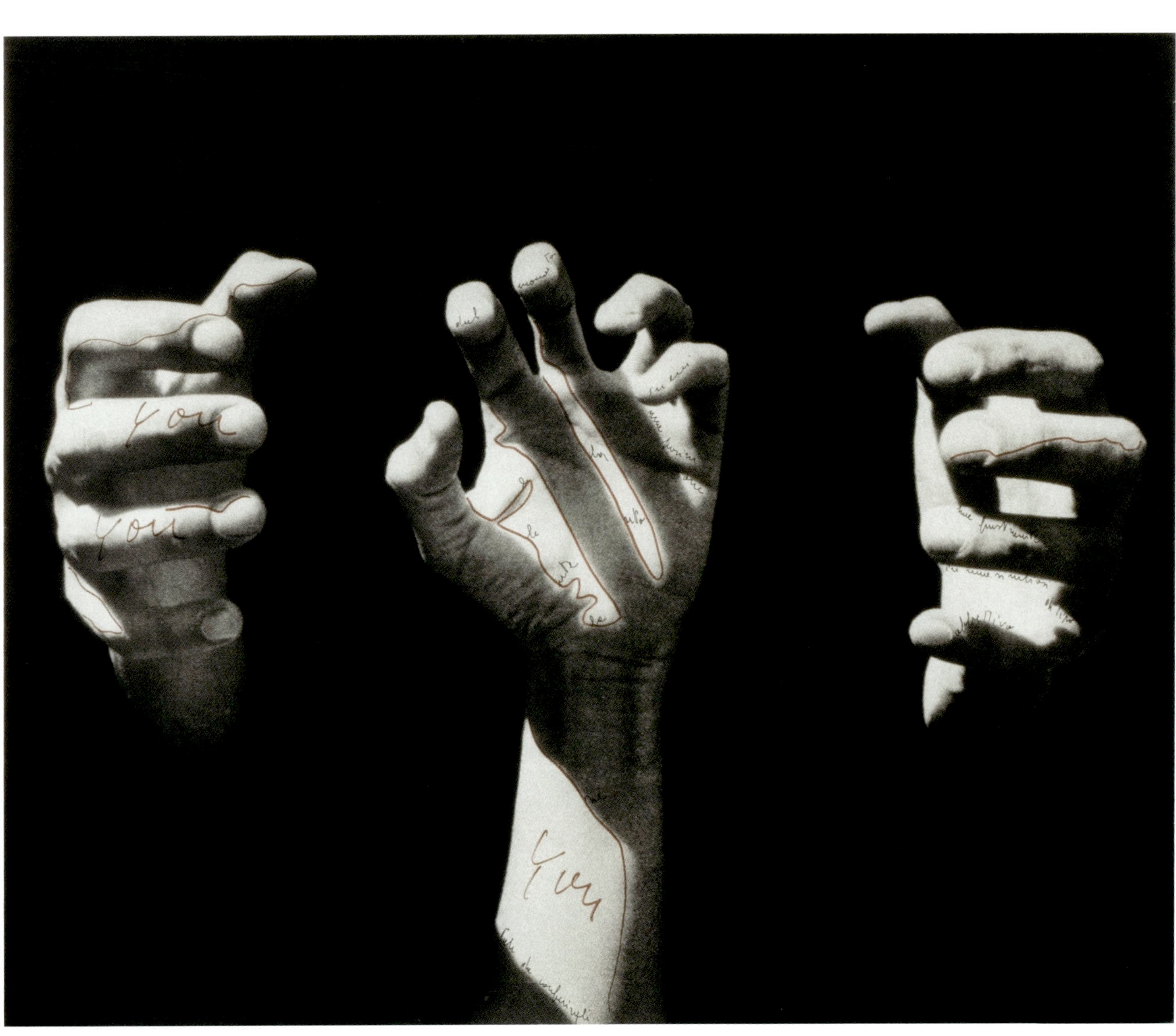

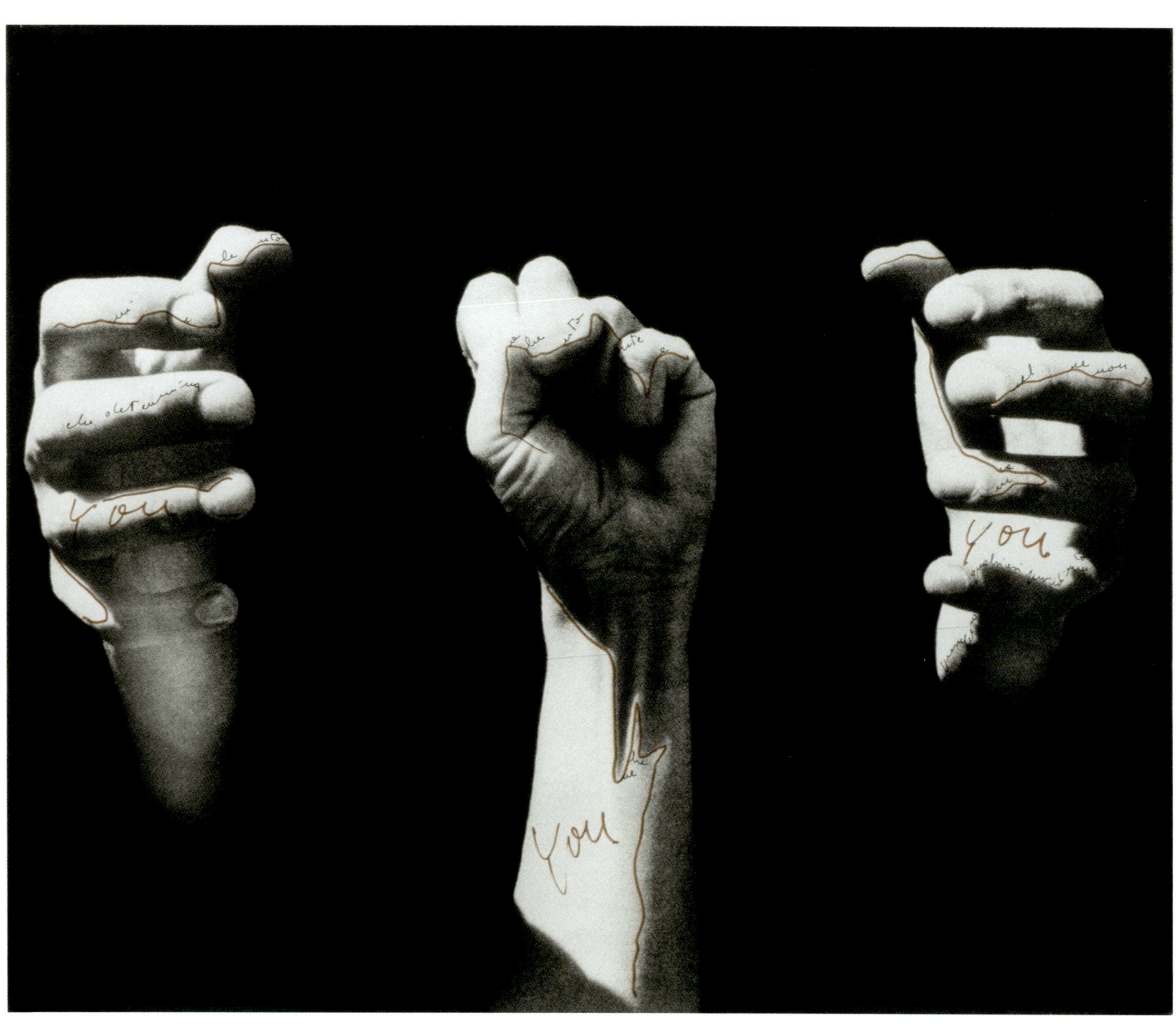

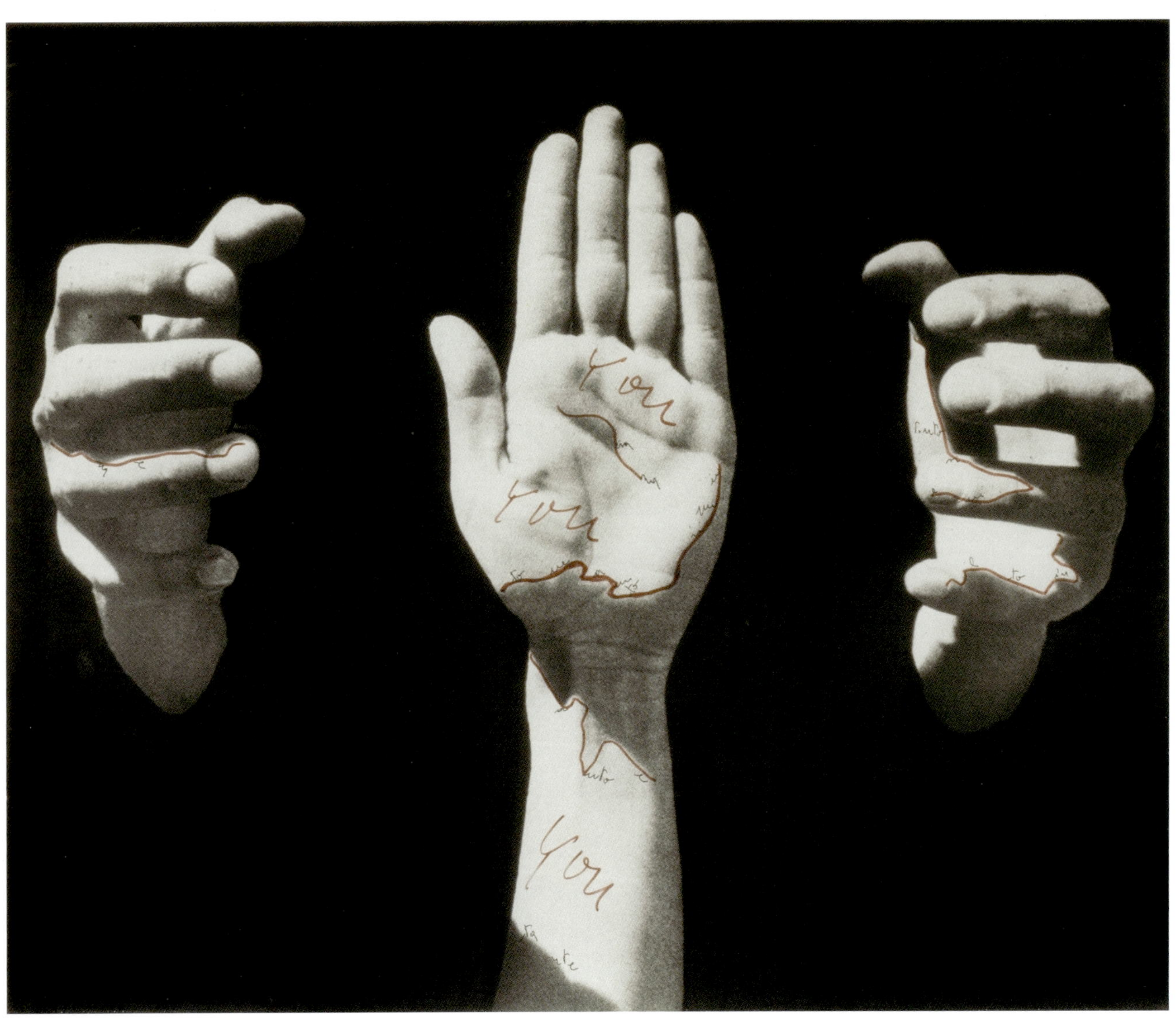
you
you
you

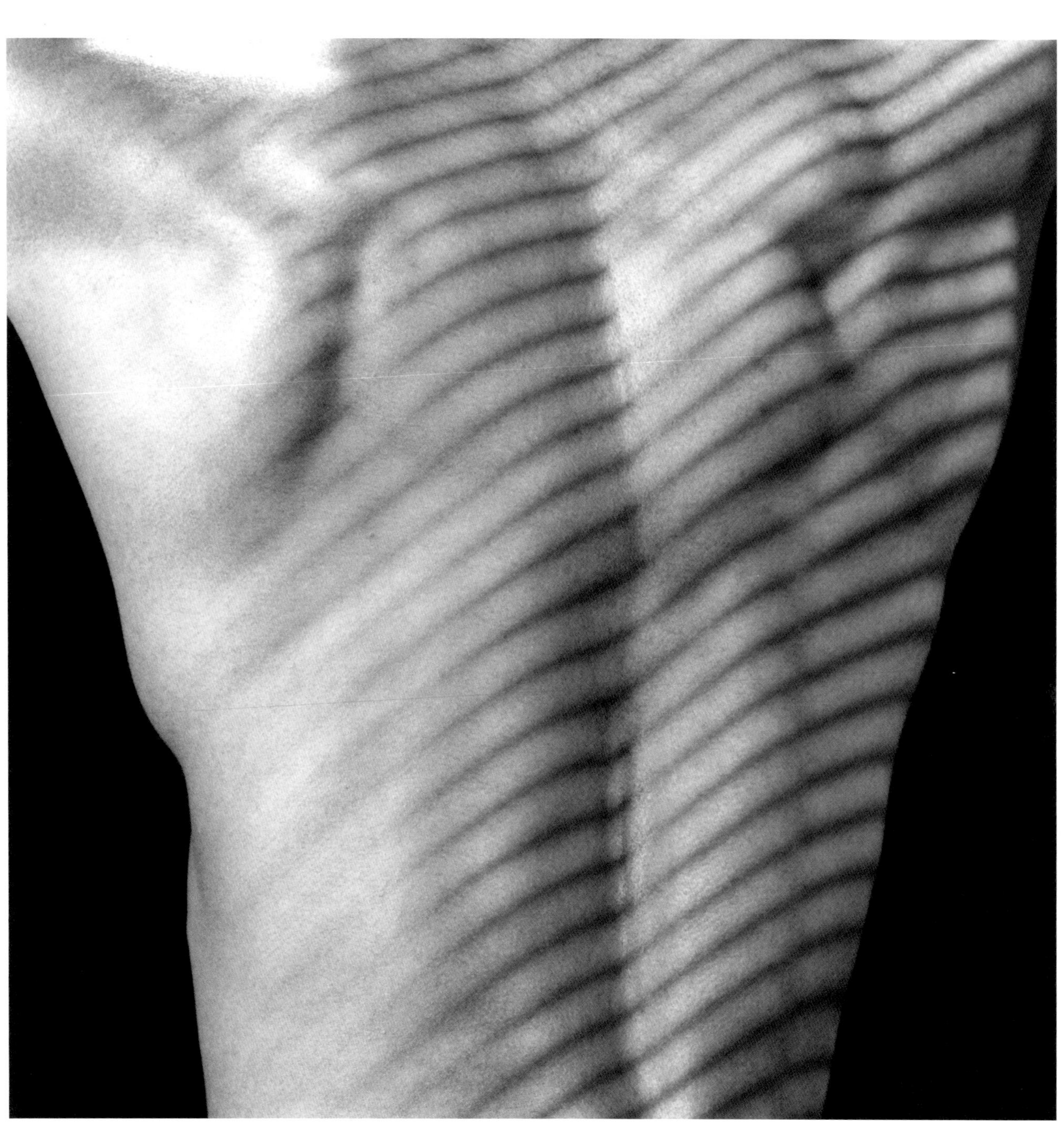

18   Robert Mapplethorpe, *Thomas/Back,* 1986

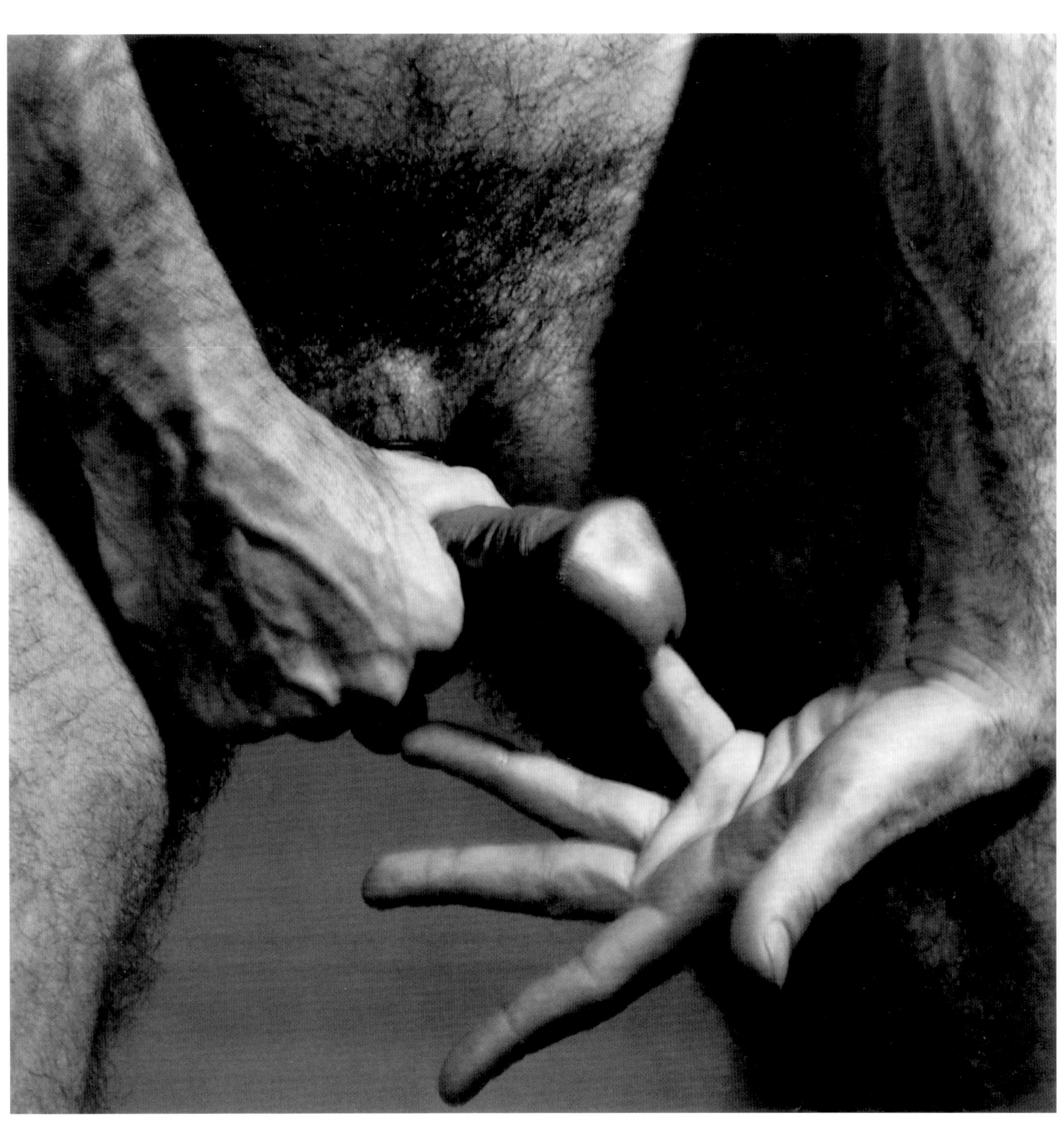

19   Robert Mapplethorpe, *Lou, NYC,* 1978

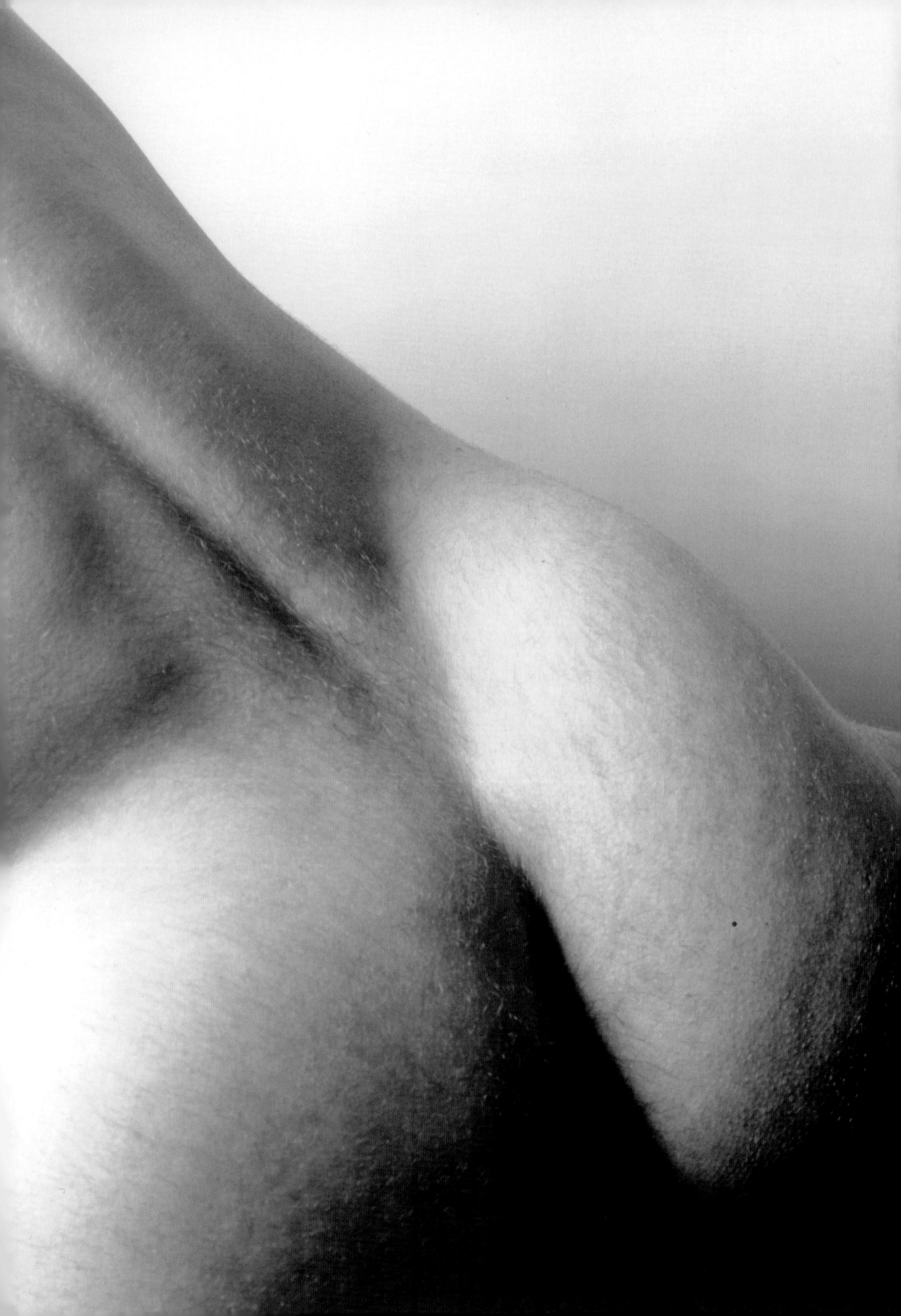

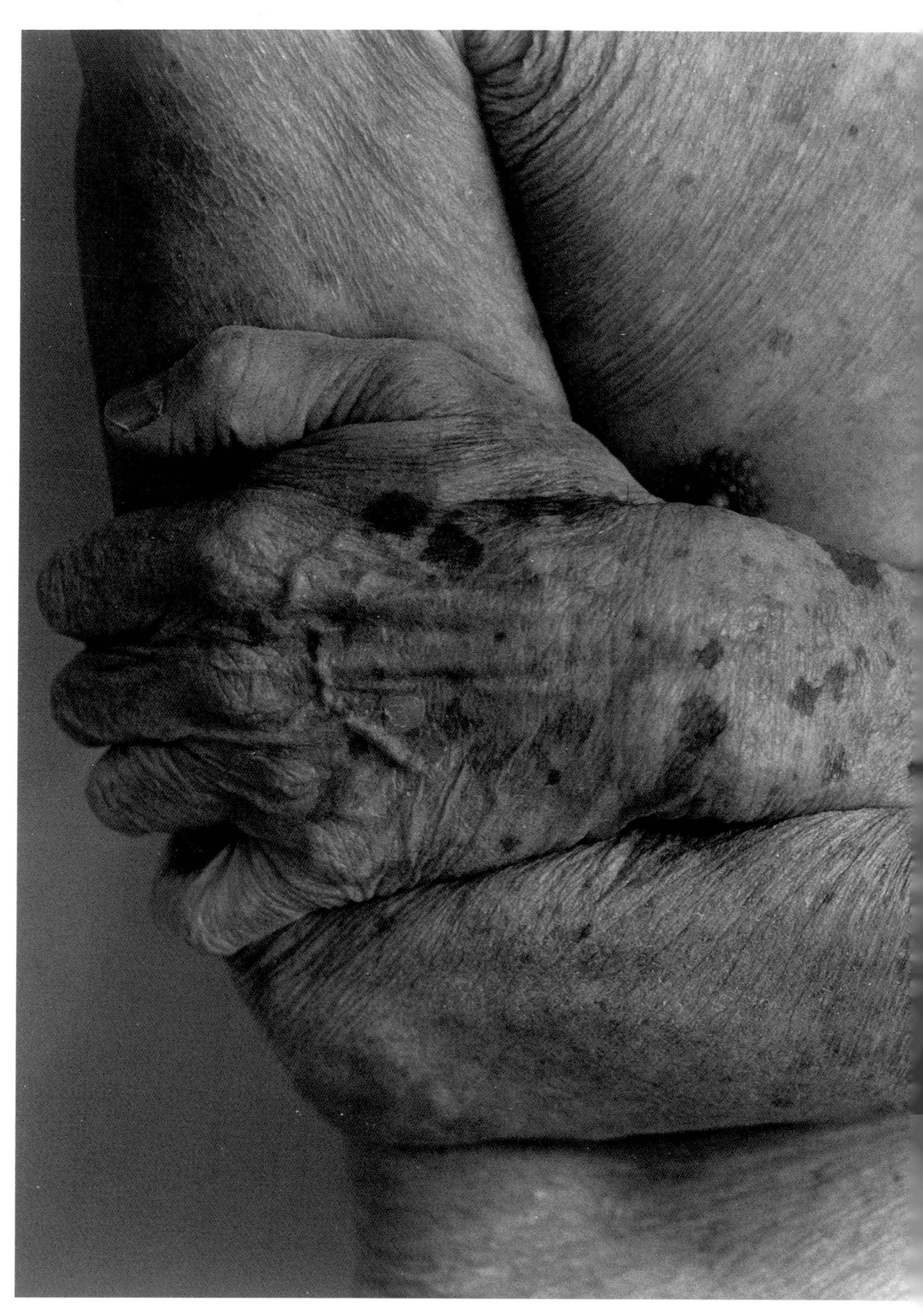

21 Miyako Ishiuchi, *1906 to the Skin, #17*, 1991–1993

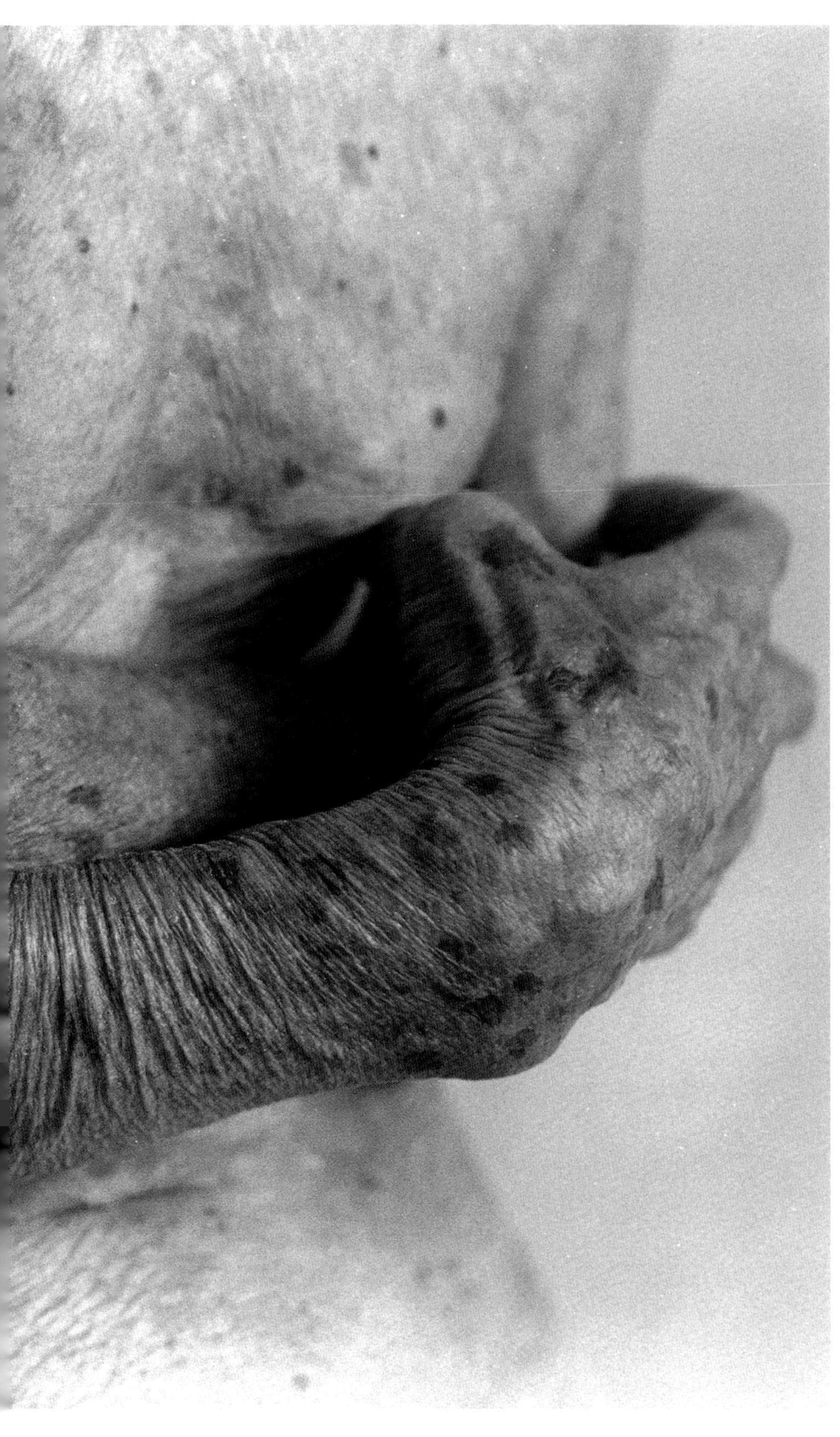

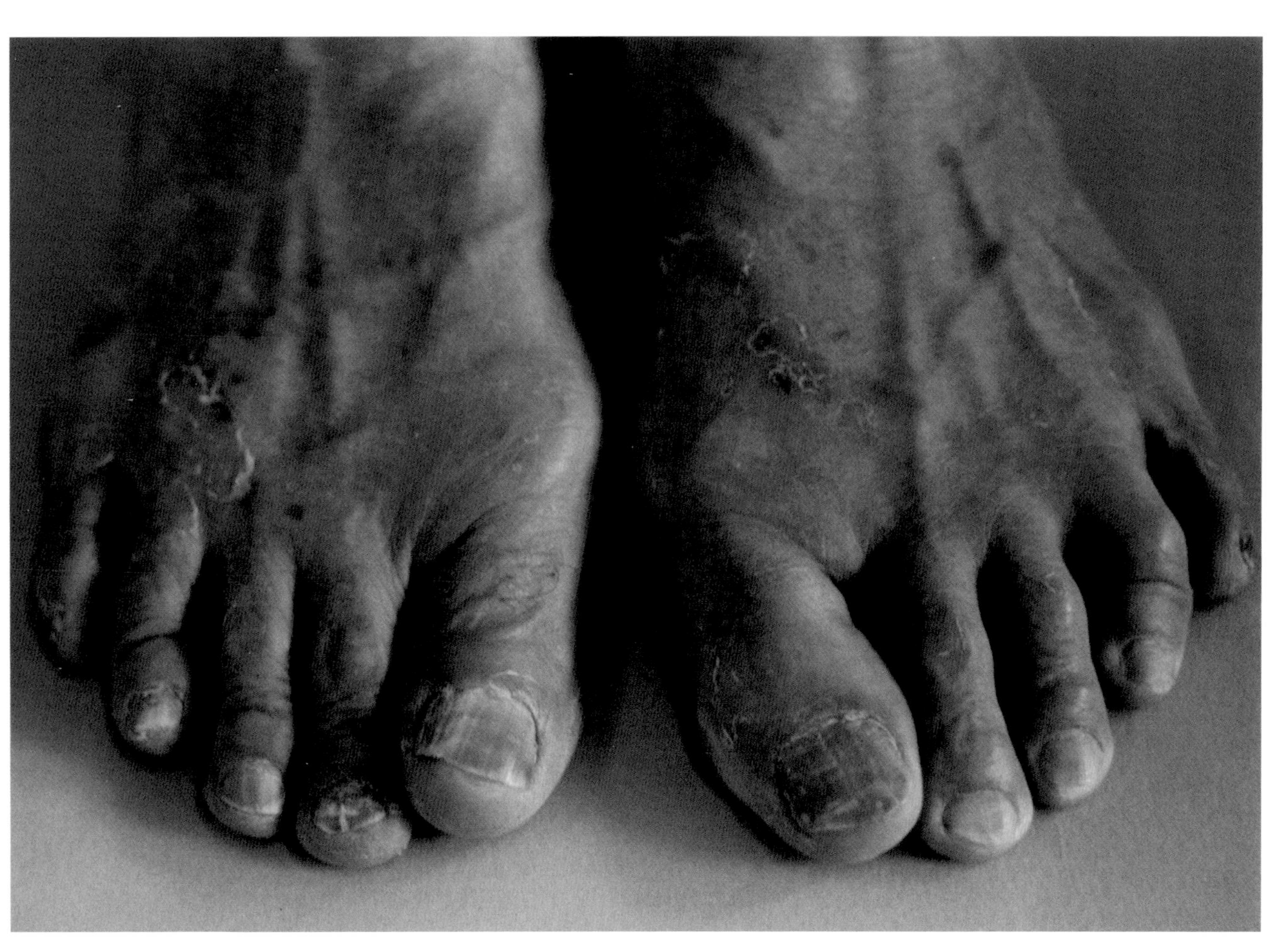

22   Miyako Ishiuchi, *1906 to the Skin, #55,* 1991–1993

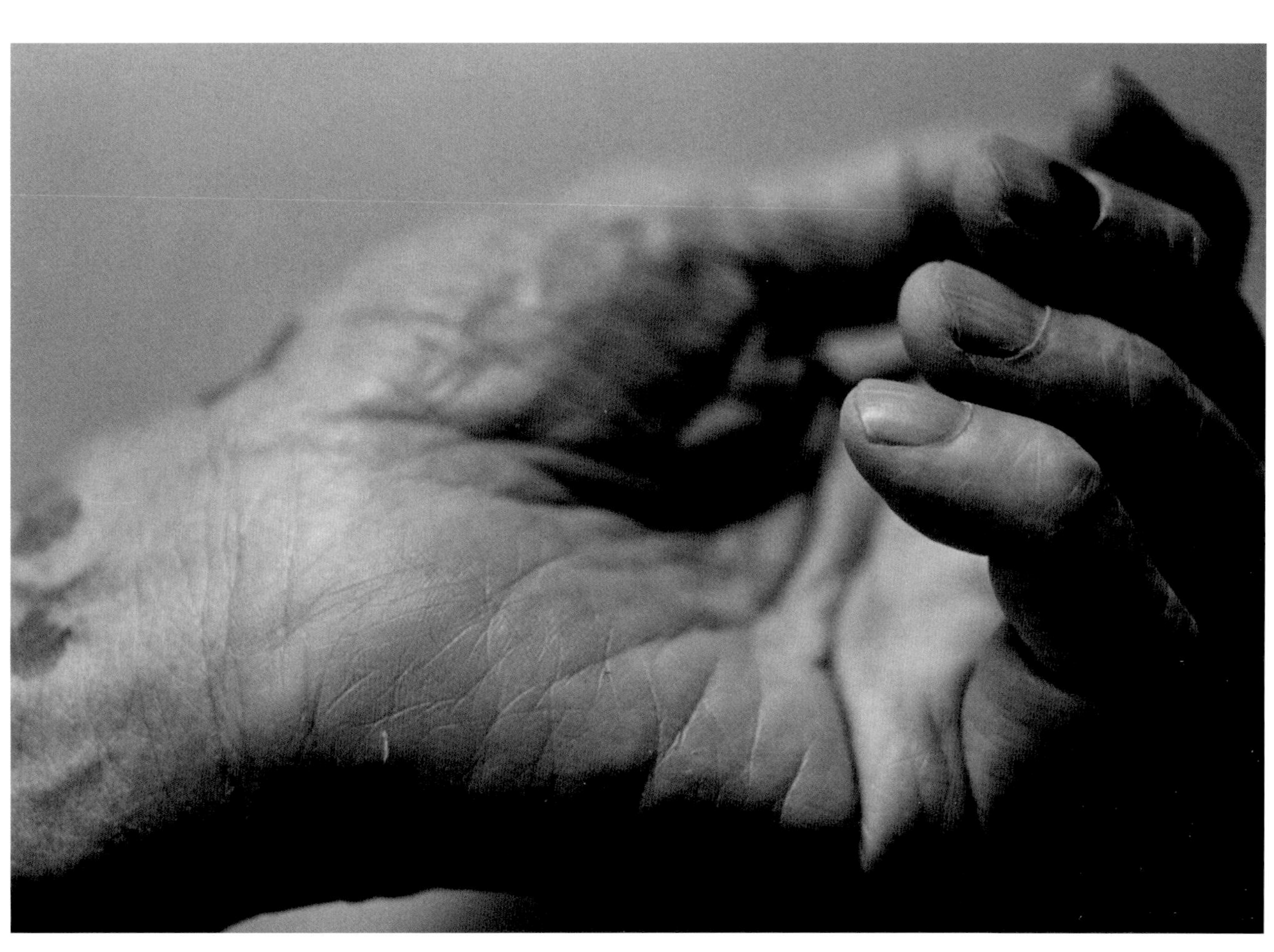

23　Miyako Ishiuchi, *1906 to the Skin, #39*, 1991–1993

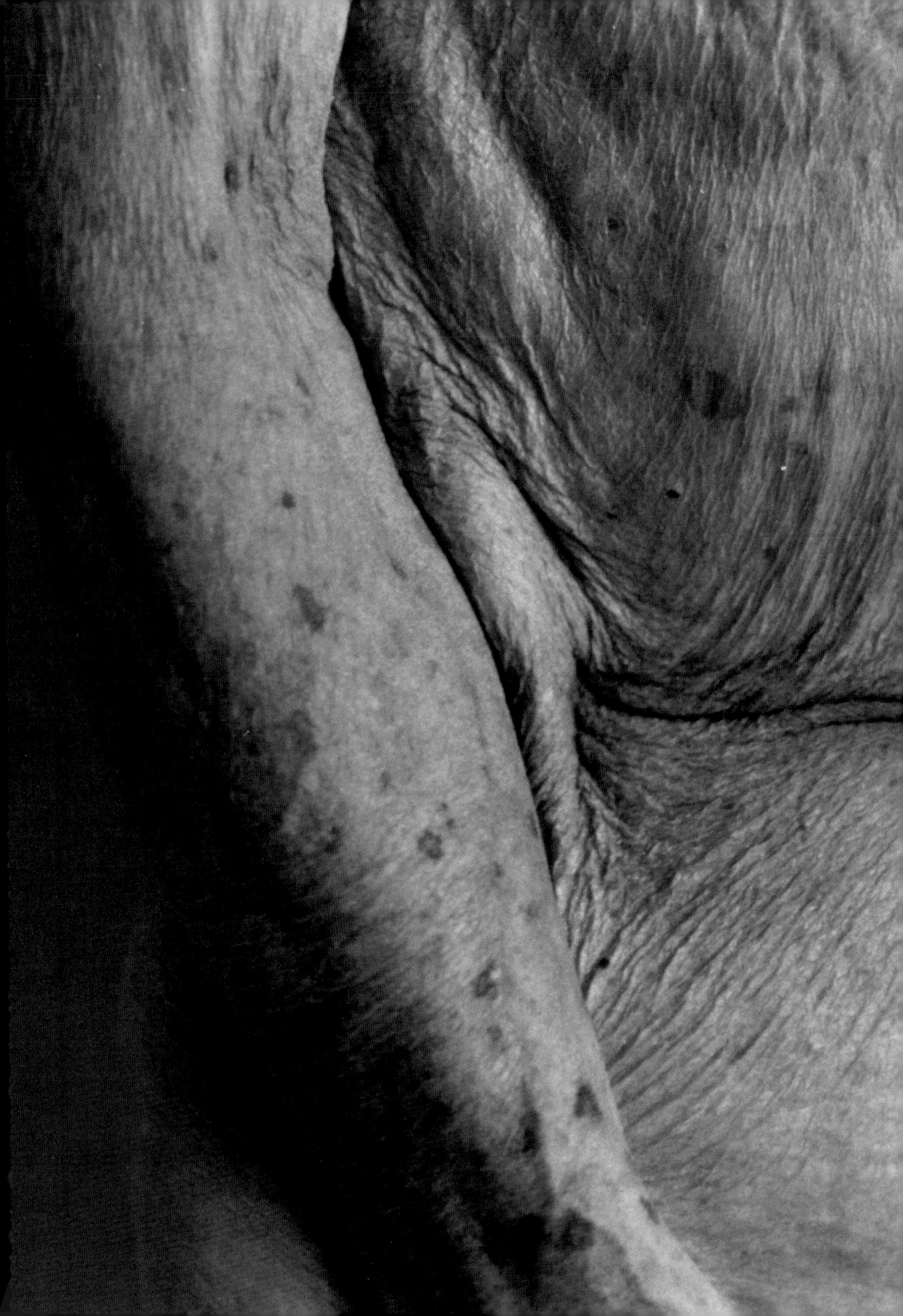

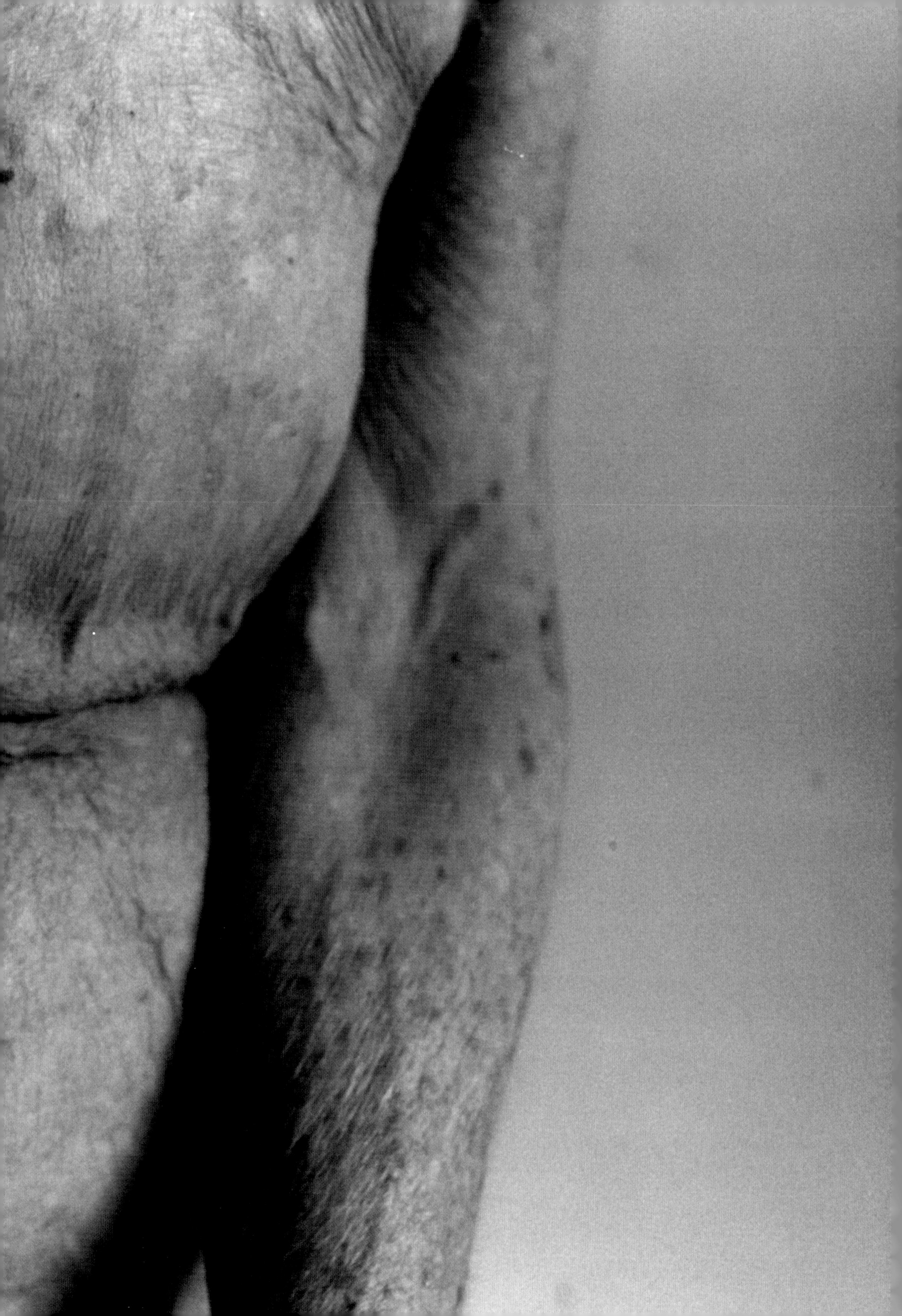

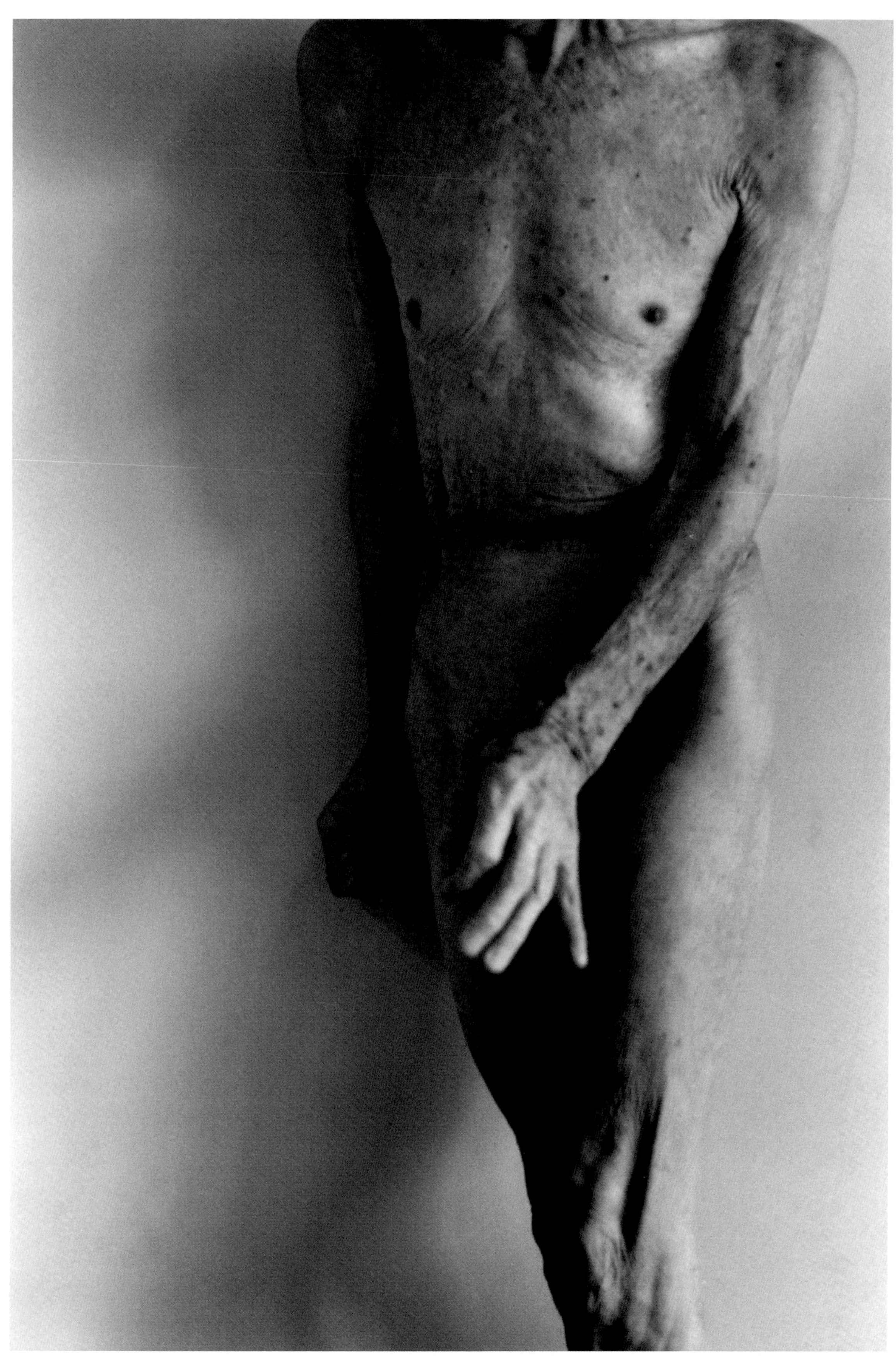

25   Miyako Ishiuchi, *1906 to the Skin, #60,* 1991–1993

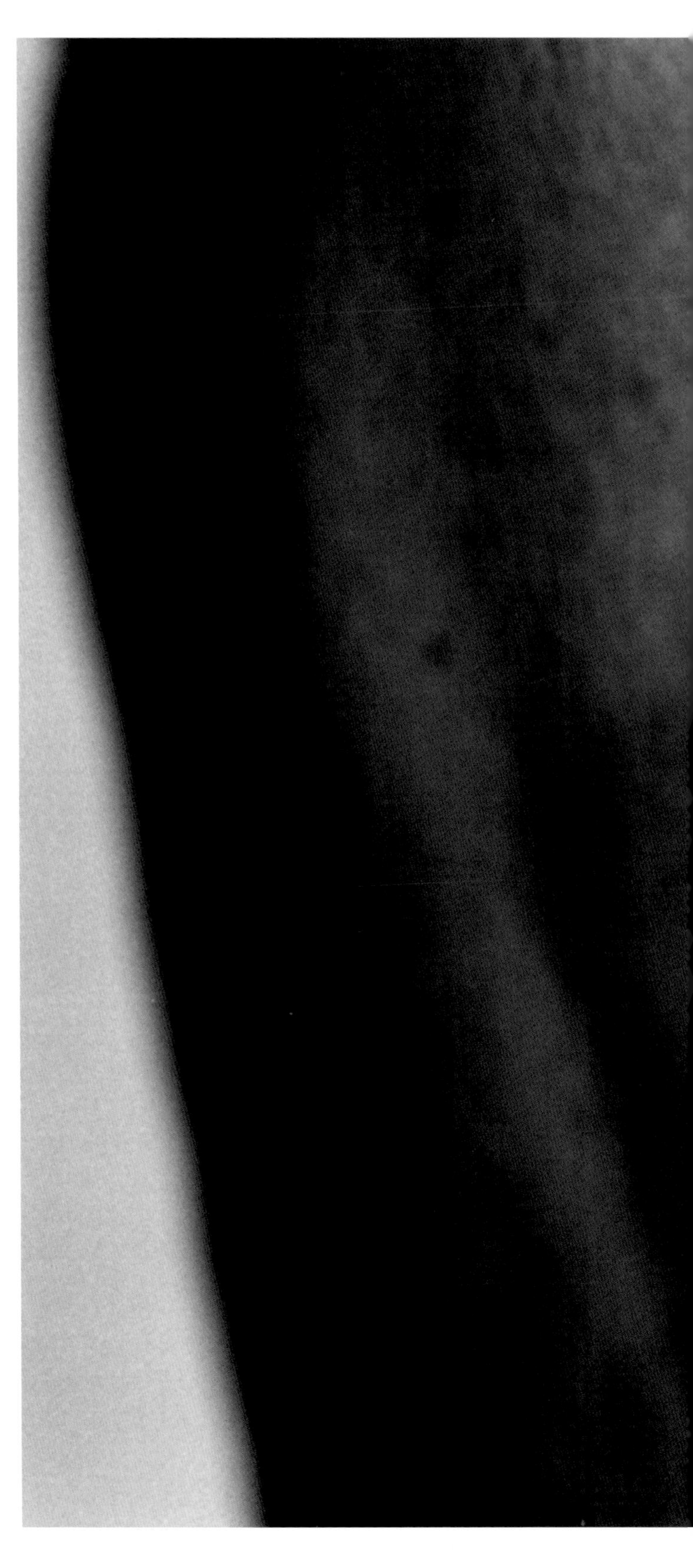

26   Miyako Ishiuchi, *1906 to the Skin, #38,* 1991–1993

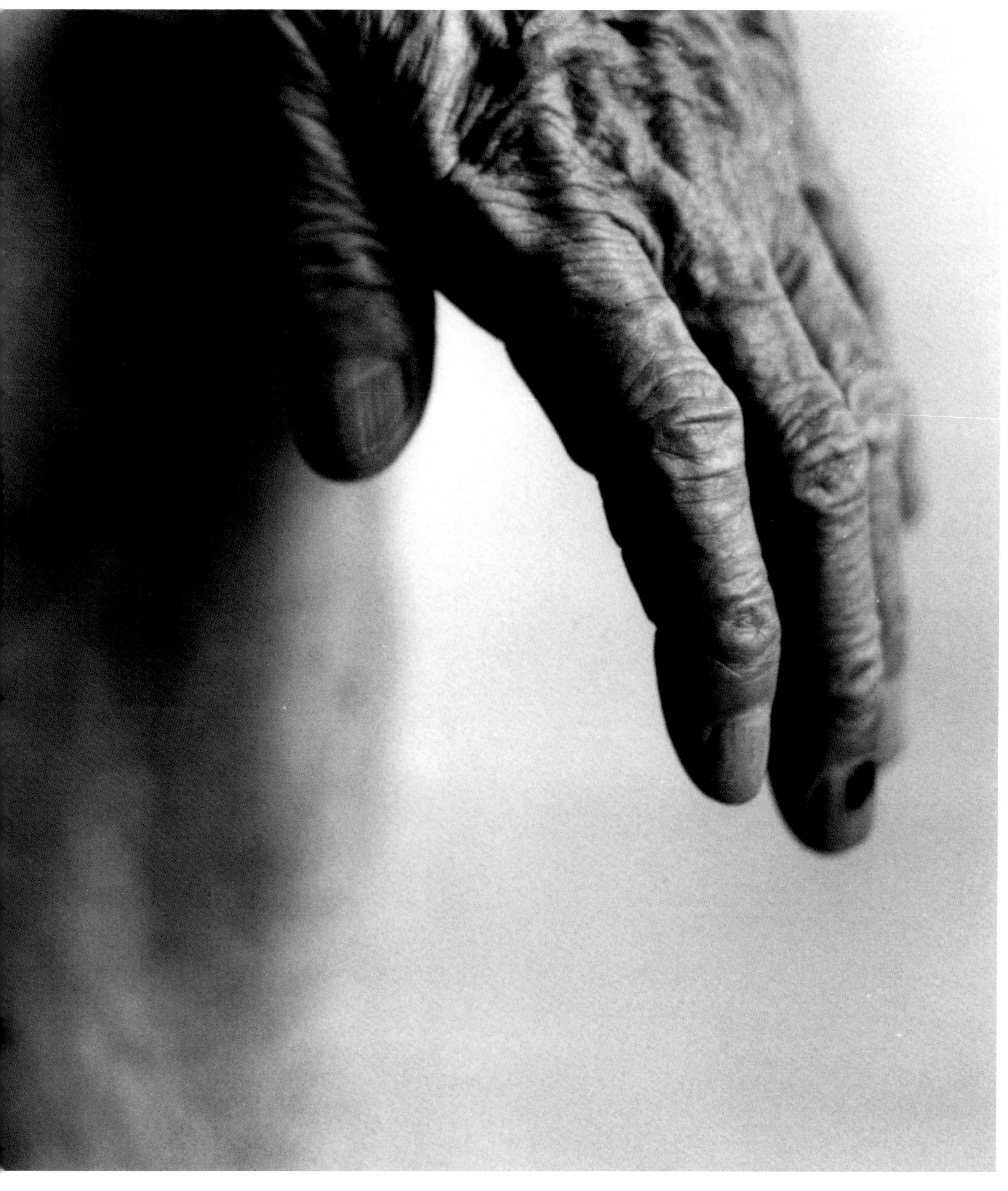

Liste der abgebildeten Werke List of Plates

1
Bruce Nauman
Thighing (Blue), 1967
4:36 min, Farbe, Ton, 16-mm-Film
auf Video 4:36 min, color, sound,
16mm film on video
Courtesy Electronic Arts Intermix
(EAI), New York

2
Hannah Wilke
Gestures, 1974–1976
Basierend auf der gleichnamigen
Videoperformance von 1974
(35:30 min, s/w, Ton) Based on the
1974 video performance of the
same title (35:30 min, b&w, sound)
Silbergelatinepapier Gelatin silver
paper
9 Blatt 9 sheets,
je 12,7 x 17,8 cm each

3
Vito Acconci
Openings, 1970
14 min, s/w, ohne Ton,
Super-8-mm-Film auf Video
14 min, b&w, silent, Super 8mm
film on video
Courtesy Electronic Arts Intermix
(EAI), New York

4
John Coplans
Hand, Two Panels, Vertical, 1988
Silbergelatinepapier Gelatin silver
paper
130,5 x 105,5 cm
Albertina, Wien Vienna

5
John Coplans
Interlocking Fingers, No. 6, 1999
Silbergelatinepapier Gelatin
silver paper
85 x 68 cm
Albertina, Wien Vienna

6
John Coplans
Interlocking Fingers, No. 17, 2000
Silbergelatinepapier Gelatin
silver paper
85 x 68 cm
Albertina, Wien Vienna

7
John Coplans
Back with Arms Above, 1984
Silbergelatinepapier Gelatin
silver paper
106,6 x 81,2 cm
Privatsammlung Private
collection, Innsbruck

8
John Coplans
Frieze No. 6, 1994
Silbergelatinepapier Gelatin
silver paper
6 Blatt 6 sheets,
je 61 x 78 cm each
Albertina, Wien Vienna

9
John Coplans
Self-Portrait, Six Times, 1987
Silbergelatinepapier, auf Karton
montiert Gelatin silver paper,
mounted on cardboard
87 x 230 cm
Albertina, Wien Vienna

10
John Coplans
Fingers, Front, 1999
Silbergelatinepapier Gelatin
silver paper
85 x 68 cm
Albertina, Wien Vienna

11
John Coplans
Hand with Buttocks, 1987
Silbergelatinepapier Gelatin
silver paper
58 x 76 cm
Albertina, Wien Vienna

12
John Coplans
Toes on Foot, Five Panels, 1989
Silbergelatinepapier Gelatin
silver paper
5 Blatt 5 sheets,
je 53 x 43 cm each
Albertina, Wien Vienna

13
Bruce Nauman
Studies for Holograms (1–5), 1970
Serigrafie Screen print
Je 66 x 66 cm each
Museum Ludwig, Köln Cologne,
Graphische Sammlung

14
Hannah Villiger
Block XXX, 1993/94
C-Print, Polaroidfotografie, auf
Aluminium montiert C-print,
Polaroid photograph, mounted
on aluminium
Darstellung der 6 Fotografien
Dimensions of the 6 photographs:
254 x 377 cm
The Estate of Hannah Villiger

15
Hannah Villiger
Block XXXI, 1993/94
C-Print, Polaroidfotografie, auf
Aluminium montiert C-print,
Polaroid photograph, mounted
on aluminium
Darstellung der 6 Fotografien
Dimensions of the 6 photographs:
254 x 377 cm
The Estate of Hannah Villiger

16
Ketty La Rocca
Untitled (Craniologia), 1973
Radiografie mit überblendeter Foto-
grafie Radiograph superimposed
with photograph
70 x 50 cm
SAMMLUNG VERBUND, Wien
Vienna

17
Ketty La Rocca
You You, 1974
Silbergelatinepapier Gelatin
silver paper
Serie von 10 Fotografien Series
of 10 photographs,
je 50 x 60 cm each
Courtesy Georg Kargl Fine Arts,
Wien Vienna

18
Robert Mapplethorpe
Thomas/Back, 1986
Silbergelatinepapier Gelatin
silver paper
61 x 51 cm
The Robert Mapplethorpe
Foundation

19
Robert Mapplethorpe
Lou, NYC, 1978
Silbergelatinepapier Gelatin
silver paper
50,8 x 40,6 cm
The Robert Mapplethorpe
Foundation

20
Robert Mapplethorpe
Vincent, 1981
Silbergelatinepapier Gelatin
silver paper
41 x 50,8 cm
The Robert Mapplethorpe
Foundation

21
Miyako Ishiuchi
1906 to the Skin, #17,
1991–1993
Silbergelatinepapier Gelatin
silver paper
77 x 106,5 cm
Courtesy The Third Gallery
Aya, Osaka

22
Miyako Ishiuchi
1906 to the Skin, #55,
1991–1993
Silbergelatinepapier Gelatin
silver paper
27,9 x 39 cm
Courtesy The Third Gallery
Aya, Osaka

23
Miyako Ishiuchi
1906 to the Skin, #39,
1991–1993
Silbergelatinepapier Gelatin
silver paper
27,9 x 39 cm
Courtesy The Third Gallery
Aya, Osaka

24
Miyako Ishiuchi
1906 to the Skin, #61,
1991–1993
Silbergelatinepapier Gelatin
silver paper
77 x 106,5 cm
Courtesy The Third Gallery
Aya, Osaka

25
Miyako Ishiuchi
1906 to the Skin, #60,
1991–1993
Silbergelatinepapier Gelatin
silver paper
39 x 27,3 cm
Courtesy The Third Gallery
Aya, Osaka

26
Miyako Ishiuchi
1906 to the Skin, #38,
1991–1993
Silbergelatinepapier Gelatin
silver paper
27,9 x 39 cm
Courtesy The Third Gallery
Aya, Osaka

Astrid Mahler # Artist Biographies

Vito Acconci
Born 1940 in New York

The works of Vito Acconci revolve around the self, the body, and, not least of all, space. Accordingly, after performances and installations he became increasingly interested in architecture and landscape architecture. Acconci studied literature at the College of the Holy Cross, Worcester (Mass.), completing his studies in 1964 at the University of Iowa. In the course of his numerous teaching positions, he taught art theory at various institutions in New York, while also publishing articles in magazines. In the late nineteen-sixties he began creating performances and video works involving his body as the central element. Around the mid-seventies he developed audiovisual installations that made use of his recorded voice. The interaction between artwork and viewer would become an important aspect of his work in which he practiced a social and political critique.

John Coplans
1920 London – 2003 New York

Coplans worked as painter, journalist, writer, and curator until, at the age of sixty, he began making photographs. After serving in the army Coplans studied painting in London. In 1960, due to his interest in the contemporary art scene, he relocated to San Francisco, teaching for a year at the University of California, Berkeley. In 1962, along with Philip Leider and John P. Irwin, Jr., Coplans was a co-founder of the art magazine *Artforum*. From 1971 to 1977, while based in New York, he served as the magazine's editor-in-chief. From 1967 to 1970 he worked as a curator at the Pasadena Art Museum. In 1980 he was the director of a small museum in Akron, Ohio, relocating back to New York at the beginning of the following year. He had already turned to photography in Ohio, producing portraits of couples, which he exhibited at the Art Institute of Chicago. In 1984 he began making self-portraits with the help of an assistant operating the shutter release. In the nineteen-eighties he realized a series of his hands and feet, and assembled his pictures into multipartite large-format tableaus. Coplans died in 2003 in New York.

Astrid Mahler # Künstlerbiografien

Vito Acconci
Geboren 1940 in New York

Die Werke von Vito Acconci umkreisen das eigene Ich, den Körper und nicht zuletzt den Raum. Demzufolge beschäftigte er sich nach Performances und der Umsetzung von Rauminstallationen zunehmend mit Architektur und Landschaftsarchitektur. Acconci studierte Literatur am College of the Holy Cross, Worcester (Massachusetts), und beendete sein Studium 1964 an der University of Iowa. Im Laufe seiner umfassenden Lehrtätigkeit unterrichtete er zunächst Kunsttheorie an verschiedenen Institutionen in New York und publizierte Artikel in Magazinen. Ab den späten 1960er-Jahren entstanden Performances und Videoarbeiten, in denen er seinen eigenen Körper als zentrales Element einsetzte. Gegen Mitte der Siebzigerjahre entwickelte er audiovisuelle Rauminstallationen, wobei er seine aufgenommene Stimme nutzte. Die Interaktion zwischen Kunstwerk und Betrachter sollte ein wichtiger Ansatz seiner Arbeit werden, in der er soziale und politische Kritik übt.

John Coplans
1920 London – 2003 New York

Coplans arbeitete als Maler, Publizist, Autor und Kurator, bevor er im Alter von 60 Jahren zu fotografieren begann. Nach seinem Dienst in der Armee studierte Coplans Malerei in London. 1960 übersiedelte er aus Interesse an der zeitgenössischen Kunstszene nach San Francisco und unterrichtete ein Jahr lang an der University of California, Berkeley. Zusammen mit Philip Leider und John P. Irwin junior gründete Coplans 1962 das Kunstmagazin *Artforum*. Von 1971 bis 1977 fungierte er als Chefredakteur der Zeitschrift mit Sitz in New York. Von 1967 bis 1970 arbeitete er als Kurator im Pasadena Art Museum. 1980 leitete er ein kleines Museum in Akron, Ohio, doch zu Beginn des darauffolgenden Jahres übersiedelte er wieder nach New York. Bereits in Ohio wandte er sich der Fotografie zu; es entstanden Porträts von Paaren, die er am Art Institute of Chicago ausstellte. Ab 1984 fertigte er unter Mithilfe einer Assistentin, die den Auslöser betätigte, Selbstporträts an. In den 1980er-Jahren verwirklichte er Serien seiner Hände und Füße und kombinierte seine Bilder zu mehrteiligen großformatigen Tableaus. Coplans starb 2003 in New York.

Miyako Ishiuchi
Born 1947 in Gunma Prefecture, Japan

The central themes of Miyako Ishiuchi's work are time, memory, and the signs that these leave behind on human skin or on objects. Ishiuchi studied textile design at the Tama Art University and started making photographs in the mid-nineteen-seventies. Beginning in 1977 she realized three related series of works in and about Yokosuka, the city in which she spent her childhood and youth. At the beginning of the nineteen-nineties she became interested in close-up details of the body, focusing on hands and legs. The result was a series on women of around the same age as the artist, as well as works on her grandmother, and later also her mother. If in her earlier works she concentrated on the female body, she now turned to the male body. She made photographs showing fragments of the body of the dancer Kazuo Ohno as well as the poet Ito Hiromi. In 2005 Ishiuchi represented Japan at the 51st Venice Biennale.

Robert Mapplethorpe
1946 New York – 1989 Boston

Mapplethorpe's oeuvre—or more specifically his explicit treatment of homoerotic and sadomasochistic themes—has for decades been the source of controversies. From 1963 to 1969 Mapplethorpe attended the Pratt Institute in Brooklyn, where he studied graphic design, painting, and sculpture. Around the end of the nineteen-sixties he worked on collages using images taken from magazines. At the beginning of the seventies he began making photographs with a small Polaroid camera, which led mainly to a series of self-portraits. At the same time he became enthusiastic about historical photography and began to collect. Mapplethorpe soon switched to a large-format Polaroid camera. He moved in the artistic milieu around Andy Warhol, which led to commissioned work such as portraits of high-society figures and members of the cultural scene, especially musicians, artists, and actors. Toward the end of the nineteen-seventies he created the controversial studies of the male body mentioned above, as well as flower still lifes. From very early on his work found private support, which led to an active national and international exhibition schedule. In 1988 the Whitney Museum of American Art in New York held the first large retrospective of his work. In 1986 Mapplethorpe was diagnosed with AIDS. Three years later he died from HIV-related complications.

Miyako Ishiuchi
Geboren 1947 in der Präfektur Gunma, Japan

Die Themen Zeit und Erinnerung und die Zeichen, die sie auf der menschlichen
Haut oder auf Gegenständen hinterlassen, sind die bestimmenden Themen in
Ishiuchis Arbeit. Die Künstlerin studierte an der Kunsthochschule Tama Textil-
design und begann Mitte der 1970er-Jahre zu fotografieren. Ab 1977 verwirklichte sie drei zusammenhängende Werkgruppen in und über Yokosuka, jene
Stadt, in der sie ihre Kindheit und Jugend verbrachte. Anfang der 1990er-
Jahre begann sie sich für Körperdetails zu interessieren und fokussierte aus-
schnitthaft auf Hände und Beine. Es entstanden Serien von Frauen, die im
selben Lebensalter wie die Künstlerin standen, sowie Arbeiten über ihre Groß-
mutter und später auch über ihre Mutter. Konzentrierte sie sich in den vergangenen Werkgruppen auf den weiblichen Körper, wandte sie sich nun dem
männlichen zu. Sie fotografierte fragmentarische Körperbilder des Tänzers
Kazuo Ohno sowie den Dichter Ito Hiromi. 2005 vertrat Ishiuchi Japan auf der
51. Biennale in Venedig.

Robert Mapplethorpe
1946 New York – 1989 Boston

Mapplethorpes Œuvre beziehungsweise seine explizite Auseinandersetzung
mit Homoerotik und Bondage-Sadomaso-Motiven ist seit Jahrzehnten umstrit-
ten. Von 1963 bis 1969 besuchte Mapplethorpe das Pratt Institute in Brooklyn,
wo er Werbedesign, Grafik, Malerei und Bildhauerei studierte. Gegen Ende
der 1960er-Jahre arbeitete er an Collagen, in denen er Bilder aus Zeitschriften
verwendete. Anfang der Siebzigerjahre begann er, mit einer kleinen Polaroidkamera zu fotografieren; es entstanden vor allem Selbstporträts. Gleichzeitig
begeisterte er sich für historische Fotografie und begann zu sammeln. Mapplethorpe wechselte bald zu einer großformatigen Polaroidkamera. Er bewegte
sich im künstlerischen Umfeld Andy Warhols: Es entstanden Auftragsarbeiten
wie etwa Porträts von Mitgliedern der High Society und der kulturellen Szene,
besonders von MusikerInnen, KünstlerInnen und SchauspielerInnen. Gegen
Ende der 1970er-Jahre schuf er die bereits erwähnten kontroversen Körperstu-
dien von Männern und Blumenstillleben. Sehr früh wurde seine Arbeit privat
gefördert und eine rege nationale wie internationale Ausstellungstätigkeit begann. 1988 zeigte das Whitney Museum of American Art in New York eine
erste große Retrospektive seiner Arbeit. 1986 wurde bei Mapplethorpe Aids
diagnostiziert, drei Jahre später starb er an den Folgen der HIV-Infektion.

Bruce Nauman
Born 1941 in Fort Wayne, Indiana

Nauman is internationally one of the best-known conceptual artists. His work is often concerned with socio-cultural and aesthetic questions, and involves a broad range of artistic techniques. From 1960 to 1964 Nauman studied at the University of Wisconsin, Madison—initially mathematics and physics, later fine art. In 1964 he transferred to the University of California, Davis. After graduating he began teaching at the San Francisco Art Institute in 1966. It was at this time that Nauman abandoned painting to work first on fiberglass sculptures and later increasingly on installations and performances. His work was quick to find a reception and to be exhibited. As early as 1972, the first retrospective of his work toured through America and Europe, beginning at the Los Angeles County Museum of Art. In the mid-nineteen-eighties he began using self-produced video recordings, which he incorporated into his installations. An important aspect of Nauman's work is the interaction between artist and viewer. At the end of the seventies he moved to New Mexico, where he lives and works today.

Ketty La Rocca
1938 La Spezia – 1976 Florence

Ketty La Rocca is a major figure in Italian conceptual art. The basic element of her art is language. In her early works she interrogated body images and ideals of beauty by combining textual elements and cut-out photos to form collages. In 1967 her work began to focus on the relationship between word and sign. La Rocca turned to video, installation, and performance. She developed a sign language, using the hands of women and men to portray certain gestures. She inscribed this "hand alphabet" with words. In 1972 she participated in the Venice Biennale. In her last work, La Rocca, by this time suffering from a brain tumor, made use of X-ray images of her head. She died at the age of thirty-eight in Florence.

Bruce Nauman
Geboren 1941 in Fort Wayne, Indiana

Nauman ist einer der international bekanntesten Konzeptkünstler. In seinem
Werk behandelt er vielfach soziokulturelle und ästhetische Fragen und setzt
verschiedenste künstlerische Mittel dafür ein. Von 1960 bis 1964 studierte
Nauman an der University of Wisconsin, zunächst Mathematik und Physik und
später bildende Kunst. 1964 wechselte er an die University of California, Davis.
Nach seinem Abschluss unterrichtete er ab 1966 am San Francisco Art Institute. Nauman gab die Malerei zu jener Zeit auf und schuf zunächst Fiberglas-
skulpturen, bevor er sich zunehmend mit Installationen und Performances
beschäftigte. Früh wurde sein Werk ausgestellt und rezipiert: Bereits 1972
wanderte, ausgehend vom Los Angeles County Museum of Art, eine erste
Retrospektive seiner Arbeit durch Amerika und Europa. Mitte der 1980er-
Jahre verwendete er erstmals selbst produzierte Videoaufnahmen, die er in
seinen Installationen einsetzte. Wichtiges Mittel für Nauman ist die Interaktion
zwischen Künstler und Betrachter. Ende der Siebzigerjahre zog er nach New
Mexico, wo er noch heute lebt und arbeitet.

Ketty La Rocca
1938 La Spezia – 1976 Florenz

Die Künstlerin La Rocca ist eine herausragende Vertreterin der italienischen
Konzeptkunst. Die Sprache stellt das wesentliche Moment ihrer künstlerischen
Arbeit dar. In ihren frühen Werken kombinierte sie ausgeschnittene Fotos und
Schriftversatzstücke zu Collagen und thematisierte so Schönheitsideale und
Körperbilder. Ab 1967 stand das Verhältnis von Wort und Zeichen im Zentrum
ihres Schaffens. La Rocca wandte sich dem Video, der Installation und der
Performance zu. Sie entwickelte eine Zeichensprache und setzte die Hände
von Frauen und Männern dazu ein, bestimmte Gesten zu vollführen. Dieses
»Handalphabet« beschriftete sie mit Wörtern. 1972 nahm sie an der Biennale
in Venedig teil. In ihrer letzten künstlerischen Arbeit verwendete die an einem
Hirntumor erkrankte La Rocca Röntgenaufnahmen ihres Kopfes. Sie starb mit
38 Jahren in Florenz.

Hannah Villiger

1951 Cham, canton of Zug – 1997 Auw, canton of Aargau

Villiger's best-known works are the series in which details of her own body
are fragmented and assembled into almost abstract tableaus. The Swiss
artist studied art at the Kunstgewerbeschule (School of Applied Arts) in
Lucerne. Around the mid-nineteen-seventies she worked on large sculptural objects made of organic materials and photographed her objects and
installations. In 1980 Villiger contracted open tuberculosis. The lung disease
would repeatedly break out anew and have a major influence on her work.
In 1983 she made her first enlarged Polaroid images. Photography became
Villiger's almost exclusive means of artistic expression. During this time
the main motifs of her work were fragmentary urban images, such as the
view from the window of her apartment and her own body. From 1992 to
1996 she taught "spatial design" at the Schule für Gestaltung Basel (Basel
School of Design). In an international context her intense gallery exhibition
schedule reached a climax in 1994 when, together with Pipilotti Rist, she
represented Switzerland at the Bienal de São Paulo. Villiger died of heart
failure at the age of forty-six.

Hannah Wilke

1940 New York – 1993 New York

Hannah Wilke's best-known works revolve around her own body and involve
autobiographical elements. From 1956 to 1961 Wilke studied at the Tyler
School of Art of Temple University in Philadelphia. In 1965 she took on a
teaching post at Plymouth-Whitemarsh High School in Plymouth Meeting.
In the same year she received a teaching position at White Plains High
School, New York, which she held until 1970. Two years later she began
teaching—until 1991—at the School of Visual Arts, New York. In the late
nineteen-fifties Wilke developed a "female iconography" based on organic, often vaginal, forms that she wanted to set against the male phallus.
During the seventies she began working with latex, creating objects and
sculptures. At the same time she worked in the fields of video-performance,
body art, photography, and installation. In 1987 Wilke contracted lym-
phoma. She subsequently produced an unsparing visual document of the
transformation of her disease-ridden body. Hannah Wilke died in 1993 in
New York.

Hannah Villiger
1951 Cham, Kanton Zug – 1997 Auw, Kanton Aargau

Villigers bekannteste Arbeiten sind jene Werkgruppen, in denen sie Details
ihres eigenen Körpers fragmentiert und zu beinahe abstrakten Bildtafeln zu-
sammenfügt. Die Schweizer Künstlerin besuchte an der Kunstgewerbeschule
Luzern die »Fachklasse für Bildnerische Gestaltung«. Gegen Mitte der 1970er-
Jahre arbeitete sie an großen skulpturalen Objekten aus organischen Materialien und fotografierte ihre Objekte und Installationen. 1980 erkrankte Villiger
an offener Tuberkulose. Die Lungenkrankheit sollte immer wieder aufs Neue
ausbrechen und großen Einfluss auf ihre Arbeit nehmen. 1983 entstand die
erste vergrößerte Polaroidaufnahme. Villiger begann, die Fotografie fast ausschließlich als ihr künstlerisches Ausdrucksmittel zu verwenden. Ausschnitt-
hafte Stadtbilder wie der Blick aus dem Fenster ihrer jeweiligen Wohnung und
der eigene Körper wurden in dieser Zeit zum Hauptmotiv von Villigers Arbeit.
Von 1992 bis 1996 unterrichtete sie »Räumliches Gestalten« an der Schule für
Gestaltung Basel. Ihre intensive Ausstellungstätigkeit in Galerien erreichte
1994 ihren Höhepunkt in einem internationalen Kontext: Gemeinsam mit Pipilotti Rist vertrat sie die Schweiz auf der Biennale in São Paulo. Villiger starb
mit 46 Jahren an Herzversagen.

Hannah Wilke
1940 New York – 1993 New York

Hannah Wilkes bekannteste Werkgruppen umkreisen ihren eigenen Körper
und beschäftigen sich mit autobiografischen Elementen. Wilke studierte von
1956 bis 1961 an der Tyler School of Art der Temple University in Philadelphia.
1965 nahm sie eine Lehrtätigkeit an der Plymouth-Whitemarsh High School
in Plymouth Meeting auf. Im selben Jahr erhielt sie an der White Plains High
School, New York, einen Lehrauftrag, den sie bis 1970 ausführte. Zwei Jahre
später unterrichtete sie – bis 1991 – an der School of Visual Arts, New York.
In den späten 1950er-Jahren erfand Wilke eine »weibliche Ikonografie«, die auf
organischen, oftmals vaginalen, Formen basierte, die sie dem männlichen
Phallus entgegensetzen wollte. Im Laufe der Siebzigerjahre begann sie mit
Latex zu arbeiten und kreierte Objekte und Skulpturen. Gleichzeitig arbeitete
sie in den Bereichen Videoperformance, Body Art, Fotografie und Installation.
1987 erkrankte Wilke an Lymphdrüsenkrebs; die Veränderungen ihres von
Krankheit gezeichneten Körpers setzte sie schonungslos ins Bild. Hannah
Wilke starb 1993 in New York.

Diese Publikation erscheint anlässlich der
Ausstellung
This catalogue is published in conjunction
with the exhibition
Körper als Protest
The Body as Protest
Albertina, Wien Vienna
5. September – 2. Dezember 2012
September 5 – December 2, 2012

Herausgeber Editors
Walter Moser, Klaus Albrecht Schröder

Lektorat Copyediting
Jasmin Holbein, Hatje Cantz
(Deutsch German)
Joann Skrypzak (Englisch English)

Übersetzungen (Deutsch–Englisch)
Translations (German–English)
Benjamin Carter

Grafische Gestaltung und Satz
Graphic design and typesetting
Andreas Platzgummer, Hatje Cantz

Schrift Typeface
Akzidenz Grotesk

Herstellung Production
Heidrun Zimmermann, Hatje Cantz

Reproduktionen Reproductions
Repromayer GmbH, Reutlingen

Druck Printing
Dr. Cantz'sche Druckerei Medien GmbH,
Ostfildern

Papier Paper
Galaxi Keramik, 150 g/m²

Buchbinderei Binding
IDUPA, Owen/Teck

Erschienen im Published by
Hatje Cantz Verlag
Zeppelinstrasse 32
73760 Ostfildern
Germany
Tel. +49 711 4405-200
Fax +49 711 4405-220
www.hatjecantz.de

Informationen zu dieser oder zu anderen
Ausstellungen finden Sie unter
www.kq-daily.de
You can find information on this exhibition
and many others at www.kq-daily.de

Hatje Cantz books are available internationally at selected bookstores. For
more information about our distribution
partners please visit our homepage at
www.hatjecantz.com

ISBN 978-3-7757-3423-3

Printed in Germany

Umschlagabbildungen Cover illustrations
Ketty La Rocca, *You You,* 1974 (vorne front)
John Coplans, *Back with Arms Above,* 1984
(hinten back)

Frontispiz Frontispiece
John Coplans, *Interlocking Fingers, No. 6,*
1999

Abbildungsnachweis Photo Credits

Kat. cat. 1, 3: Courtesy Electronic Arts In-
termix (EAI), New York; Kat. cat. 2: Marsie,
Emanuelle, Damon and Andrew Scharlatt,
The Hannah Wilke Collection & Archive, Los
Angeles; Kat. cat. 4–12, Abb. figs. 1, 2, 7, 10
(Moser): The John Coplans Trust; Kat. cat. 13:
Rheinisches Bildarchiv, Köln Cologne; Kat.
cat. 14, 15: The Estate of Hannah Villiger;
Kat. cat. 16: SAMMLUNG VERBUND, Wien
Vienna; Kat. cat. 17: Courtesy Georg Kargl
Fine Arts, Wien Vienna; Kat. cat. 18–20: The
Robert Mapplethorpe Foundation; Kat. cat.
21–26: The Third Gallery Aya, Osaka; Abb.
figs. 3–6 (Moser): Fotosammlung Öster-
reichisches Filmmuseum, Wien / Kaderver-
größerungen: Georg Wasner Photography
Collection of the Austrian Film Museum,
Vienna / frame enlargements: Georg
Wasner; Abb. fig. 9 (Moser): David Hockney
Inc.; Abb. figs. 1, 4, 5 (Natlacen): museum
moderner kunst stiftung ludwig wien; Abb.
fig. 2 (Natlacen): Archiv Arnulf Rainer; Abb.
fig. 3 (Natlacen): Sammlung Fotomuseum
WestLicht, Wien Vienna; Abb. figs. 6, 9
(Natlacen): Albertina, Wien Vienna; Abb. fig. 7
(Natlacen): Fotosammlung Österreichisches
Filmmuseum, Wien Photography Collection
of the Austrian Film Museum, Vienna

Partner der Albertina
Partners of the Albertina

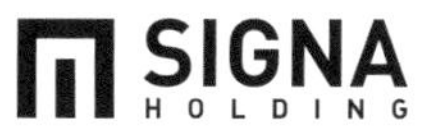

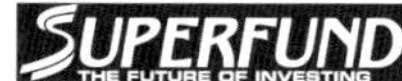